THE NEW DEMONSTRATING
TO WIN!

The Indispensable Guide for Demonstrating Complex Products

ROBERT RIEFSTAHL

ISBN: 0615477097
ISBN-13: 9780615477091
2910 Terranova Court
Colorado Springs, Colorado 80919
USA

Demonstrating to WIN!, LLC believes that the information described in this publication is accurate and reliable, and much care has been taken in its preparation. However, no responsibility, financial or otherwise, can be accepted for any consequences arising out of the use of this material, including loss of profit, indirect, special, or consequential damages. There are no warrants that extend beyond the program specified.

The customer should exercise care to assure that use of the information in this publication will be in full compliance with laws, rules, and regulations of the jurisdictions with respect to which it is used.

The information contained herein is subject to change. Copying or duplicating any portion of this documentation without the prior written permission of Demonstrating to WIN!, LLC is prohibited by law.

Trademarks

Microsoft®, NT®, Microsoft PowerPoint® and Microsoft Word® are either registered trademarks or trademarks of the Microsoft Corporation the United States and other countries.
NxTrend® is a registered trademark of Infor Global Solutions.
IBM® is a registered trademark of IBM Corporation.
ScreenCam® is a registered trademark of Lotus Development Corporation.
UPS® is a registered trademark of United Parcel Service of America, Inc.
Federal Express® is a registered trademark of Federal Express Corporation.
Sesame Street® is a registered trademark of The Sesame Workshop.
Tinker Toys® is a registered trademark of Playskool.
Wiffle Ball® is a registered trademark of The Wiffel Ball, Inc.

DEDICATION

To my wife Suzanne and my sons Trent and Bennett, thank you for your support as I traveled the world spreading these ideas that have come from so many.

TABLE OF CONTENTS

ACKNOWLEDGEMENTS

I have many colleagues and friends to thank, especially Ross Jacobsen, Niel Powers, Rusty Bond, Patrick Becker, Jeff Hatten, Andrea Marboe, Doug Walker, Guy Lammle, Ross Elliott, Russ Cram, and Randy Hughes. Similarly, many former customers have been a tremendous help, most notably Al Jones, Paul Harlow, Dave Gillies, Doug Fanning and Kay Mason. Finally, I wish to thank my wife Suzanne for her undying encouragement.

BIOGRAPHY

Robert (Bob) Riefstahl sold and demonstrated software products for more than 20 years. As a sales manager he witnessed hundreds of demonstrations. He became keenly interested in demonstration techniques as he watched some demonstrations soar while others failed. The question was "what differentiates a good demonstration from a bad one?" This book breaks the code and answers that question.

In the first print of the book, Mr. Riefstahl provided his readers with a unique look at what makes some demos succeed while others failed. Shortly after publication, Mr. Riefstahl and his first partner Ross Jacobsen, started 2WIN! Global. Since the book first went to print much has changed as his firm soared to success across the world. Their clients have included global organizations such as Microsoft, Oracle, Adobe, SolidWorks, SAP, HP and IBM. This version of the book provides the reader with new insights that incorporate the global experiences of Mr. Riefstahl's team.

Born near Chicago, Illinois, Robert Riefstahl graduated with honors from Northern Illinois University with a Bachelor of Science degree in Marketing. Upon graduation in 1980, he immediately began demonstrating technology equipment and software as a territory salesperson for the Burroughs® Corporation in Jacksonville, Florida. His position sent him into a Florida territory selling accounting and billing software to small government agencies. After leaving Burroughs in 1982, he joined a small start-up firm that created and sold physician-billing software. This continued successfully until 1990 when he joined a fast growing software firm called NxTrend® Technology. NxTrend was acquired by Infor Global Solutions in 2004. Prior to acquisition, NxTrend created and implemented enterprise wide software for distributors.

In 2001, Mr. Riefstahl started the firm 2WIN! Global. His organization has experienced tremendous growth. They have successfully completed thousands of training workshops on demonstrating, selling and presenting techniques to pre-sales, sales, marketing and services professionals in over 40 countries around the world.

FORWARD

I was first introduced to the book Demonstrating To WIN! many years ago as part of my team's development and focus around this topic. When I turned to Chapter 4, The Demo Crime Files I instantly knew we had found an expert that truly understood the fine aspects of demonstrating a complex solution. In fact, we took it one step further and leveraged 2WIN! Global's expertise to bring their innovative thinking to our team. Needless to say, the results were dramatic.

Since my first experience with the book several years ago we have seen dramatic changes in the technology, solutions capabilities, and go-to-market strategies for the software industry at large. More presentations and demonstrations are being performed on the web. Discoveries with clients are shorter, more prescriptive and controlled by the prospects. Software has become more complex and difficult to demonstrate. And to top it off, sales engineers are deeper into their careers and all of us could use new energy and tactics on our collective quest for innovation and continual improvement.

The New Demonstrating To WIN! arrived just in time! Bob and his team have leveraged their global experiences from the largest software companies in the world to bring the reader the latest ideas and techniques that address today's challenging and complex demonstration environments. In this version of the book, he refines discoveries and addresses current trends. His web suggestions are precise and effective. Finally, the new Demo Crime Files chapter has some additions you won't want to miss.

Beyond the tactical benefits that the book has provided us, our association with 2WIN! Global has enabled us to improve our connection with our clients and enhance the credibility, awareness and passion of our people.

If you are in the business of selling and demonstrating complex solutions be it software, technology, medical devices or financial products, I am confident your team will benefit from this quick but comprehensive read.

Ken Crovetti
National Vice President, Solutions North America

SAP America, Inc.

PREFACE

It was a warm summer day in Atlanta, Georgia as I walked from the IBM® parking garage off Peachtree Street to the IBM® Tower. I had my laptop, documentation, implementation manuals and my prospect's requirements list. I had spent several days with the prospect to learn all about their business structure and processes. I knew the names and personalities of everyone attending the demonstration. Best of all, I knew where our software would score a home run and where I could expect to strikeout.

During the next two days, my teammate and I joined hands with our prospect and led them through our software. We carefully demonstrated how, by using our software, they'd improve their individual jobs and overall corporate operations. Sure there were rough parts, but we recovered from them quickly because we were prepared to attend to our shortcomings. We were awarded the business and the customer, with our software, grew to become one of the best-known industrial distributors in the United States. Our successful demonstration was *the* clear factor in our victory.

This demonstration was a turning point for me. Knowing this, I began to analyze demonstrations and technical presentaions as a sales concept. Why are some successful while others fail? How is it you can finish a demonstration and be told by the prospect "it went fine," only to learn later you lost the business to a competitor who performed better in front of the customer? What is it that makes one presenter perform better than anyone else you know? These questions and more are answered in this book.

In my 20 plus years of selling software, I've given or witnessed hundreds of demonstrations and technical presentations. During that time, I've been amazed at how inconsistent and non-compelling some of them can be. Why is that? I believe it's due to a lack of training. While there are some excellent training programs that focus on presentation techniques, sales strategy and contract closing, none provides a complete picture of what's necessary to succeed at demonstrating or presenting software.

The common belief is that successfully demonstrating software is an *art* rather than a *science.* I find that thought ludicrous! No, demonstrating software isn't for everyone. And yes, there'll always be gurus who have a natural talent for wooing an audience. They just seem to *feel* their way through a presentation, knowing precisely what to say, to whom, how and when. They're naturally smooth. I don't happen to be one of those people. Sure, I've been successful. But for me, it's been a long process filled with "demo crimes," blown sales opportunities and disappointed prospects. I'm not a natural salesperson, nor am I an unusually quick learner. So, what's my secret? I'm a hard worker and I'm analytical. I watch other presenters and demonstrators and make note of their techniques, mirroring the things they do well. This book is a compilation of the best techniques I've learned over the years so you can perform truly effective demonstrations and technical presentations.

The process of demonstrating *effectively* is a journey, not a point in time. I can speak from personal experience; more than my share of demonstrations have missed the mark. I've included lots of my experiences in the book, both good and bad. Because my primary background is demonstrating and selling business application software, many of my examples come from this industry. However, no matter what type of software you sell or marketplace you serve, the principles of demonstrating are the same. In fact, the same principles and techniques apply to software demonstrations, technical presentations, even proof of concept and conference room pilot exercises. Any time spent in front of a customer is precious and you want to enter each opportunity fully prepared.

It's my sincere hope this book will make your journey to successful demonstrations shorter than mine, collapsing it from a round-the-world flight to an express trip from New York to Boston!

INTRODUCTION

It's now ten years since the first publication of Demonstrating To WIN!, and the last decade has seen amazing transformations take place in the software industry. Mergers and acquisitions have resulted in fewer choices for the customer, tougher competition for new deals, and a more complex collection of products and solutions to be mastered by the sales team. There are fewer "net new" or "green field" opportunities, and more competition for market share. As a sales team, you're working harder to displace competitors while simultaneously working to ensure that your position in existing accounts is strengthened. Sure, you're still demonstrating software to new prospects, but an increasing amount of your time is spent bringing new products and new releases to existing customers.

Customers and prospects have also changed. They're much more sophisticated buyers than they were just ten short years ago. They've seen the aftermath of poor decisions and complex implementations, and they're determined not to repeat those experiences. They demand value, and they want it in a short timeframe. If the value isn't evident, they simply allocate their capital to other projects. The CFO is now a major stakeholder in software decisions, and you have new competitors that have nothing to do with software or technology. Your biggest competitor may be other uses of capital or resources within an organization. So the 'no decision' result has become more common as CFOs move budget money and resources to other, non-technical initiatives.

And, of course, the software itself has changed. Software has become stronger both in terms of capability and flexibility. This is obviously great for the user, but it's made the job of presenting and demonstrating software solutions that much more difficult. Software companies can have hundreds, if not thousands, of products across multiple markets.

All of these changes have been taken into account in this edition of the book. But, as the old saying goes, the more things change, the more they stay the same. And that is certainly true when it comes to the fundamentals, techniques and demo crimes discussed in the original Demonstrating To WIN! In fact, the changes in the industry make the techniques in this book even more valuable. It was never very effective to simply show up and demonstrate the features of your software, but now it can be an absolute deal killer. Between the increased expectations of the customer and the increased flexibility in the software, a poorly structured or feature-heavy demonstration will fall very flat and can easily harm the deal.

Today, prospects and customers expect a clear, strong value message and they expect to have it reinforced at every step in the sales process and by every member of the sales team. They expect sales professionals to avoid demo crimes (mistakes made in customer facing events), and present a clear, compelling demonstration that's directly applicable to them.

So what can you expect in this new edition? First, a greater emphasis on Discovery. If you're going to create a high-value demonstration applicable to a sophisticated customer, you'll need to learn more about that customer. Fortunately, the resources available to you to learn about a customer or prospect continue to grow. Second, you'll need an updated crime list. As connectivity has improved and software has changed, a few of the crimes are not as common as they once were. But technology has also led to a few new crimes, and those have been documented. You will see a wider range of demonstration techniques that include specialized and innovative tactics and strategies for web presentations. Finally, as Demonstrating To WIN! reached a wider audience of software professionals, we applied our comprehensive experiences and included examples for system engineers working with very technical products.

Of course, there's been one other change we should talk about. The first publication of Demonstrating To WIN! was based on my twenty-plus years of selling and demonstrating software. Since that time, we have taught thousands of workshops in over 50 countries around the world. During those sessions, my team at 2WIN! Global has had the pleasure of sharing our knowledge with thousands of software professionals in just about any area of the software industry that you could name. Household names like Microsoft, SAP, Oracle, SunGard, IBM and HP have experienced the benefits of our strategies much as you are about to experience them in this book. During our travels, we have learned that with minor cultural adaptations, the concepts in this book have improved sales efforts globally. I trust that you'll find those experiences reflected in this new edition of Demonstrating to WIN!

CHAPTER 1
Demonstrating is a Responsibility

If you've chosen a sales or sales-support career in the software industry, or are asked to participate in software demonstrations, you have a great deal of responsibility. First, you have an obligation to your company. They've hired you to represent the company's products effectively and professionally. Many people's livelihoods depend on you. It's your obligation to be the best you can be at presenting your software. If you truly believe in your products and services, you owe it to all the people within your company to provide your prospective customers a compelling view of your products.

Second, you have a responsibility to your prospects. They need a proper and realistic image of the capabilities of your software. They'll witness demonstrations from a number of competitive products. If they're to make an informed decision, they need an effective demonstration from you. You may have the best product on the market, but if you can't represent it effectively, they'll be the worse off for it.

YOUR COMPANY

Your company expects a great deal from you. You might find yourself in planes, trains and automobiles. You work long hours. Your knowledge base is constantly eroding. You're always in need of training, which requires even more of your time. You're expected to adapt to organizational change, and go above and beyond the call of duty on a regular basis. But, your daily challenges pale in comparison to what your company expects out of you during a software demonstration or presentation.

- The programming staff thinks the software is so good it will sell itself.

- The CEO believes on top of the outstanding product functionality, you have an army of customer support people that make your job *easy.*

- The salesperson expects you to just show up next Tuesday and "do what you normally do" with no preparation and no additional information about the prospect.

- The marketing people believe that they have constructed the perfect messages and put them in the perfect presentation deck to make your preparation *easy.*

- The implementation staff thinks you make the software sound much better than it really is (as in stretching the truth from time-to-time).

- The accounting staff thinks you invent contract and payment terms to get your commission check quicker.

- What are you thinking? *Please, shoot me now and put me out of my misery!*

Everyone I just mentioned expects you to be an expert software demonstrator and presenter. You don't have the luxury of mediocrity. It's your job to take your software and make it beautiful.

YOUR PROSPECT

Have you ever been on the receiving end of a mediocre demonstration or presentation? How about one that's *really* dismal? Do you remember feeling trapped and claustrophobic? Did you wonder if this was what it felt like to be in jail? Let me describe a software demonstration environment. See if you can relate. The demonstration begins at 9:00 a.m. You look at your watch and its only 9:35. You fidget in your chair, daydream and wish you were anywhere but in this miserable presentation. Thoughts run through your head: you have phone calls to catch up on, the grass to mow and there's the weekend! You look at your watch again. Oh no, it's only 9:42. It's only been seven minutes since you checked your watch last and there's more then three hours to go!

What's the ultimate problem? Sure, as the person receiving the demonstration, your time is being wasted. But even worse, you're not getting the presenter's message! You're not connecting with them or their product/service. Allow me to share an experience when I was the prospect. My company hired a respected firm (recommended to us by an industry acquaintance) to train our sales team on how to contact the top officer in a company. The success of the course was crucial. Getting to the right people in sales calls had always been a challenge for our people…myself included. We really *needed* this training. It was a full-day session. We flew all our salespeople in from across the US and Canada for the meeting. Not only was this costly from an out-of-pocket expense perspective (airfare, hotels, meals, etc.), it also cost us one full day of productivity. We anticipated a great presentation and anxiously awaited the refreshing ideas, techniques and materials. Unfortunately, here's what transpired:

8:00 Two presenters arrived. Sadly, they knew nothing about our business. Prior to the session, there had been no attempt to learn about our company, processes or people. They had no idea what value our software added to our prospective customers' business.

8:10 They introduced themselves by reading from a script, word-for-word. Then they turned on an ancient overhead projector and started feeding old-fashioned transparencies through an automatic feeder that jammed every third foil. They attempted (very ineffectively) to play off each other during the session.

9:15 Our salespeople (the audience) began to look around the room.

10:00 The salespeople started heckling the presenters.

11:15 The dialogue between the audience and presenters became argumentative.

12:00 Celebrations erupted over the relief of a lunch break. Everybody made as many phone calls as possible so they didn't have to return to the training.

13:30 The room started to get openly hostile.

15:00 Everyone gave up, shut up and slouched in their chairs, hoping if they said nothing, the misery would soon end.

Afterward   After expressing our dissatisfaction, the presenters offered to come back and perform the session again. No way. Had I allowed them to return, our CEO would've had my head!

What's the bottom-line? They came to conquer and left defeated. Amazingly, the subject matter and techniques they recommended were excellent! I still use some of them when calling on top executives. However, this was only accomplished because of a conscious effort on my part to carefully re-shape the material to fit my needs. Since none of the other salespeople use the material or techniques today, the training was essentially a waste of time and money.

The reputation and quality of your software and company *makes no difference* if your demonstration is inadequate. When a demonstration is going poorly, the prospects will check out. They'll no longer think about their friends (your clients) who love your software. The consultant who highly recommends you will be forgotten. It's bad enough that individuals in the presentation will be upset that you're wasting their valuable time. What's worse is when the owner comes to the shocking realization you're wasting the time of *everyone* in the room!

It's your *responsibility* to make sure this never happens to your prospect. You owe it to them to show your software in the best possible light. You owe it to them to demonstrate how *they* can use the product in their business. If they manufacture vinyl siding, they don't want to know how your software can help them manufacturer desks and chairs. Nor do they want you to show them features *you* think are really good but mean absolutely nothing in their business. They want to know how your products and services will help make *them* more productive, competitive and profitable. That's it. Nothing more. Nothing less.

EFFECTIVENESS

What's an *effective* demonstration? Some sales profession-als think it's when you've taught your prospect about all 500 features in your software. These folks consider an effective presentation a dump of knowledge. "If, at the end of the dem-onstration, they know how to run our system, I'm well ahead of my competition." *Wrong!*

Has something like the following ever happened to you? You specialize in automating $30 – $100 million-dollar fur-niture manufacturers. Your company has what most con-sider the leading software package in the industry. You own 40 percent of the market. Your prospect is a $55 million dollar furniture manufacturer. They're right in your strike zone. Three of the prospect's competitors have your system installed. You give a full-day demonstration. The room is full of people who sit quietly throughout the day. They ask some good questions. Along the way, you proudly provide affirmative answers. It's a little quiet after lunch, but you pick up steam again about 2:30. You get some disagree-ments from the crowd but work your way through them. People in the room manage to nod their heads from time-to-time. You're getting approval. You've taught them all they need to know for one day. You pack up and on the way out ask your sponsor, "Bill, how do you think it went today?" Bill responds, "I think everyone now has a full understand-ing of what your software will do." On the way to your car, you begin to smile. You jump in the car, call the boss and tell him how well the demonstration went. Three weeks go by before you get a form letter from the prospect. You're shocked to learn you haven't even made the short list of three finalists! Sound familiar? What went wrong?

You're not there to *teach* your prospect about your software. Their *understanding* your software isn't the mark of an *effective* demonstration. It's not an educational session in the traditional sense. You're presenting your software for the sole purpose of providing them with a *vision* of how it can improve their company. That's it. An effective demonstration "bridges" the gap between how the prospect does things today and how your product will help them do it *faster, better or cheaper* in the future. An effective demonstration means they discover how your software will help them, *not* how it works!

You are likely thinking, "Wait a minute. Why shouldn't we be teaching our prospects how to use our products? That's what they say they want!" In many cases prospects and customers approach a buying decision by wanting to learn everything possible about your solution. That is why so many prospects insist on detailed technical presentations and a proof of concept or conference room pilot. But even in those situations, your role needs to remain clear and consistent: You are there to help the prospect see how the software will benefit their organization. No prospect will ever use every feature and capability in the software they buy. They will concentrate solely on what helps them in their work. You are there to bring focus to those areas and help them see how the advantages they will realize if they implement your solutions.

CHAPTER SUMMAR'

In all situations, effective demonstr*
bility. While every organization needs
between sales and technical sales, it '
that will be in front of the prospec
responsibility for the outcome of th*

CHAPTER 2
Demonstrating Is Not an Art!

People have a bad habit of assigning the word *art* to any human activity that, by all appearances, is accomplished in a seemingly effortless fashion. "Do you remember the way Michael Jordan played? He was an artist with a basketball."

Implying someone can do things in an *artistic* fashion suggests those with natural talent are the best in their given field. Let me go ahead and burst your bubble. This statement is *absolutely true!* The people who are the very best in any endeavor tend to have a great deal of *natural* talent. However, many other successful business people, leaders and athletes have more courage than natural talent. Famous people like Bill Gates, Mother Theresa and Nelson Mandela are but a few examples of courageous talent. These superstars succeeded because they focused on the *fundamentals,* not simply because of their raw, natural talent.

DEMONSTRATION ANXIETY

Do you get nervous before a demonstration or presentation? Is your opening less than inspiring? Do you find yourself searching for the right words and begin rambling? These are all classic symptoms of demonstration anxiety. In one fashion or another, I've experienced each of these anxieties in my career. I can't think of a single presentation I've done where I wasn't nervous at the beginning! It's perfectly normal to be nervous before and at the beginning of a demonstration. However, there's a big difference between being nervous and being crippled by anxiety. Being nervous simply shows you respect the significance of the task you're about to begin. When you become anxiety-crippled, you're ineffective.

For most of us, anxiety can be linked to a fear of the unknown. We lack knowledge about our current or pending situation. What's the solution? Learn as much as you can about your situation. Break it down. Analyze it. In the case of a software demonstration, that means learning about your:

1. Prospect's Company.

2. Prospect's Industry.

3. Prospect's Niche.

4. Product Knowledge.

5. Competition.

6. Audience (individually and as a group).

7. Prospect's Operating and Technical Environment.

8. Equipment.

9. Prospect's Processes and Workflows.

10. Your Product's Strengths.

11. Your Product's Weaknesses.

1) Prospect's Company - It's crucial to learn all you can about the company to whom you're about to provide a demonstration. There are many things to learn about your prospect. You need to know their history, the principals of the company, their primary competitors, customers and vendors, and their goals and initiatives. Identify everyone who will attend the demonstration. Determine their job titles, positions in the decision process, job histories (both with the existing company and prior careers) and the three primary goals they have for the demonstration or presentation. Send your sponsor an Attendee Checklist well in advance (see below). Have them gather the information on this form for everybody attending the demonstration. This survey form captures the names, backgrounds, interests and needs of the attendees for the demonstration. You need this basic data in order to understand something about the players involved in the demonstration. Do not skip this step just because this prospect happens to also be a current customer. You need to understand the circumstances of this particular opportunity even if you have done business with this customer before. This powerful information will:

- Enable you to convey an image of partnership.

- Help you gain their trust and confidence.

- Allow you to address their specific issues.

DEMONSTRATION ATTENDEE CHECKLIST

Session _____

Attendee _____ Title_____

Primary Responsibility _____

Attendee's Top 3 Interests In Demonstration (What do they want covered?)

   1. _____
   2. _____
   3. _____

Session _____

Attendee _____ Title_____

Primary Responsibility _____

Attendee's Top 3 Interests In Demonstration (What do they want covered?)

   1. _____
   2. _____
   3. _____

Session _____

Attendee _____ Title_____

Primary Responsibility _____

Attendee's Top 3 Interests In Demonstration (What do they want covered?)

   1. _____
   2. _____
   3. _____

This checklist is just the beginning of your "Discovery Process" (or Discovery for short). Discovery should be appropriately structured to match the nature of the opportunity. If your demonstration will be at the prospect's location, I highly recommend spending extra time at your prospect's place of business. If you are conducting a web demonstration, Discovery will more likely be done over the phone. But every demonstration should be preceeded by Discovery activities. As you become more familiar with your product, industry and competition, you can usually perform your Discovery the day before the demonstration. Until that point, schedule Discovery interviews at least one week in advance. This will give you ample time to incorporate what you learn into your presentation. If you are given the opportunity to perform Discovery interviews on-site, try to hold your meetings with people in their normal working environment. Avoid being confined to a conference room when conducting interviews. You want to see them perform their jobs using existing tools (or lack thereof). Why? First, you'll get a better appreciation for what they need and want. Also, you might uncover activities that are important as it relates to your demo, but the prospect doesn't even give them a second thought. Use a questionnaire to help with your fact-finding.

I always, always, always ask each individual, "If it was completely up to you, what three things would you change about your existing system?" Then ask, "What are the three best things about your existing system?" If appropriate, ask, "What are the three things you'd like demonstrated when I come back?" Basically, these are three ways of asking the same question, right? Why ask it three different ways? I've found if I only ask one question, I get responses like, "I would like the system to be much faster." Sure, better response time will be a nice thing to highlight, but you need to dig deeper. Two or three variations of the same question will uncover *real* issues. You will get truly meaningful information.

Your goals in the Discovery are many:

- Learn more about the organization. (Note that the internet is a great source of information about the company, their financial details, and their industry.)

- Establish a relationship with the people to whom you'll be presenting and what's important to them.

- Determine the issues that are really important to your audience. What are their current issues, desired outcomes and the impact of making those changes?

- Identify your weaknesses so you can prepare and provide responses during the demonstration.

- Establish credibility by showing that you *care* about them, as individuals and as a company, by investing your own time learning as much as you can.

Keep in mind that the Discovery Process is important with all demonstrations, regardless of length or format. Your activities might be in person, by phone or even e-mail, but the purpose and the value are the same. You'll learn more about the Discovery Process in Chapter 5, which I've devoted to this critical, but usually neglected, step in a demonstration.

2) Prospect's Industry - Your prospect belongs to a certain industry. Most prospects fall into what is referred to as a Standard Industry Classification or SIC code. The prospect's SIC code defines their primary business. Why is this important to know? If your prospect sees that you understand (or are trying hard to learn) something about their industry, they'll be more likely to respect and listen to you. Think about a time that you met somebody from another country who was visiting your country. Did you respect and admire them for trying to learn your language? I bet it also made you want to help them.

Another advantage of knowing something about their industry is it helps you demonstrate how your software can address their real problems. Start by learning the common terms used in the industry. The web is a wonderful source for industry information. You can find industry associations and publications, free or inexpensive industry training, and access to industry experts with a few simple searches. Also, find out if you have any existing customers in your prospect's industry (SIC code). In addition to providing you industry information, they'll hopefully allow you to use them as a reference.

There was a time when you could skip understanding the prospect's industry if you were selling technical software – infrastructure and middleware products. Decisions were made at CIO level and below, and CIO's were technical them-selves. Those days are largely gone. As business users have become more technology savvy, CIO's have become more business savvy. With very few exceptions, you will be present-ing to a mixed technical *and* business audience, and you will need to speak credibly about business and industry concerns. Even if your *direct* audience is technical, you will need to sell your advantages "up the chain" to business decision makers. If you understand the business and the industry, you can better provide them what they will need to sell internally.

3) Prospect's Niche - No two prospects are exactly alike, even if they're in the same industry. They all have a niche you need to recognize and understand. I'm sure you're thinking, "Make up your mind. First you tell me the indus-try is important. Now you're telling me everybody is differ-ent!" Guilty as charged. Here's an example. If you're selling physician-billing software, never make the mistake of thinking a doctor is a doctor. A pediatrician is nothing like a plastic surgeon. Sure, they're both doctors, but their interests and needs in a new billing system are likely to be very different. In order to know your prospect's niche, you need to go beyond memorizing the terminology and acronyms of the industry. You want to know "insider information." Again, customers in the same industry, even if they are not in your prospect's exact niche, can usually give you some clues. Industry trade journals and web resources are also excellent for this kind of information. Many times, the information is free and available to anyone willing to spend a little time on-line.

4) Value Drivers – All organizations have key metrics by which they measure themselves. Your prospect is no different. Knowing those metrics is necessary in order for you to build a strong value case for your solution. Every prospect has a long list of projects and initiatives they would like to address, but their capital is limited. A good way to think about this is that you are not competing solely with other solution providers, you are competing with every possible use of this prospect's capital. Knowing the prospect's key value drivers gives you the opportunity to shape your benefit statements and messages around their needs. This helps you beat all other competitors.

5) Product Knowledge - Knowing your product is obviously important. I'm talking raw product knowledge rather than demonstration techniques. This is a meet-minimum expectation your prospect has of you. Have you learned what is *practical* to know for this demonstration? Are you prepared to focus your product on your prospect's specific needs and interests? If you're not knowledgeable enough to explain and d- ˈate the raw features, functions and advantages of uct, you have one of two options. Either determine what you don't know and learn it before the demo or bring somebody along who does know.

Gauge your product understanding by performing a self-evaluation with the assistance of your supervisor. The Knowledge Index below will help you identify areas where you need additional training or practice. I strongly recommend creating a Knowledge Index for you and your colleagues.

Another good exercise is to practice with your software in front of a video camera. This exercise will do wonders when you have a serious case of pre-demonstration butterflies.

	Accounting	Purchasing	Process Flows	Corporate Overview	Internet Products	User Interfaces	Education Tools	Integration	Electronic Catalogs	Dashboards	Data Warehousing	Sales Analysis	1/1 Total
Pre-Sales													
Steve Anderson	2	2	4	4	4	4	4	3	4	2	4	2	39
Mike Peters	3	2	3	4	4	4	3	3	3	2	4	2	37
Bill Stevens	0	0	1	1	2	1	1	1	0	0	1	0	8
David Andrews	0	0	2	1	2	2	1	0	0	0	2	0	10
Jerry Collins	1	1	3	4	4	2	2	2	3	2	4	0	28
Base Total	6	5	13	14	16	13	11	9	10	6	15	4	122
Base Average	1.2	1.0	2.6	2.8	3.2	2.6	2.2	1.8	2.0	1.2	3.0	0.8	
Outside Sales													
John Davidson	3	4	2	3	5	4	2	3	4	3	2	3	38
Bob Riefstahl	4	4	2	5	5	4	3	3	4	4	5	3	46
Mike Davis	4	4	3	4	4	4	4	1	3	2	4	2	39
Jason Waters	2	2	3	2	2	4	1	1	2	2	3	1	25
Doug Smith	3	3	4	5	4	4	4	3	4	4	4	3	45
Gary Desmond	4	1	3	2	4	4	2	4	4	4	4	0	36
Base Total	20	18	17	21	24	24	16	15	21	19	22	12	229
Base Average	3.4	2.8	3.0	3.6	3.8	4.0	2.8	2.4	3.4	3.2	4.0	1.8	
All Sales Total	2.3	1.9	2.8	3.2	3.5	3.3	2.5	2.1	2.7	2.2	3.5	1.3	31.3

Product Topic

KEY:
0 = No knowledge
1 = Elevator Pitch
2 = PowerPoint Presentation
3 = Screen Cam Demo
4 = Live or Web Demo
5 = Teach & Material Development

6) Competition - "Who's my competition?" Always ask your prospect this important question. Don't be afraid to ask the question, especially if you have an insider in the organization. They're usually not opposed to sharing this with you. I find 80 percent of the time, if I know an insider, they give me this information without me even having to ask. If you do get some resistance, here's a little trick. Ask them about *their* competition. After discussing their competitive situation (which can be valuable information itself), they'll be reminded that *everybody* has competitors. More than likely, they'll give you the information you need.

After identifying your competition, *always* research them. The best source of competitive information I've found is the Internet. It still amazes me how much a competitor's Web site can teach me about them, their strategies, their key customers and sometimes even their employees! Research is important even if you think you know all about them. In today's technology world, your competitor can quickly reinvent themselves, their products and their strategies. Don't get lulled to sleep with confidence and old knowledge. Review competitive information before every demonstration.

Your prospect's market niche may determine your competitors. It may also vary depending on geography and what products you're trying to sell. Like most marketplaces, you probably have one or two primary competitors. Given the consolidation in the marketplace, you probably meet the same competitor repeatedly, often across different product lines. Some suggestions for profiling them:

- Don't focus solely on features of their products because those have a tendency to change quickly. Look at the financial health of the company, their revenue, number of employees, ability to deliver service, reference accounts and the sales representative you constantly compete against.

- In situations where *competitors* have acquired products, look at their reputation and track record at integrating and supporting acquired products. Understand the reputation and position of the product pre- and post-acquisition.

- Look at the industry and technical standards supported by the competitor. Evaluate the competitor's position toward standards in general and particular standards that they seem to focus on.

- Think in terms of positioning. Does your competitor compete on price, technology, services or software functionality?

- Create a separate competitor version of the Knowledge Index to store all this information. This will help you anticipate the "traps" your competitors will be setting for you. It will also help you set traps for them. Remember that a trap demonstrates the benefit of a feature in your product, service or company you know your competitor can't match. You've placed a perfect trap if your prospect demands one of your unique capabilities in all future software they evaluate.

Often, your prospect will ask, "Why are you better than your competitor?" If they ask you this question, you should be prepared with an "Elevator Pitch" which is a rehearsed answer for an anticipated question. You must deliver it in a minute or less. A competitive "what differentiates you" question is one you *must* anticipate. So, imagine you're traveling in an elevator with your prospect. You're on the first floor. They ask what differentiates you from your competitor. Then they press the button for the tenth floor. Before you get to the tenth floor, you need to give them a diplomatic, professional and concise answer. Avoid being emotional. Be matter-of-fact. This is your opportunity to be aggressive against your competition. Take advantage of it. Did they get a similar opportunity? You bet they did! This is a tremendous selling opportunity, but it won't present itself if you don't ask about your competition.

7) Audience - The personality of a organization typically follows that of its leadership. This is true with every organization I know. If the CEO or key executive is low-key, so is the organization. If the CEO or key executive is well organized, so is the organization. With this in mind, you generally want to establish the tone of your demonstration based on the personality of the organization's leader(s). You can anticipate the personality of key executives without ever meeting them through the interviews you conduct during your Discovery.

A sales colleague shared the following story that supports this idea. During his Discovery, he learned the CEO of the company was very religious. Offensive language, sexual connotations, and religious references were strictly forbidden in his company. Accordingly, this salesperson took no chances. He stressed with his demonstration teammates the need to be conscious of and sensitive to this information. His competition was not quite as careful. In the end, he won the business as much because of his sales team's professionalism as the merits of his software.

Obviously, executives won't be the only people in the audience. You should profile separately all the individuals scheduled to attend the demonstration. Again, the Attendee Checklist discussed above will assist you with this process. By profiling the audience, you'll assess their needs, desires and personalities. This will allow you to focus specific software benefits on individuals rather than a faceless, nameless audience.

8) Prospect's Operating and Technical Environment - Who are the prospect's best customers, suppliers, and partners? What are their key product lines or services? What is the nature of their current technical environment? Are they a "Linux shop" or a "java shop"? If you know specific examples of their data or architecture and are prepared to use them in your demonstration, you put your prospect on familiar territory. This simply makes it easier for them to concentrate. Because it's their data, they won't question its validity thus they will be free to concentrate on how your software can improve their business and technical operations. For example, let's say your prospect does all their shipping with UPS®. Don't show them shipping integration examples from Federal Express®. Chances are, the shipping method makes no difference to your software and the point you are trying to make. So why show the prospect an unfamiliar environment? Use something the prospect can relate to. This is one of the important aspects of the Bridge-Building concept that we'll discuss in Chapter 3, *Important Demonstration Concepts*.

9) Equipment – Do yourself and your prospect this favor: know how to operate the equipment you bring to your demonstration! It's extremely distracting to your audience when you can't get your laptop to connect to your projector, get your wireless connection to work, or use the fancy pointing device your brought! If your equipment does malfunction, keep a cool head and have a contingency plan. For example, if you normally demonstrate your software over the Internet, be prepared to show or simulate it on your laptop should you have problems with the connection. If you commonly demonstrate remotely over the web, remember that you have a responsibility to ensure the smooth operation of not just your equipment, but the prospect's as well. Today's corporate security and firewalls can wreak havoc on your ability to demonstrate over the web. Make sure the prospect knows what they will need to make your demonstration a success, and whenever possible, help them test the full environment before the demonstration.

10) Prospect's Processes and Workflows - I'll spend a great deal of time on process and workflow when we discuss the Discovery Process in Chapter 5. Process flows are one of the most important aspects of your demonstration. Learn the processes and workflows your prospect uses to perform their business and technical tasks today, without your software. Everybody has routines. They make our lives manageable. Get familiar with your prospect's routines. Then prepare, practice and demonstrate how they'll process-flow their jobs using your software without disrupting any of their routines (unless one of their objectives is to shake things up). Keep in mind that you need to understand both automated and human workflows as they currently exist. Many important process steps are "hidden" behind automated and integrated workflows. You certainly can't afford to miss one of these and have it come up as a question or objection during the presentation.

To illustrate this point of familiar routines, try this experiment. Assuming you wear a wristwatch, take it off and put it on your other wrist. Leave it on that wrist for several hours. After just a couple glances at the wrong wrist, you'll experience the frustration of having one of your routines disrupted! That's a simple example of a daily process flow (routine) and how important they are to us.

Now let's apply the same concept to a software demonstration. Assume you presenting accounting as part of your ERP software. Your prospect wants a new system with lots of checks and balances. Because their old software has none, they've lost thousands of dollars due to errors. Here's the kicker. Your software can be configured with all the checks and balances in what you call "automatic-post-mode." In automatic-post-mode, the software handles all the checks and balances behind the scenes. The user doesn't have to do a thing. All of your customers love automatic-post-mode. They've convinced you the old-fashioned checks and balances method is a waste of time. So, which method do you show them? Unless you want to be shown the door, show them what fits into their routine. It doesn't matter if you can show a whiz-bang feature. If your prospect can't visualize the process flow, they won't connect with you or your software.

Process flows are key to a successful demonstration. They're the *routines* of the business world. Ignore them and your demonstration will inevitably fail. Exploit them and your demonstration will soar.

11) Your Product's Strengths - It seems obvious you should know your software's strengths. The problem is many salespeople have trouble prioritizing them during a demonstration. Consider this scenario.

Most software today includes some sort of dashboard or graphical overview capability. For example, let's assume you're demonstrating the great new process dashboard in your Business Process Management (BPM) system. You want the customer to see the powerful capabilities that this graphical overview can provide. Your demonstration dialog goes something like this: "You can see here a number of indicators as to how our order processes are performing. Here we can see the number of orders in each stage of the process, including picking and shipping. Here we can see the number of backorders being created and the number being cleared over the last hour timeframe." So far, so good. But dashboards are very powerful and very configurable. So you continue. "If we right-click here and select 'Configure', we can change this from a dial gauge to a thermometer style. Great. Now let's change the information that we are monitoring to be in dollars, and margin as opposed to gross. And from there we can move the gauge to the upper left, then insert a drill-down box here showing the top ten orders at all times." You continue, "Once we have the drill down in place, we may want to go over to our backorder area and change both timeframes and refresh rates...." Thirty minutes later you conclude with "...so that's the BPM dashboard. As you can see it is a very powerful feature of our software."

What was a really powerful feature of the software? The demonstration began by showing how you could quickly see the status of your sales processes. This feature quickly mushroomed into a number of other *so-called* strengths. Are you trying to point out that your software is flexible? That may very well be a strength that is relevant to your prospect. If so, you'll definitely want to show it. Just finish your first strength (monitoring the processes) before you move on to the next (software flexibility).

Your Discovery will help you identify the strengths of your software that are important to your prospect. Because each prospect is unique, strengths will change from one demonstration to the next. Once you've listed the relevant features for this prospect, prioritize them and organize the demonstration accordingly. Just make sure to demonstrate strengths one at a time, focusing on process flow and benefits.

12) Your Product's Weaknesses– There are two types of product weaknesses. The first is the type your competitor will attempt to highlight. It may be product or service related. Perhaps they pick on you because you're small, or perhaps large and unresponsive. Maybe your training is complex when compared to theirs. Your product might not have a "bell" or "whistle" offered by the competitor. Whatever the weakness, you know them well, and you're tired of having them come up all the time. It aggravates you because the competition has managed to come up with a huge and convincing story about why no company should operate without this feature (that your software is missing). Unfortunately, they've figured out the perfect *trap* to set for you and they do it every time! If they've gained that type of advantage over your product, you need to bring it to the attention of your development department immediately. I can't tell you how many times I've been pounded by a competitor only to find out my development colleagues can give me a quick response in the form of an enhancement.

The second type of product weakness is one of fit within your prospect's business. Identify these during your Discovery. You have several options for addressing the situation.

- Prepare a work-around answer ahead of time and practice presenting it repeatedly. You want this alternative to look effortless and smooth. This isn't a sleight-of-hand trick. Rather, it's a realistic demonstration of how a company, once adept at the software, will solve this problem on a daily basis.

- If your company offers the option of modifying the software for a customer, either directly or through a partner channel, prepare a mock-up screen, report or other visual aide to show how it could work with the modification(s) in place.

- If you have a compelling argument against using the software in the way the prospect wants it to work, plan a discussion of the issue. Make it convincing, but not aggressive. Don't dig in if you meet resistance. Test the discussion ahead of time on the telephone. This is a very powerful technique for diffusing a weakness in your product and minimizing the amount of modification (always a good idea!) needed to satisfy the prospect's needs.

It's all right to admit your product has weaknesses. A sign of a successful demonstration is when a prospect is so excited during your conclusion they comment, "Your software is great and you do such a good job showing it. However, I have to believe it has some weaknesses. Can you please give me a couple of examples?" What a dream question! It opens up a great opportunity for you to gain additional credibility for your company, product and services. If you're lucky enough to get this question, turn it into a trap for your competitor. Be prepared with an Elevator Pitch. Here's an example of a well-prepared answer. "Weaknesses? Let me think for just a moment. Some people think our training is too comprehensive. However, whenever a product is very capable and sophisticated, extensive and thorough training (including the assurance of our back-up support) becomes a key to the successful use of the product." That so called weakness sounds pretty darn good to me!

You have weaknesses. In any given situation, all software does. Don't ignore them or constantly try to cover them up. Prepare a response and move on. A good Discovery will uncover your weaknesses (relative to each prospect) so they won't surprise you during the demonstration. By properly planning for your perceived weaknesses, you can minimize their impact. On occasion, you can even turn a weakness into strengths!

CHAPTER SUMMARY

Demonstrating software is not an art. No, a winning software demonstration is the right blend of preparation, knowledge, and technique. Know everything you can about your product, competition and prospect. You gain this knowledge with a thorough Discovery. You apply this knowledge with solid demonstrating techniques. Your journey into winning demonstrations has just begun.

C H A P T E R   3
Important Demonstration Tactics

 ## *BRIDGE-BUILDING*

The "Bridge-Building" concept is the most important funda-mental you can learn about demonstrating. This concept involves bridging the mental gap between how your prospect performs their job today and how they'll perform it with your software in the future.

Your prospects perform their job day-in and day-out using their existing methods, procedures and software (assuming the job is already automated). It's a habit they've formed over a great deal of time. Their existing methods have the power-ful force of *inertia* behind them. Webster's dictionary defines inertia as "…an object retains its state of rest or velocity along a straight line so long as it is not acted upon by an external force." In business speak, that means *change is hard*. Your prospect has an inner physical or mental force that says, "I don't want to change." In fact, my experience has taught me the only person who likes change is a two-year-old child with a dirty diaper, and even he needs to be coerced!

Unless this is your second time through the book, you're no doubt asking yourself, "How can this be? After all, my prospect sent out an RFP (request for proposal), assembled a selection team, hired a consultant, set a timeline for a decision and established a financial budget for a new system. Clearly this is someone who wants to experience change. Right?" *WRONG!*

Sure, prospects receiving your demonstration have a desire to improve their operations. But deep down, they don't want to change. Change is risky. It requires sacrifice, disruption and dedication. Why do you think 95 percent of the wealth in the world is controlled by only five percent of the people? One big reason is because 95 percent of us are averse to change. Now, you could get lucky and have one of the "five percent folks" in your demonstration, but the odds are against it.

In all likelihood, change is being *forced* on your prospect. They're probably facing some compelling or significant event. It's your job to identify this event, especially as it relates to the ultimate decision-maker. Compelling events come in many shapes and sizes. Some examples include:

- A change in ownership or management, including merger or acquisition activities.

- A change in financial condition (i.e. computer lease is expiring or support services have become unreasonable).

- Support for their software or has been discontinued or the underlying technology has become obsolete.

- Their existing software vendor is out of business or no longer supporting or enhancing a particular product line.

- A customer, vendor, or regulatory requirement that their existing system can't fulfill.

Think of a deep canyon. At the beginning of the demonstration your prospect is on one side of the canyon (with their software or solution). You're asking them to move to the other side (to your software). The prospect knows there's good reason to cross this canyon (compelling event). However, they're not very excited about it (fear of change).

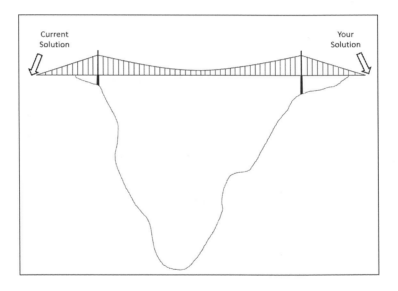

How are you going to get them across the canyon? You need a bridge, right? If you think the prospect will build a bridge them self, *you're fooling yourself*. After all, how many people are willing to be a construction worker on a bridge over a deep canyon? (Maybe five percent, right?) It's your job to build a Demonstration Bridge (or Bridge for short).

What do you use to construct your Bridge? You'll build it with knowledge and technique, specifically:

- A knowledge of your prospect and their needs.

- A knowledge of your software.

- The technique of demonstrating how your software will address and improve their process flow requirements.

To complicate matters, almost all prospects are afraid of heights. In spite of this fear, they insist on looking down. This will happen many times during your demonstration in the form of objections and points of clarification. You've no doubt heard the cries from the audience such as, "Wait a minute! Do you mean we're going to have to …?" or "Hold on a minute. Can you please go through that process again? I didn't quite get it the first time." You know what your prospect is really doing? They're telling you they're scared. What are you going to do about it? Just like helping somebody with a fear of heights across a bridge over a deep canyon, you're going to take them by the hand and *lead them* across. You need to help them close their eyes and *visualize* being on the other side of the Bridge (using your software). They'll be hesitant at first (beginning of your demo or presentation), but if they trust you (you've built credibility), they'll follow you across the Bridge to your software. In fact, if you do a really good job on the first half of the Bridge, some of your demonstration audience, but probably not all, will let go of your hand and walk the rest of the way on their own. If that happens, feel good about yourself. You'll have developed into a highly skilled Demonstration Bridge builder!

My first major defeat as a salesperson was with a chainsaw distributor in North Carolina. At the outset, we were sure to win the business. My company had the experience of successfully installing another well-respected chainsaw distributor in Florida. The distributor in Florida was a close personal friend of our prospect in North Carolina. I swooped into North Carolina knowing I would *knock their socks off* with our software. For the next two days, my teammate and I showed them every feature and function in our software. After the demonstration was finished, we were told they preferred an older product sold and supported by a local competitor because "they seem to understand our business better." What went wrong? I had dumped all of my high quality bridge pieces in front of my prospect and assumed they would know how to put it together. My much smarter and more experienced competitor had inferior materials to work with, but actually built the Bridge for the prospect so it was easy for them to walk across. Most demonstrations focus on features and functions and ultimately become a training session. This style of demonstrating is totally ineffective. You're asking your prospect to both change and take all the risk. Don't do this to your prospect. Don't ask them to build the Bridge to your software by themselves. Remove the risk of change by taking them on a knowledge (not a feature) journey. Fearlessly build and lead them across the Bridge.

Ask yourself this simple question: "Have I ever lost a deal to an inferior product?" If your answer is yes, I'll guarantee that one of the prime reasons for your defeat was because your competitor was a more effective Bridge-Demonstrator.

THE TELL-SHOW-TELL TECHNIQUE

I'd like to thank Michael Bloomfield, a software consultant from New York, for first bringing this technique to my attention.The concept is simple. It's the ability to *tell* the prospect what they're about to see, *show* them what you just told them they'd see and finally, *tell* them what they just saw. Though this may seem like a very simple concept, it is one of the most difficult to practice in a demonstration. Many of the demonstration mistakes discussed in Chapter 4, *The Demo Crime Files,* are caused by not following this simple technique. Anyway, Michael helped me realize that this is much more than a demonstration technique. It's an important life skill. He pointed out that it's the same method employed by the producers of Sesame Street™, the popular children's television show. If you've ever watched this show, you know they teach a lesson every day through repetition and reinforcement. For example, how do they teach children the letter "C?" They start by introducing the letter "C" as the topic the kids will be learning that day (tell). Then they sing songs about the letter "C"; "…C is for cookie that's good enough for me, cookie, cookie, cookie, starts with C" (show). They finish the lesson with a summary of the letter "C" (tell).

OK, let's apply this technique to a software demonstration situation. "Bill, at this point I'm going to show you how quickly service reps can access customer information. When a call comes in, the customer's name and number appear automatically. When the service rep accepts the call, all of the customer's information, including a call history, automatically displays on-screen. We simply have to accept the call (tell). *You now demo the software accepting the call and displaying the information* (show). Did you see that? It still amazes me how fast and easy it is to get the information. Just think about how much faster it it will be for your service people and how pleased customers will be with not having to constantly repeat information (tell)."

Notice how it's simple and to the point. You demonstrated a single feature of your software and combined it with a single benefit for the prospect. This technique makes it easier for the prospect to absorb your feature along with its corresponding benefit. Prospects want to learn all about the great features of your software, but not all at once. If your demonstration flow is well organized and logical, you'll have ample opportunity to use this same technique on many other features of your software. Unfortunately, what happens far too often during a demonstration is a demonstrator wanders off into tangents after the first "tell." They never get to the point (show) or deliver the benefit (second "tell"). This frustrates the prospect. It prompts numerous questions and objections that lead to confusion about the basic workflow of the software. By not using this technique, the software appears disorganized and difficult to use.

Here's how the same demonstration dialogue might sound when the Tell-Show-Tell technique is *not* used: "Bill, at this point (menu is pulled down, selections are made, screen changes three times) I'm going to show you how customer information displays automatically for an incoming call. *You now simulate receiving the call.* Bill, if the system doesn't recognize the number for the customer, you can always look it up manually. (Screen changes again). In fact, there are many ways to look up a customer (Lookup window appears). It might be by name, or postal code, or a product serial number. Additionally, if you can't find the customer, you can always add them to the system by opening this 'New Customer' window. (New Customer screen is selected.) From there you can collect their information as well as the product information they are calling about. Can you see how the automated call recognition can be helpful? By now Bill is thinking about a number of problems with your software. He's wondering:

- Why is it so complicated to take a service call?

- How many customers will be frustrated by service reps bouncing around screen to screen?

- Is it a good idea that anybody and everybody can just add customers whenever they want? Won't that cause problems later?

- Maybe this automated answering system isn't all that reliable. Otherwise, why make a big deal out of how to go around it?

- The list of problems is endless!

The more technical and detailed your presentation, the more critical the Tell-Show-Tell technique becomes. Take the example of "demonstrating" something like an advanced integration system – an Enterprise Service Bus (ESB). This is a complete departure from a process based software solution. The most you can demonstrate is the *effect* of the software, not the operation of it. More likely, you won't demonstrate anything, you will use a technical presentation to talk about the operations and capabilities of the product. So if you just start right into the detail, you will quickly confuse and lose your audience. If you use the Tell-Show-Tell technique you can easily break down the presentation into small segments that help your audience fully grasp the importance and the benefit of everything you are presenting.

Simplify and clarify your demonstration by using the Tell-Show-Tell technique. Prospects will get a better understanding of the powerful features and benefits of your software and you'll drastically reduce objections and problems during the demonstration. If it's good enough for Big Bird™, it's good enough for you and me!

ENGAGING ~~Business Discussion~~

There's nothing more discouraging than starting a demonstration at 8:30 a.m. and by 10:30, no one in your audience has uttered a word. When this happens, you're in trouble. I'll be the first to admit some prospects are just quiet or ultra serious, and audience expectations vary by country and culture. In these situations, probably more than any other, it's critical to engage your audience during the demonstration. But whatever you do, don't make the mistake of challenging your audience with comments like, "Boy, are you all quiet!" Keep in mind, it's not *their* problem they're quiet…it's *yours*.

Engaging is a technique that gets your prospect integrated and involved in the demonstration or presentation. It's important because most individuals retain a very small percent (usually less than 20 percent) of what they simply hear in a demonstration. That should alarm you! In order to increase retention, you need them *actively listening*. That happens when they're asking (and answering) questions, making comments and participating in discussions. When your audience is doing this, retention levels increase dramatically. Here's another benefit: by engaging in the demonstration, your prospect will begin to assume some ownership of the information being presented.

One of my sales colleagues, Rusty Bond, is the best I've ever seen at engaging an audience. He addresses each individual attendee by their name, no matter how many people are in the room. Rusty knows people love to hear their name and it makes them perk up when you call them out. He also takes advantage of his southern heritage (Rusty was born and raised in Moss Point, Mississippi), using southern colloquialisms throughout his demonstration. One of Rusty's most powerful "engaging" techniques happens when he demonstrates taking a sales order over the telephone. Here's how it goes. "Y'all need to pay attention to this next section of the demonstration. I'm gonna show you how I can take an order over the telephone. Then, at the end of this session, I'm gonna ask you a few questions." A test? Is he crazy? Without fail, the prospects sit forward as he starts the demonstration. Why? They hope he'll trip up! They want to see him crash. (Sounds like a stock car race!) Some interrupt him during the demonstration, but Rusty politely says something like, "Now y'all can't stop me in the middle of this or I'll really mess up. Seriously, I'll cover all your questions and then-some when I'm done." You see, Rusty knows in order for the audience to cross the Bridge with him, they need to see the process flow without interruptions. Sometimes the same person will insist on interrupting again, so Rusty politely fends off the question a second time. Quite often, the rest of the people in the room tell the individual interrupting to shut up until poor Rusty finishes! In the end, Rusty asks them some questions. "Did anyone see what I did that improves customer service?" Almost every time, someone wants to "take the test." But if nobody jumps in, Rusty simply provides the answer and moves on to the next question. "Ok, did anyone see how I was able to answer a question for the customer while I had them on the telephone?" Pretty soon, the whole group is participating in some form or fashion. It's impressive (and fun) to see how they *engage* in Rusty's demonstration. You may think this sounds staged and corny. Believe me, Rusty felt the same way the first couple of times he used this technique. But the prospects love it!

A technique I like to use for engaging the audience involves taking their *temperature*. This technique means learning how they feel about the software *at various points in time*. After demonstrating a process or feature, I ask an individual (by name) if she can see how this feature will benefit her. To keep from becoming redundant, I ask these temperature questions in many forms. Some other examples include, "Karen, does this make sense to you?" or "Karen, can you see how your people will use this to save time?" In addition to engaging the audience, these questions help me gauge how my demonstration is going.

Another technique for engaging your audience is to introduce topics that aggravate them today. Typically, you learned about these during your Discovery. What you want to do is discuss them a bit before you demonstrate your solution to the problem. Pour a little gas on the fire before you put it out! "Karen, you explained that you have trouble entering orders over the telephone when some of the products the customer needs aren't in stock. You don't really have a quick way of entering that information. Is this correct?" Karen replies, "That's right. It's driven me crazy as long as I've been here!" Although it may not sound engaging, Karen is now paying attention. She also knows, as does everybody else in the room, you listened to her during the Discovery. You're on the road to establishing credibility and trust. But you don't need to limit this technique to those presentations where you have a full Discovery. You know the problems prospects typically have and you know the aggravation they cause. Use this to your advantage. Ask specific people in the audience about these areas. Best case, you get them engaged in your solution. Worst case, you discover which problems will resonate with the audience and which will not.

Prizes are another excellent way to engage the audience and have fun at the same time. For example, I like to use rubber sponge balls with a corporate logo printed on them. Whenever someone asks a good question, answers an objection for me or provides a suggestion, I toss them a sponge ball. I make sure by the end of the demonstration everyone in the room has a sponge ball!

Finally, one of the simplest but best ways to engage the prospect is to *relate* to them. Whenever possible during your demonstration, incorporate examples from *their* world. In order of preference, I like to use examples from the prospect's:

- Business.

- Colleagues in their industry they know and respect.

- Industry in general.

- Computing world.

I will often get questions about engaging audiences in a web demo. Too often, presenters assume that web demos cannot be engaging, so they don't even try. They just plow through the material, assuming that the invisible audience out there is still paying attention. *Wrong!* If anything, you need to be *more* engaging when you cannot see your audience. Almost all of the techniques that work with a live audience also work with a remote audience. Sure, you can't throw sponge balls at them, but you can ask questions of them, you can relate to them through stories and industry references, and you can reflect back to them what you learned through Discovery and how it applies to the demonstration. And you can *always* use the Tell-Show-Tell technique to break up the monotony of just going screen to screen to screen.

After I wrote the first edition of "Demonstrating To WIN!" I read an article that advocated showing the most exciting areas of your software first. In many cases, I completely agree. If you have the executive decision maker and her supporting cast in the room at the beginning of your demo, don't make them wait to see the most compelling part of your software. Show it right away. However, make sure you don't commit the "I love this part of my software" crime (see Chapter 4) and make sure it leads them across the bridge. If that demonstration sequence goes well and your software or your prospect's needs have some degree of complexity, you'll have more work to do. It is now that your demonstration fundamentals become particularly important. As you progress through this book, it will become apparent as to why it takes more than effectively showing a few exciting features of software to win the demonstration. But then again, you intuitively know that don't you?

Engaging an audience increases their retention levels. It keeps them from turning to stone during your demonstration or turning to their e-mail during a web presentation. An audience that is engaged will feel as if they're part of the solution you're offering. They won't be bored, and they may actually start rooting for you! Put most simply, engaging your audience will help them cross your Demonstration Bridge.

TRUST

Imagine if your demonstration went something like this:
- At the beginning, you get questions like, "Bob, how do I enter a sales order with notes attached to it? Can you show me, please?"

- You answer the question by showing him that you can enter notes on any business document and that, even though it would probably never be necessary, you can actually add *1,000 pages* of notes per document.

- The questions keep coming, but they soften in tone. You have to write a couple down to research later, but for the most part, you answer them in the context of the prospect's business.

- After a couple hours, you respond to a question with, "Would you like me to show it to you?"

- Rather than wanting to see anything, your prospect says, "No, we believe you. Go ahead and move on."

Congratulations. You have gained their trust! The best way to build trust is by establishing credibility. This is best done through knowledge of their business, knowledge of your software, confidence, customer references and, most important, your ability to build a Demonstration Bridge. When you combine these aspects into a demonstration, you simply can't be touched by your competition.

Here's another way you can gauge if you have the trust of your audience. Observe what happens when someone new enters the room. For example, let's say a new person comes into the above demonstration at the point you transition from sales orders to purchase orders. After a few minutes, this new person asks if notes can be entered on a purchase order (same basic question as was asked above). Two things can happen. First, you might be expected to answer the question again. If that's the case, you haven't yet earned the audience's respect. Or, somebody could jump in and say, "They sure can post notes. In fact, the note can be 1,000 pages long!" When you get a comment like this, you've gained their trust. It should also be comforting to know they're retaining the material!

CONFIDENCE

If they're going to cross the Bridge, your prospect needs to have confidence in you. Nothing builds confidence more than the way you address their questions. Notice I said *address*, not answer. Don't confuse confidence with pure knowledge. Sure, prospects want all their questions answered on the spot. That's human nature. Plus, they've invested their valuable time in your demonstration and they want their time to be used well. Obviously, clear, concise answers to their questions will provide value and efficiency. If your knowledge is impressive, they'll be impressed. However, unless your software is extremely simple or you've been working with it for years, you can't expect to answer every question in every demo. Thus the importance of addressing questions in a manner that instills confidence, even when you don't know the answer.

Since it's a difficult situation, let's look at when your prospect asks a question and you *can't* provide an immediate answer. Here's what I do. I pause, think for a moment and then respond honestly with, "I'm really not sure. I have a suspicion I know, but I'd prefer to provide you with a precise answer. Would it be ok if I write that one down and follow-up with you in a day or two? Now, to make sure I've got it right, let me repeat the question."

Let's examine what took place in that exchange.
- I took some time (five seconds or so) to think about the question. This shows the prospect I was really listening to the question.

- I openly admitted I was *not* confident of an answer and, therefore, didn't want to guess. Honesty is truly a virtuous character quality. They will respect you for telling them the truth.

- I wrote down the question for further research. If you want to shatter their confidence in you, don't write it down. It galls me when a demonstrator says they'll check into something and never writes anything down. When you don't know the answer, writing it down shows you're thorough, thoughtful and conscientious.

- I *reflected* their question back to them by repeating it. They will be able to mentally "move on" if they're sure you know what they need. Plus, the last thing you want to do is waste your valuable time researching the wrong question. Make sure you've got it right.

Now, let's assume you do know the answer to their question. If you know the answer, give it to them. Product knowledge is king. However, should you just launch into it, full speed ahead? No. The most effective thing you can do is pause. Spend a moment thinking about each question before you deliver your answer. Here's why:

- The pause establishes cadence with your prospect.

- As you proceed through the demonstration, they'll know you'll give them a well thought-out answer whenever a question is asked. This will encourage them to ask more questions, which is always a good thing. (Remember our discussion above about *engaging* the audience).

- When tougher questions come along, it won't seem as awkward when you take more time to formulate and deliver your answer.

- Pausing *forces* you to allow them to finish their question. You'll avoid the "Cutting Off a Question" demo crime (Chapter 4).

- It gives you an opportunity to organize your response. Do you have all the information you need to answer the question? If not, your response should begin with another question.

A key factor in establishing trust is the confidence your prospect has in you. Keep this in mind when you respond to their questions. How you address them, whether with or without an answer, is one of your most important confidence-building activities during a demonstration. It ranks right next to product knowledge itself.

THEME DEMONSTRATING

Every demonstration or presentation, no matter how short or long, needs a theme. Why? Prospects like organization, form and structure. When they're about to cross the Bridge with you during your presentation, it's helpful to take their minds off the fact that they're afraid of heights. A theme is an excellent way to accomplish this.

Whenever possible, you want to come up with a unique theme for each prospect demonstration. However, if you're having trouble coming up with something unique, ask your colleagues what worked for them. Many of our clients have created a repository of workshop themes on their internal portal. During our global travels, we have worked with organizations that require the use of standard marketing messages and presentation decks. If that's the case with your company, you can use those messages as a backdrop to your own creative the

Your entire demonstration should wrap around your theme. Here are a couple suggestions:

- Introduce it when you open the demonstration. Even if it is only a 30 minute web demo, always open with a theme.

- Lace your theme into as many aspects of your initial presentation as possible.

- Tie the value (the benefits) of what you are showing back to that theme, helping to reinforce it.

- A theme should differentiate you from your competition, thus becoming a competitive advantage.

- Don't pick a theme you can't build a story around.

- Pick a theme you're personally passionate about.

For example, assume that you are selling a software product for Business Intelligence (BI) and you have selected the theme "Better Information for Better Decisions". Craft an opening that gives an example of how better information did, or would have, led to a better decision. The example might be from another customer or might not be from the software industry at all. History is full of examples where decisions would have been different if information was more complete or better known. Then, when you are presenting the capabilities of your software, continue to emphasize the improvements in information availability and visibility. In each case, ⁓ie this to the impact that this information would have on ⁓aking for your prospect. At the end of the day, ˈˌck to the theme and make sure that your ⸴ how better access to *their* information decisions in *their* organization. Bring it to completion by ensuring that the prospect sees the impact of those improved decisions.

The proper theme needs to be applied to the proper prospect. For example, if you learn in Discovery or from your sales lead that your prospect has a relaxed atmosphere, you can be more creative with your theme than if your prospect is very conservative.

I remember a demo in Munich, Germany where the client's sales lead (a German) told his pre-sales professional (an American) that he should be very conservative with his prospect. The sales lead insisted that the theme be simple, quick and neutral in terms of emotion. His pre-sales resource insisted on using props and drama to illustrate the pain of the prospect. He had learned to always do that in a demo skills workshop (not ours). The pre-sales person won the argument and produced a dramatic skit that illustrated the pain in this prospect's existing supply chain. Needless to say it went over like the Hindenburg's last flight. If the team had stayed with a conservative, short theme, the outcome would have been positive as the software was an excellent fit.

A theme is a powerful tool that wraps around your entire demonstration. If constructed correctly and applied appropriately, it will help your prospect to remember, understand, know and respect both you and your company.

EFFECTIVE TIME UTILIZATION

The key to time management during a demonstration is control. If you want your prospect to cross the Bridge, you need to manage the timing and content of the information delivered in the demo. Assuming you've performed a Discovery, you know what they want and need to see. So take control. Show it to them.

Unfortunately, many demonstrations become a tug-of-war over who has control of the presentation, you or the prospect. A clear indication you're losing control is when your prospect becomes frustrated and starts asking you lots of questions, taking you in too many directions. But don't simply relinquish it to them. That's not what they want (though they probably don't know it). They're simply *starving* for information, and you're not providing it to them fast enough or in a form they can relate to.

Here's an illustration. Assume for the moment you're extremely hungry and you love cheeseburgers. You go to a local restaurant and order a giant cheeseburger and savor it. The next day you go back to the same restaurant for another cheeseburger. The same thing happens a third day, forth, fifth…the feast continues for two weeks. Are you tired of cheeseburgers yet? You bet! Here's the point: satisfying hunger isn't always a matter of simply eating your favorite food. It's also about variety. In a demonstration, you have control over the menu. The Discovery is key. It reveals the information you'll need to maintain control. If you find out they like steak, don't put vegetarian selections on the menu, even if you're a fantastic vegetarian cook! Mix it up a bit. Keep the menu interesting by giving them some steak soup as an appetizer to the T-bone you'll be serving for the main course.

If you cannot, for some reason, perform a proper Discovery and find yourself being pummeled with unanticipated questions during a demonstration, you have to put the brakes on and regain control. How? Turn the tables and start *asking* questions. In other words, make the Discovery part of the presentation. Ask the prospect to help you list on a flipchart all the things they want to make sure your software will do during the demonstration. Once you've finished, tell them when you'll be covering each item and note that on the flipchart as well. Leave the flipchart in plain view during the demonstration. This will serve as a reminder to your prospect that you won't skip these items.

The agenda is a time management tool that can be used either to your advantage or disadvantage. You rarely use the agenda recommended by the prospect. Naturally, it's important to develop your agenda around the prospect's desires, but you'll also want to work in *your* key points. Therefore, you will likely need to negotiate an agenda that meets both of your needs. The final agenda will be based upon your Discovery, but should also include key selling features and issues that differentiate you from your competitors. If your prospect provides you an agenda that perfectly fits your goals for the demonstration, buy a lottery ticket on the way to their office. It means your prospect wants to see exactly what you want to show them. If they know that much about your software, company and services, they need a contract, not a presentation!

If you're dealing with a rigid consultant, a highly structured selection team or a tightly scripted demonstration, I'd recommend adhering to the prospect's agenda. By not following their agenda you may risk offending them. Even so, bring your own private agenda that quietly inserts your key points in strategic places within their agenda. They're happy, but you still make your points!

If your demonstration is longer than 90 minutes, you will need to plan on breaks. Breaks can disrupt your demonstration flow, and subsequently your control. They are a dilemma. The challenge is that by taking breaks you run the risk of your audience leaving you (physically or mentally) for an extended period of time. Once people take a break and get on their mobile phone or start checking their e-mail, you can count on them being gone for at least 20 minutes. That's why I recommend taking breaks of 15 minutes or less; long enough for biological relief but too short for serious telephone time. Another trick for maintaining control of breaks is to demonstrate a really exciting feature both before and after the break. Select features that solve a pain-point your prospect identified during the Discovery.

- Preceding a break with a key Bridge-Building feature helps you influence the break time by giving your prospect something to talk about during the break. You want to hear this type of conversation during the break: "You want me to grab you something to drink? Man, wasn't that great how they could just answer the telephone and all of the customer information and history was instantly available."

- Launching into a key feature after a break should provide you some control over the length of the break. That's especially true if you baited them with this information just before the break began. Imagine your prospect checking their watch and saying, "Hey, let's get back in there. I want to make sure to see the automated desktop integration capabilities. We spend way too much time re-entering information today."

Time management is a matter of control. The control of the demonstration is yours to win or lose. A thorough Discovery is one key to maintaining control. Your ability to address questions will signal how well you're doing. Proper handling of the agenda and breaks is another key to managing your message and your audience. Both you and your prospects will feel better if you maintain control throughout the demonstration.

CHAPTER SUMMARY

When you started this chapter, you were probably looking for a suggestion or two for improving your demonstrating skills. In golfer's terms, you were only looking to remove the slight fade from your shot. What I may have told you is your grip's wrong, your knees aren't bent, your back swing is too quick and your weight-shift is off! Don't worry. In the remainder of this book, we'll focus on one demonstration skill at a time, much like a good golf pro works on one element of your golf swing at a time.

CHAPTER 4
The Demo Crime Files!

Please forgive me. I'm normally optimistic and maintain a positive outlook. This chapter, however, is devoted to the negative aspects of demonstrations and sales presentations. It's important to point out the common "crimes" made in demonstrations because most people don't recognize them.

Just like in real life, some crimes are minor offenses while others carry the death penalty. I'm not suggesting *any* demo crime is acceptable. Crimes aren't acceptable in society, nor should they be when presenting or demonstrating software. However, unlike in society, there are no pre-established right and wrong demonstration crimes.

Don't be intimidated by the number of times you catch yourself committing demonstration crimes. They can be corrected with just a small dose of preparation, focus and practice. So, go easy on yourself. Most software professionals (myself included) have committed every one of these crimes and never even realized it. That is, until now!

I used to end my demonstrations by asking my audience, "How do you think it went today?" Early in my career, they'd typically respond, "You did a good job in describing what your software does." For years, I thought they were giving me a compliment. In some ways they were. After all, I taught them a great deal about my software. They understood how it worked. However, when I found out a few weeks later that I didn't even make the short list of finalists, I was always stunned. When I'd ask why, a typical reply went something like, "Well, no specific reason. We liked you and your company. Your product was good but the other products just seemed to fit us better." This is hardly a satisfying answer! Where do you begin to improve your product, services, company or approach based upon a politically safe comment like that?

Can you relate to this story? If you can, your prospect is telling you that you're a good teacher, but someone else made a connection. Your competitor got them excited. They helped them cross the Bridge to their system. Your software was in standard definition while your competitor's was in HD! But be aware that most prospects won't point out your crimes. You have to be lucky enough to have a prospect like Al Jones. Al was a prospect of mine in Atlanta, Georgia. His company was on a system search, and he knew the potential our software offered compared to my competitors. Unfortunately, my competitor won the demonstration. Al was kind enough to point out to me why I almost lost the sale. I've never forgotten the lesson. Here's what he told me. "Bob, you have a much better product than your competitor, and I think it would serve us much better. However, the users think the competitor is amazing because he really understands our business. He provided specific solutions to our everyday struggles." Al went on to give me an example of a situation my competitor used in a demonstration. They asked the users, "Have you ever cut a 12 foot copper pipe and wondered what you were going to do with the remnant? Well, with our product you simply…" Al explained, "Bob, you guys are demonstrating widgets and ABC companies, while the competition is talking in our lingo. The users simply can't relate to your software." Of course! That was a turning point for me. From that moment on, I've always focused on bringing each prospect's business, products and situations into my demonstrations!

The crimes in this chapter are all examples of things that we do that hampers that Bridge crossing that we are looking for. Don't be concerned with how many times you can relate to the crimes in this chapter. Highlight your problem areas and focus on correcting them one at a time. To make it a little easier, I've grouped the crimes by type.

GROUP #1 – FEATURING CRIMES

This is the collection of crimes that are most common in demonstrations. We learn the software feature by feature, so we tend to present the software feature by feature! These crimes tend to overwhelm or confuse the prospect, affecting both the confidence and the motivation for them to start the journey across that Bridge.

THE FIELD BY FIELDER

The teacher in us wants our prospects to learn all there is to know about our software. After all, the more they know, the more they'll like you and your product. Right? Demonstrating static information files, configuration options, and administration settings is about as exciting as watching your email synchronize. Imagine the following demonstration of a hospital information system. "This is our patient demographics file. By simply entering a number in the patient number field, which by the way is 18 characters long, you can set up a new patient. From here we enter the patient's name. The patient name field is 48 characters. That should be plenty big enough to handle even your biggest patient names. There are multiple address fields that should help with those lengthy addresses." Blah, blah, blah.

"But wait a minute," you say, "if my prospect doesn't know where their demographic files are located in the system and with what those files contain, how can they possibly understand how the rest of the system works?" Simple. Most people assume you store basic information and have basic administration capabilities, just as they have in their current solutions. Demonstrating or explaining such capabilities does nothing to help your prospect. What will help them is an understanding of how they'll use the system on a day-to-day basis and how streamlining existing tasks will help them get their jobs done. They want to understand how software features *they can relate to* can add to their company's bottom line. They want to hear how you can solve some of the problems and aggravations they face today. They want to know if you can take them forward. They don't want to hear about file maintenance and administrative capabilities!

There are two common causes behind the "Field by Fielder" crime. The first is simply a lack of comfort. The act of reading screens (or slides) is a very common error when you feel uncomfortable with your material. You may be thinking, "How much trouble can you get into when you're discussing the fields in the master files or administrative settings?" The truth is, plenty! Not only will you put your prospects to sleep, but you also run the risk of hitting a roadblock that's impossible to overcome. For example, what if your patient name field is limited to 40 characters as compared to their existing name field of 50 characters, and they think they need all 50? How do you dig out of that hole? What if you can't find, or worse, don't have that key setting that they think they need? How will you answer the question? The second common cause behind the crime is demonstrating without a plan. Your goal is to show prospects how the software will benefit them by smoothing process flows, automating manual processes, reducing the possibility of errors. If you have no plan as to how to show this, it becomes easy to fall back to a field by field method of demonstrating or presenting.

If I'm unfamiliar with my software or presentation, I still catch myself reading screens. Even after 20 years of demonstrating. I'm like an insecure child clinging to his stuffed animal. When you're on new or uncomfortable turf with no definitive demonstration plan, it's easy to explain fields instead of showing process advantages and software flow. A lack of knowledge, whether industry, software, prospect or process flow related, is typically the major reason demonstrators commit the "Field by Fielder" crime. Other times, it's just a bad habit.

DATA DUMP

Have you ever caught yourself rambling from one software feature to another? When you do this you're performing a "data dump" on your prospect. You know the situation. You start out showing someone a particular software feature, and it quickly manifests itself into six related but different features. By the time you finish (fifteen minutes later), you look at your bewildered prospects and they have no idea what you were just attempting to demonstrate. You just committed the "Data Dump" crime.

Assume for the moment that you're selling a nurse's information system. The primary purpose of your software package is to allow nurses to enter products and services they have provided to a patient in the hospital. You're about to demonstrate a feature in your software that allows you to scan the patient's chart in order to begin the process of entering the products used for billing purposes. You start by saying, "At this point, I'm going to show you how you can walk up to a patient's bed and accurately and efficiently enter materials against her bill. What I can do is pick up the patient's chart and scan their ID number. I could also scan the ID number from a wristband. If I need to, I can enter their numbers on the keypad or find them by name. In fact, from this same hand-held unit, you can find any patient in any bed across the entire hospital chain! Anyway, now that I've entered the correct patient into the system I can begin entering the materials against their hospital bill. If the patient is still in the room, I enter the products by scanning them. However, if I get interrupted during the process, I can stop what I'm doing and begin entering nurses' time cards if I need to." At this point, the prospect stops you and says, "Wait a minute, I would never allow a nurse to enter time cards for other nurses. Why in the world would you let them do that?" You now begin playing defense, and 20 minutes later the prospect has no idea what you set out to demonstrate to them!

Data dumping has a number of causes. First, as demonstrators, we feel compelled to show anything and everything our software can do *right now* because:

- This is our one and only chance to impress this prospect with our software.

- Our prospect might interrupt and ask us to explain the software more thoroughly.

- Our competitor has all these features so we better explain we have them as well.

- The prospect might not be impressed with the feature we set out to demonstrate, so we feel compelled to reach further and show more.

- Our software is designed to be very flexible with a capability to go anywhere and do anything at any time. We want to make sure the prospect sees that flexibility.

Second, data dumping comes from a lack of proper preparation. If you don't know what is or is not important to your audience, how can you possibly focus your demonstration on their primary needs? This is one reason why some form of Discovery must be done prior to each demonstration.

Third, data dumping can be a byproduct of sheer excitement. You're so excited about the depth of features in your software you discuss each one of them at every possible opportunity. Your knowledge of the software isn't in question. Your prospect knows you understand the functionality of your software. They simply can't digest it all.

Finally, data dumping is caused by not following a feature with a benefit. Remember our Tell-Show-Tell technique?

Data dumping is actually becoming more common. Software designs have changed to actually promote this behavior. Advanced interface methods make it easy for you to go from any one feature or capability to any other with just a click of the mouse! That is great for the user, but it is just plain confusing in a demonstration. It confuses the prospect and stops them from crossing the Bridge during your demonstration. We've all been there, haven't we? Once your prospect responds to one of your extra features with, "Wait a minute, we would never want to do that," you'll waste valuable time playing defense.

It's counter-productive to data dump on your prospects. Set out to show a feature of your software and demonstrate *only that feature*. You spent hours preparing for a reason. Stick with your original plan.

WOULD YOU PLEASE JUST FINISH THAT THOUGHT?

Want to know something that's even worse than data dumping? How about when you start to show a feature, but start jumping to completely different places in the software in a stream of your own consciousness? If you're data dumping, at least you're presenting in one logical area of the software. Contrast that with the rambling and meandering that occurs when you don't even finish a thought.

This crime is driven by a fear that you won't have another opportunity to show them other important features later on in the demonstration or presentation. You may be baited into committing this crime because you think they'll surely under-stand the benefits of the breadth of your software. This is no way to showcase your software. People can't relate to this kind of meandering thought. They need concise thoughts, benefits and closure.

For example, assume you're demonstrating an order-entry system to Chris who is the telephone sales manager for an auto parts retailer. Chris's company has many locations across the country. His telephone salespeople usually sell parts from local stock but they can also sell from other locations. On occa-sion they'll even authorize one of their suppliers to ship parts directly from the manufacturing facility to their customer.

You want to support these needs by demonstrating the flexibility in your order-entry software. The dialogue might go something like this, "OK, Chris, I'm going to show you all the different ways you can fulfill a customer's request for a new water pump over the telephone. As I request the item from my inventory, *which by the way,* I can find via a part number, a manufacturer ID number, his part number or all or part of the description. *Anyway*, I find the item he wants and check my local inventory for the item. I don't have it in my local inventory. I know this because the system gives me this warning message, and if I look on the screen I see I have none available. If I have the item in stock, I can also see on the screen his price for the water pump, *which by the way,* is determined by a price matrix. Our price matrix is really powerful..."

45 minutes later, Chris finally learns how to source his water pump! What do you want to bet Chris had just a few unrelated questions along the way? Plus, he's got to be thinking, "Man, this order-entry system is really complicated!"

You set out to show Chris how he can source a water pump from either local stock, another location or direct from the factory. Demonstrate that *and only that.* Do not under any circumstance meander to other subjects. If Chris asks you the question, "Bob, how did the system determine the price for the water pump for this customer?" delay the answer with a response like, "Chris that's a good question and one I'll be covering in great detail a little bit later, if that's OK with you." Nine times out of ten they'll say, "No problem, as long as you're covering it later."

Current software designs make it too easy to slip into this crime. All software, business and technical, has moved to designs that promote flexibility in configuration and use. It's easy to jump from one point to another in the software and there can be any number of ways to accomplish a single task. That flexibility is great for the user, but can be *very* distracting during a presentation. Avoid the trap of meandering through the software. Create a plan for your demonstration or presentation and stick to it. Give the prospect a clear picture of how they'll use the software and how they'll benefit from the software.

Some key phrases will warn you that you're about to begin meandering:

- Which by the way...

- In addition to…

- Oh by the way…

- We also can…

- I forgot to mention…

- Another feature we offer is…

- Not only can we…

If you find yourself using one of these phrases, catch yourself and *STOP*! If you have trouble recognizing when you do this, ask a teammate to flash you a non-verbal signal when you start committing the crime.

Think of each capability in your demonstration or presentation as a complete thought. Concentrate on demonstrating them from beginning to end. Stick with your flow as you present a piece of functionality. Failure to do so will frequently result in taking one step forward across the Bridge and three steps back.

I LOVE THIS PART OF OUR SOFTWARE

Pretend for a moment you sell a very powerful general ledger system for small to medium sized corporations. One of the most powerful features of your general ledger system is the ability to produce sophisticated budgets. You know ahead of time none of your competitors have anywhere near your budgeting capabilities. In fact, you happen to know firsthand that this feature is usually what earns you an order when the dust settles and the smoke clears. You also know your prospect, a computer networking company, doesn't currently produce budgets nor do they plan to in the future. You've just finished a demonstration of your general ledger system and Bill, the CFO, was thoroughly impressed with your system. You have 15 minutes of allotted time remaining. You can summarize the demonstration and attempt to close the order or you can show your budgeting capabilities. You decide now is the time to bring in your big guns. "Bill," you begin, "one of the things *I love about our software* is the ability to produce, manipulate, report and graph budgets. Many of our customers think this is *the* feature that makes our software better than all the others!" Of course, Bill is thinking, "Really? Well, you idiot, we don't budget at this company and never will, and you're beginning to annoy me." After five minutes Bill reminds you once again they don't budget. "Bill, I understand you don't budget today, but if you ever decide to start, we have an awesome system for budgeting. Let me show you some more." You proceed to show him the graphs and comparison reports. You think you're on a roll. Of course, Bill is fuming because you've basically told him he's an idiot for not budgeting and insisted on ignoring his request. No matter how you summarize your demonstration, you've lost Bill as an advocate.

Rather than forcing a product feature or idea on a prospect, rearrange your presentation and strategy. Granted, you always want to demonstrate something that allows you to finish strong. However, it needs to be a feature that's meaningful to the prospect! Ignore demonstrating the features *you* love and focus on features your prospect thinks are important. This bridge-demonstrating technique will go a long way toward getting your prospect excited about your software.

TEACHING VERSUS DEMONSTRATING

We've alluded to this crime several times already. Many professionals who demonstrate software feel a responsibility to *train* the customer on their software. They think once the prospect knows how it works (versus how to use it), they'll be happy to buy your software at any price. Demonstrators who commit this crime often started their careers in training or implementation. Their background lends itself to educating people rather than bridge-demonstrating to them.

Ask yourself if the following example is bridge-demonstrating or teaching. The prospect is a manufacturer of fine furniture. Your software product specializes in automating the forecasting process. However, you've learned in your Discovery that Mike the purchasing manager has no interest in complicated lead-time (the time it takes to build a new piece of furniture) forecasting techniques. He believes the computer should simply look at the last time you built something and use that time as the new lead-time.

You're demonstrating this area of your software when Mike asks, "Julie, do you track the *lead-time* it takes to build a new set of coffee tables?" Your response, "You bet! In fact, let me show you where we do this." You go to that portion of your master files and position the cursor in the lead-time field for a coffee table. You begin a lengthy explanation of lead-time, "Mike, this is the field where the resulting lead-time is calculated by the system and then stored. Our software is very powerful. It will take the last ten times you manufactured the item and perform an exponential smoothing of those lead-times. It will also look forward against global sales forecasts and then automatically attach an alpha factor of seven on the most recent history to calculate for you the most accurate lead-time. This lead-time is then used in our MRP system to determine the most efficient quantity of product to build. It forecasts material and labor needs using the *Angola* theorem. Isn't that powerful?"

What do you think? Is this bridge-demonstrating or teaching? Obviously, you've shifted into teaching mode. By doing so, you've put your demonstration at risk. Mike may know nothing about "exponential smoothing" or the "Angola theorem." He also might be too embarrassed to ask what these mean and thus draw the conclusion, "Wow! You have to be a Nobel Prize winner to understand this complicated piece of software." Even if Mike does understand the software's formulas, he may completely disagree with the approach. Who's to say an alpha factor for lead-time should be seven? What if he disagrees with the Angola theorem? What if he's been burned by sales forecasts in the past? Perhaps your competitor placed a *trap* for you by warning Mike to "watch out for anyone who uses the Angola theorem for forecasting!" If your prospect asks you what time it is, don't teach them how to build a watch. Concentrate on your primary job: leading them across the Bridge.

You may be wondering why you shouldn't teach. After all, part of your job is to give your prospect as much information as possible to help them make an informed decision. If your product has more features and functions than your competitor's, it seems logical to *teach* them as many of these features and functions as possible. What if your competitor makes a big deal out of the capability to support exponential smoothing and the Angola theory and you don't? What if you happen to know Mike is a big proponent of these lead-time techniques? Isn't now the time to educate him on your adherence to these same techniques? The answer to all these questions is no, No, NO!

Usually, criminals don't start off committing the most serious crimes. They whet their appetite on misdemeanors. For example, people don't start out robbing banks. They begin by shoplifting. They're enticed. A similar thing happens to demonstrators. Before they become a hardened "teacher" in their demonstration, they tend to commit some the following minor offenses.

 a) Part of Your Job - Some may argue you're responsible for knowing as much about your software as is humanly possible. They believe you should be able to translate this knowledge at a moment's notice to your prospect. How impressive that would be! To a certain degree, this is true. It is important to know as much as you can about your software. Product knowledge is a terrific, irreplaceable asset and is a must when demonstrating. However, what's more important is delivering the information your prospect needs *in the proper manner*. Focus on building the Bridge. If Mike likes simple lead-time calculations, show him a simple lead-time formula! Again using our Mike example, what does he need to know *right now* to feel comfortable with your lead-time techniques? "Mike, we store lead-time on every item you manufacturer so you can always forecast needs for your products. Our software will keep the lead-time current with the last time an item was manufactured. As we discussed in my Discovery interview, you can switch to a more complex method if necessary, but your current lead-time forecasting seems to be working great for you so why change?"

b) More Relevant not More Features - Have you ever lost a deal to a competitor who had an inferior product with less features and functions than yours? If not, please send me your card with the name of your favorite candy bar written on the back, and I'll send it to you. You'll be the only software demonstrator I've come across who can make that claim! Demonstrating isn't a contest of *more*; it's a contest of *more relevant*.

Here's an illustration. You want to buy some tomatoes from the supermarket. You only need six of them for your recipe. You walk to the produce section of the supermarket and find the tomato section. In front of you are 500 tomatoes from which to choose. You're having trouble finding them. You want them ripe but firm. They need to be evenly red, but not bruised. Luckily, the produce manager walks up and asks how she can help. You explain your situation, and she explains how a worldwide disease has harmed the appearance of tomatoes but, she then proceeds to quickly pick out six perfect tomatoes for you. Are you happy? You bet! You ignore the 494 so-so tomatoes in the bin because you've got the six you need. Regardless of how many were in the bin, those six perfect tomatoes are all you need and the produce manager delivered them to you.

You run the risk of demonstrating *more features* versus *more relevance* when you fall into teaching mode. Remember that this is not a contest of who has more. It's a contest of whose is most *relevant*. You need to be like the produce manager during the software demonstration. You need to quickly assist your prospect by giving them exactly what they want. You don't need to try and convince them to take 500 features when all they need for their business are six perfect ones!

c) They Have It; You Better Have It Too - What if your competitor has lead-time forecasting features like you do? Should you quickly explain to the prospect you have these same features? No. This accomplishes nothing other than making you appear "me-too." Besides, Mike told you he doesn't want to use sophisticated forecasting techniques, so why suffocate him with your theories?

d) They Asked For It - The usual objection to the "Teaching" crime is that the prospect asked to be taught. The RFP was structured that way, the demo script was structured that way, and the prospect indicated that they "want to learn everything they can about the software." So if they wanted to learn, I should teach them, right? Wrong. This is an area where you need to do what's right, not what you were asked to do. Most software systems remain in service for twelve years. This results in inexperienced buyers. Prospects don't need to know the details of how it works. Instead, they need to know what the software is capable of and why it will make their work simpler, more efficient, more profitable, etc. It's your job to help them gain that knowledge. That's what demonstrating is all about.

SO WHAT?

Train yourself to internally ask the question *"So What?"* after every software feature you demonstrate. This is a *very* important element of successful demonstrating. Here's the bottom line: don't make statements of functionality without following with some type of benefit.

Forgive me if I'm making this sound like Sales 101. We all know the importance of connecting features to benefits. The problem is, there's something mysterious about demonstrating software. It draws salespeople into a *teaching* role and we leave the benefits behind. Remember, your prospect is contemplating spending all this time, money and effort on a demonstration with the expectation that your software is beneficial to them. If you don't outwardly explain the benefits of your software during the demonstration, they'll likely miss many of the key reasons for purchasing your software.

One of the best sales managers I've ever worked with is a good friend, Doug Walker. Doug has an interesting way of reinforcing this concept when he's in the audience at a demonstration. He sits in the back of the room with a big piece of paper that says *"So What?"* Whenever the demonstrator presents a feature without a benefit, the sign gets held up! It's rather intimidating, but gets the point across.

Here are a few examples of statements *without* associated benefits:

- "In this field in the software, you can identify the order as a *rush* item." *So What?*

- "With this one portal view, you can see the status of all of the servers and the traffic they are handling." *So What?*

- "By simply touching a key, you can have the patient's chart right before your eyes." *So What?*

- "Here you can see the monthly average as well as up to two standard deviations over or under the average." *So What?*

Now let's try a few of these same statements *with* associated benefits:

- "In this field in the software, you can identify the order as a *rush* item, thus enabling your order staff to provide the warehouse important notice for these types of orders. This feature will help to alleviate the problem you have now of rush orders not being expedited properly."

- "With this portal view, you can see the load on all of the servers and determine which servers are experiencing delays or problems. This proactive approach means you spend less time and money chasing problems and the business doesn't suffer from poor or disrupted service."

- "By simply touching a key, you can have the patient's chart right before your eyes, whereas now you go searching through file cabinets. With your new software, you'll save significant time over your present chart searching methods."

If there's no benefit, why bother making the statement and wasting the prospect's time? The fact is you shouldn't. Let's take a look at our last example from above, "Here you can see the monthly average as well as up to two standard deviations over or under the average." "*So What?*" Is it particularly important to have two standard deviations? If not, skip the statement. It's not a meaningful feature of your software for this prospect. It's simply fill-in time for your demonstration. *Stop* showing features with no real meaning or benefit to your prospect.

On occasion you'll get lucky and your prospect will say something like, "Wow, you can see two standard deviations?" However, I can count on one hand the number of times a prospect stopped me over some small feature to tell *me* the benefits they're going to derive from it. You're more at risk of them saying, "What's the value of that? What I really want to see is a moving average with configurable timeframes. Do you have that? Is the standard deviation method the only way I can analyze the sales information? I'd like to see the other formulas. This sure looks complex and inflexible." Oh, the holes we can dig for ourselves!

I make it a point to ask myself the question "*So What?*" after each software feature. You should too. It will help you:

- Get your points across.

- Establish the value of your software to your prospect.

- Bring your prospect across the Bridge. If a feature has no *benefit* to the prospect, there's no sense in demonstrating it.

SUMMARY

The "So What?" crime helps to summarize this section on "Featuring" crimes. Our goal is always to make software capabilities understandable and relevant to the prospect. With every "featuring" crime, we stray from that goal. Applying the "So What?" test will eliminate most of these crimes from your demonstration.

GROUP #2 - ALIENATION CRIMES

As you read this title, you are probably thinking, "What? I would *never* do anything to alienate a prospect!" It is true, nobody sets out to alienate a prospect, but it happens over and over again. Inadvertently, we often confuse or frustrate the very people we are trying to convince. These crimes may be a little more subtle than the "featuring" crimes, but do not be surprised if you find yourself nodding your head as you read about these serious crimes.

IF YOU THINK THAT'S COOL, WAIT TILL YOU SEE...

Imagine you're demonstrating to a sports apparel company that sells clothing to hiking enthusiasts. In the room are Lisa, the chief executive officer, Mark, the chief financial officer, Andy, the director of information systems and Sheila, the vice president of sales. They sell primarily through catalogs and the web to a regular group of specialty sports stores. You complete a demonstration of how you can target coupons, specials, and new product introductions to existing customers based on their buying patterns and demographic information. The demonstration went very well. In fact, Sheila, the vice president of sales says, "That's fantastic. We can increase our sales 30 percent if we implement this feature!" What a great reaction! You have them just where you want them. Unfortunately, rather than summarizing your capabilities in this area, you feel compelled to continue selling. "If you think that's hot, I can reduce your credit card fees by 20 percent because now your customers can pay for the material using alternatives to traditional credit cards or in-house accounts!" Lisa, the chief executive officer, jumps in, "Really? I just read an article about a catalog house being sued for $300,000 by a customer whose system was infected by a virus based on an alternative payment system. Can you imagine? There's a whole website dedicated to such horror stories!" Mark, the chief financial officer, says, "Lisa, I also read in *Credit and Collections Monthly* about the battle going on between bank merchant accounts and these newer alternatives. It looks like there will be a lot of changes coming over the next few years." Andy, the director of information services, adds, "Hey, I read in *Internet Retailing Quarterly* that virtually everyone who currently accepts alternative payment systems over the Internet is dropping the capability due to the massive losses from fraud and complaints."

Congratulations, you've just placed your victory in the jaws of defeat! You now have two choices. You can either begin defending alternative payment systems for the next 10 minutes or agree with them, explain that alternative payment systems are not a good idea for them and move forward. I would highly recommend the latter.

This scenario reminds me of the "Largest Cocktail Party In The World." This event took place the night before the annual Florida-Georgia football game in the minor league baseball stadium in Jacksonville, Florida. As was the tradition, the stadium was mobbed with hard-partying students. At the end of the evening there was an incredible fireworks display and this particular year, one of the fireworks went sideways instead of up. It smashed through the window of a student's unoccupied, parked car and it exploded! Afterward, a reporter asked the student, "How did you feel when you walked out of the stadium and learned your car was blown up?" The student replied, "Man, talk about coming down in a hurry..." That's something to remember the next time you feel compelled to extend your party with fireworks without knowing ahead of time where they're heading!

DON'T ANSWER THAT!

Does the following describe you?
- You're a veteran of your software.

- You not only know the high points of the software but you have a solid understanding of your software's entire feature set.

- On a scale of one to five, with five being the highest knowledge of your software, you'd grade a three or higher across the board.

If these statements sound familiar, pay close attention to this crime. The way you answer your prospects' questions is crucial, especially when you can answer most questions quickly *and*, in a flash, demonstrate a feature that supports your answer.

Consider for a moment that you're demonstrating your state-of-the-art service configuration tool to an IT Director for a large financial services company. Your prospect, Sarah, asks a seemingly benign question. "Bill, when I'm configuring the service for deployment, can I override the standard security and integrity checks?" No problem. You've heard the question before, many times. Your software has the ability, based on someone's administrative settings, to block or allow overrides. Based on your pre-demonstration Discovery, you know the developers themselves are constantly bypassing integrity checks. You never had the opportunity to interview Sarah, but you know the answer she's looking for. You stick your chest out and say, "You bet, Sarah! Your developers can override any of the standard system checks, just like they do today." Sarah replies, "That won't help. We never want our developers to override the standard checks. That's one of the main reasons we're looking into a new system. We want to stop this practice of skipping important security and integrity steps. Our business users complain about bad services all the time and our auditors are complaining that it leaves us very vulnerable to attacks!"

Clearly your research failed you in this example. You wanted to interview Sarah during your Discovery. But because she wasn't available, you weren't able to learn her views on deployment checks and procedures. Face it, there's no possible way of interviewing everybody in the organization. Key people who will attend the demonstration may be out of town or unavailable during the Discovery. Plan for this situation.

Whenever I get questions from prospects that I didn't have a chance to spend time with prior to the demonstration, I *answer their questions with questions.* This allows us to find out many things. First and foremost, I learn what answer they're hoping for. In this case, I would ask Sarah a question like, "Well, Sarah, that depends on some system options. Would you mind telling me what your preference is?"

Experience has taught me to expect two responses. The majority of people respond with, "Our old system allows our developers to override deployment checks. This is affecting our quality, and I really need to find a way to stop this practice." That being the case, I answer with, "Good news! You can set an option preventing anyone from skipping any designated deployment check."

A few people will respond with, "I'd rather not say. Tell me how your system works." If you get this response, you're dealing with a "lay-in-the-weeds" individual (more about them in Chapter 5, *The Discovery Process*). These people are fearful of being persuaded and are concerned about your honesty.

Many times, this person will ask a question that has an obvious response. However, the obvious response is the *opposite* of what they really want. If Sarah was a lay-in-the-weeds individual, she might ask the question like this, "Our existing system lets our developers skip or override deployment steps and checks. Your system will allow that, too, won't it?" The moment you answer, "yes," Sarah's buzzing all over you like bees at a picnic. If Sarah is the CIO of the company, you're in for a long day! Why? Since the personality of the company tends to follow that of its leader, you're likely to get lay-in-the-weeds questions from all directions throughout the day.

Here's a better response to Sarah's question. "Well, that depends. Let me make sure I understand your question. What I heard you say is you want your developers to override development checks. Is that correct?" (YES or NO?) What I've done with this response is remove her ambiguity. I've just flushed Sarah out of the weeds. In almost every case, she'll tell me she doesn't want her developers to override deployment checks. Now that I know Sarah's personality, I continue to ask her questions. "Would there ever be an occasion where they'd be allowed to override the integrity and security steps? Would you allow an override with management approval?" It's only with further probing I learn what Sarah really wants. Assuming I can fill the need, I proceed with a tight, focused response. If I can't fill the need, I admit that quickly and discuss other alternatives such as a software modification. I don't try and talk Sarah out of something she thinks she wants. She will dig-in very deep on her point and, in the end, I'll lose.

The most effective method for flushing out a lay-in-the-weeds individual is by answering a question with closed-ended questions. If the prospect is willing to answer your questions, you'll quickly learn how to formulate your answers. After a while, these people will know and understand you're "on to them" and will stop trying to ambush you. This very effective technique helps maintain control of your prospect and keeps them focused. You'll also find you have fewer surprises to deal with and aren't placed in a defensive position nearly as often.

CUTTING OFF A QUESTION

The situation is pretty simple. You've been demonstrating this product for years. You understand your prospect's business because you have nine other clients with an almost identical operation. In fact, you understand virtually every need they have because six of those nine companies actually used the prospect's current software before switching to yours.

Whenever you find yourself in this situation, there's a real tendency to cut off questions and get right to a quick answer. You're under the impression the prospect will really appreciate the knowledge and understanding you have of their business. Who else could answer their question before they have finished asking the entire thing?

Here's an example. You're demonstrating to Mike, the service manager of a major outdoor equipment repair operation. Your software is already installed in other parts of the business. Now you want to sell them your service module as an upgrade. You're demonstrating how he can enter a work order for a repair on a mowing machine when he stops you to ask a question. "Steve, if I'm entering a work order on this equipment, will the system require the customer to have purchased ... " You interrupt, "Mike, let me stop you there. I've heard from many other customers their desire to only repair equipment the customer purchased from them. I can assure you the software can be set up to tell the service technician the mower was not purchased from you and then they can send the guy packing!" Mike replies, "Well, maybe some of your other customers won't repair a mower bought somewhere else, but at my company, service is the number one reason we make a profit. Why in the world would you want to put that kind of decision-making power in the hands of a mechanic anyway? I would fire the first person I ever caught doing this!"

Ouch! Can you say *retreat*? For the next 25 minutes you get to explain how this feature is really just a system option that can be turned on or off and how you appreciate where he is coming from. What a lousy position to put yourself in and all because you wouldn't let him finish his question. Had he let Mike finish the question, Steve might have heard, "Steve, if I'm entering a work order on this mower, will the system require the customer to have purchased that piece of equipment from us? The reason I ask is because we like to service anyone's equipment, regardless of where they bought it." Given this question, I suspect Steve would've provided a slightly different answer, don't you?

The key to success in these situations is patience. Slow yourself down. The more you *think* you know, the more you should slow down. You'll be perceived as intelligent, thoughtful, knowledgeable and consultative. Your prospects will quickly gain trust in you. You won't find yourself in a defensive position like you will when you're a know-it-all.

WHY WOULD YOU WANT TO DO THAT?

I recall a demonstration in Minnesota a few years back that taught me a valuable lesson about this question. I was demonstrating our enterprise-wide distribution system and we finally arrived at the general ledger (accounting) portion of the day. I was tired and so was my audience. The controller was in the room along with the operations manager and the information systems manager. I showed the controller how to post an accounting transaction into the system. He stopped me to ask, "Is there any way to *delete* an accounting transaction after it has already been posted to the general ledger?" I puffed out my chest and said, "Absolutely not! One of the benefits of our general ledger system is the ability to maintain every posting in the general ledger and never allow deletions. This is done for integrity purposes." To which he responded, "What makes you think this is so important? I need the ability to delete transactions out of the general ledger." I answered with the question, "Why would you ever want to do that? That's strictly against general accounting practices."

Good night. It was over. I never recovered. He almost went ballistic on me. How dare a salesperson question a Certified Public Accountant. Six months and a great deal of expense later he bought a competitor's system. Whether he was right or wrong was immaterial. Never ask the question, "Why would you want to do that?" This is a direct challenge and only leads to trouble. The best way to address this situation is to ask some thoughtful, probing questions.

Generally, I avoid answering direct questions with direct answers during a demonstration. Unless I'm 100 percent positive my answer is exactly what they want to hear, I'll answer with another question. The entire blow-up with the controller could have been avoided had I asked a few simple questions like, "What would you prefer the system do? Why is that important to you? Could you live with another alternative?"

In this example, I was 100 percent confident he would never want a system that allowed transactions to be deleted from the general ledger. However, once I made my initial error, retreat was the only alternative. It was pure trouble (and stupidity!) for me to take an offensive position. I should have:

- Found out why this was important to him.

- Admitted the software weakness (in his mind) and diffused his stance.

- Supported his position and made a suggestion we modify the standard system.

- The important thing was I learned from that experience. I hope you can learn from my blunder, too!

THE CONDESCENDING PRESENTER

Let's be honest: We are professionals. Over the years we have learned not just our software, but also the industry best practices related to our prospects. We understand how processes should work and how to best implement our software to help the organization. Unfortunately, our greatest strengths can quickly become our greatest weaknesses.

Several years ago, I was in Salt Lake City, Utah and had a defining moment in my demonstrating career. I was involved in a demo to a huge prospect with a unique challenge. They would take advance orders on products they did not have in inventory. When the inventory shipment arrived, they would literally take the product right off the truck and deliver it straight to customers who had placed these advanced orders. Obviously, they were focused on customer service, which was not a bad thing. They did not want to delay deliveries by taking the time to post the inventory receipt before filling orders. However, that required the computer to handle negative inventory, since the customer orders were being filled with inventory that the computer didn't think existed. From a pure accounting perspective, this is not a good practice. And for that reason, our software did not support negative inventory. So, we had a bit of a problem on our hands. The customer had a legitimate need (regardless of whether or not it followed good accounting principles) that our software could not accommodate.

The room was filled with 20 people, including the ultimate decision-maker, an executive vice president named Bill. His managers were in the room examining this problem. It was an issue only because Bill's people wanted to continue their current practice. There was no question then or today that the *right* thing was for this prospect to follow proper disciplines and not allow inventory to go negative. We tried using the "accounting principles" strategy, but it was not well received by Bill's managers. When they grew hostile over our system's lack of capability in this area, Bill actually defended us. He knew good software should never allow negative inventory. Unfortunately, the inventory expert we brought to the demonstration insisted on arguing with the crowd. To add fuel to the fire, he was very passionate about the issue of negative inventory levels. My colleague's approach became so argumentative, Bill felt obligated to begin defending his people, and he started to question the entire validity of our software.

The entire demonstration completely unraveled, and I could not call off the dogs. My expert became visibly upset. Bill was now at full tilt in the argument and was rapid-firing questions. Finally, while Bill, the executive vice president and decision-maker was asking a question, my expert placed his forefinger to his lips and said "Shhhhhh!" The room went silent. Had there been a hole in the floor, I can assure you I would've crawled into it!

This crime often starts innocently enough. We carefully line up the best experts to put in front of the prospect. We design our demonstration to match the best practices of the organization. And then, somewhere during the demonstration, we hit a snag. Perhaps someone in the audience is struggling to follow and understand something we are demonstrating. Perhaps there is a difference of opinion on the best way to accomplish something. Perhaps there is simply a communication mismatch between you and the prospect. You're getting a little frustrated, they're getting a little frustrated, and communication continues to deteriorate. Without realizing it, you soon find yourself talking *down* to the prospect. It's almost as if you're saying, "What's wrong with you? Are you too stupid to understand this incredibly basic and widely accepted concept?"

I also had a colleague who had the bad habit of starting sentences with the phrase, "You need to understand..." Can you see how this is a variation of the problem I described above? Audiences have two possible reactions to a "you need to understand" statement: shut down or start arguing. If you want to get on the fast track to being eliminated from an opportunity, this is the way to do it!

I need to be very clear here; arguing with the prospect is absolutely forbidden! This is one of the worst things you can do and simply compounds the crime of arrogance. There is no gray area on this one. You simply *do not do it*. There's nothing to be gained and everything to lose. Leave your ego at the door when you enter the demonstration room and remain professional.

You might be thinking, "Okay, smart guy, considering the fact that your software wouldn't handle negative inventory, how should the objection be handled?" The answer is "be delicate." Do everything you can to dissect and ultimately respond to the objection. The best way to accomplish this is to ask questions. In the negative inventory example, there's good reason not to allow it. Once people are in the habit of delaying the receipt of inventory, the inventory has a tendency to never be correct. If inventory levels are never reliable, people on the sales desk have no confidence telling customers the goods they want are "in stock." The purchasing people are never really sure what they should buy. The warehouse guys are never sure if the inventory is there when they get to a shelf location. The list goes on and on and on. So, ask questions that make this come to light. For example, "Steve, when a customer asks one of your people on the order desk for two of an item and the system tells you there are only two available, how confident are you the system is right? Mike, when you run a stock status report to purchase more products, do you ever feel a need to walk into the warehouse to see how much is really on the shelf? Darren, do you ever go to a location in the warehouse to get an item only to find out it's not there?"

If you sell infrastructure or other highly technical software, you're particularly susceptible to this crime. The software is complex, the standards in the industry change constantly, and it's almost impossible to avoid jargon and acronyms. Further, you're probably presenting to people with a wide range of technical skills and background. This situation makes it easy for sales engineers to unwittingly become condescending presenters. Mixed audiences and technical products represent the *most* dangerous situations, and it's your job to find a path through to success. It's my belief that a failure to understand on the audience's part is a failure to communicate on the presenter's part. Whenever I'm in front of a mixed audience, I have in my mind a number of different explanations and analogies, all designed to work from different starting points. Your goal is to take the explanation to *their* starting point, not force them to come to your starting point.

There's a lot of arrogance in the technical community, and it's a common cause of a condescending presentation. Imagine you're an expert in software design. You hold a master's degree in computer science. You've been working with application design strategies for 22 years and are quite excited about your company's approach to Service Oriented Architectures (SOA). Unfortunately, your prospect considers SOA as a passing fad and really doesn't understand the details of your approach. Can you see the train wreck waiting to happen? Be professional, understanding and patient at this point. If the "slow down" doesn't work, set the issue aside and schedule some one-on-one time for later in the day. There's never any justification for being arrogant or arguing with a prospect.

WRITE IT DOWN!

You can't possibly have an answer to every question your prospects may ask. In the event you don't know the answer to one of their questions, make sure you *always* write their questions in your demonstration notes. When you write down a question, objection or something you don't know or understand, you've provided temporary closure to their issue. Failure to do this only *one time* could prove disastrous. If you doubt this for a second, think back to a time when you were in a presentation and you had a question the presenter could not answer. The presenter may have said, "I'm really not sure of the answer to your question. I'll look into it for you." After this statement, they quickly moved on without writing down the question. How did that impact you? Did you:

- Spend the next five minutes focusing on the fact that he blew you off?

- Feel belittled? How about ignored? Irritated?

- Begin to question whether or not you would ever get a response?

- Question the presenter's credibility from that point forward?

- Remember anything about the information that was presented during the time when all those thoughts were running through your mind?

- Feel challenged to ask more difficult questions in the future?

What if the next section of your demonstration is directed at the person you just irritated? Now that you've frustrated, aggravated and possibly even belittled them by not writing down their question, you're going to show them a unique and beneficial software feature. Not a very good combination, is it?

If you can't answer their question, write it down. How hard is that? Don't guess at the answer to get around having to write it down. Failure to write down questions will almost certainly lead to future problems. Your prospects will feel ignored and irritated. They'll want to set traps for you in the future. Worse yet, they may choose to ignore the remainder of your message and *mentally* show you to the door. End each section of the demonstration by reviewing the questions and open items you wrote down, ask if you missed anything and reiterate you'll follow-up on each question. This technique will put their minds at ease.

On last note on writing down unanswered questions. It has become common practice in software demonstrations to use a whiteboard or flipchart as the "parking lot" for open questions or concerns. STOP THIS PRACTICE NOW! Why do you want to have in large, bold print everything you don't know or can't do sitting in front of the eyes of the prospect throughout your entire demonstration? Reserve these billboards for benefit statements, advantages, value statements or themes. Write all open questions or concerns on a private pad of paper. If you are in a demonstration with one or multiple colleagues, identify one of those individuals as the note taker.

LOOK HOW BAD YOU LOOK!

For those of you who have attended a sales training course, you'll recognize this crime. For years we've been taught that we must expose a prospect's pain. These experts tell us that if prospect's don't know their pain, they won't change. I don't disagree with the concept. I do however disagree with how "pain" is often presented.

I was watching a senior Solution Engineers from one of our large corporate client's perform a demo to a multimillion-dollar prospect when the realization about this crime came to me. He was starting a section of the demo with a summary of all of the prospect's pains. I watched the reaction of the prospect and saw an amazing change in their body language and demeanor. The people he was presenting the pain to were leaning back, folding their arms and frowning.

After summarizing their pains, he asked them for feedback and one of them said "Axel, we don't do things that poorly. You speak as if we don't know what we are doing around here. I'm sure you software guys have all the answers so why don't you come in here and run this place?" Ouch.

Be very careful with pain. If you address it directly, you run the risk of committing this crime. Don't start your demo or a section of the demo telling them how bad they run their operations. It can be insulting, irritating and generally puts them in a bad mood. Let your competitor who's been through the same sales training put them in a bad mood.

In Malcom Gladwell's bestselling book "Blink" he cites a study performed by John Bargh, PhD at New York University. Dr. Bargh was testing a concept that Gladwell calls "Priming". During the experiment, separate groups of subjects were asked to unscramble random words into sentences. The first group was given scrambled sentences that were primed with aggressive words like "bold, rude, and bother," while the second group was primed with kind words like "respect, considerate, and polite." This experiment lasted an entire semester. At the end of the experiment, the subjects were asked to seek out their next assignment by asking the person at the end of the hall for instruction. Unfortunately for the subjects, that person was artificially locked in a conversation with someone else, thus, the only way the subject could get their next instruction was to interrupt the conversation. Those primed with the aggressive words interrupted after an average of only five minutes. But, the overwhelming majority of those primed with polite words never interrupted at all! If they hadn't stopped the experiment at 15 minutes, they don't know how long they would have stood there!

Back to selling and demonstrating to *pain*. Consider a demo or a section of a demo that opened with a slide that contained the following phrases:

- Today, you <u>can't</u>…

- Your reporting is <u>limited</u>

- Your information is in <u>silos</u>

- Your data is <u>locked</u> into…

What am I priming them with? Can't, limited, silos and locked. Priming the prospect in this way will result in one of five outcomes:

1. They'll be convinced that they have so much pain they need to change.

2. They'll get defensive as is witnessed by their body language.

3. They'll get defensive as is witnessed by their interruptions and immediate arguments.

4. You'll make the staff look bad in front of their middle management.

5. You'll make the superiors look bad in front of their executives.

Of the five options above, you will be lucky if option 1 is the only outcome. As we have traveled the globe, salespeople and demonstration experts overwhelmingly agree that priming people with pain is a mistake.

Here's a suggestion. Try taking all these negative priming words and invert them into positive possibilities. Let your competition start off their presentation by priming the prospect into a bad mood! How? You can use positive phrases like these:

- In the <u>future</u>, you can...

- <u>Flexible</u> reporting

- <u>Collaborative</u> information across departments

- <u>Open</u> and <u>secure</u> data

Do you *feel* the difference? Now you're using positive priming words (future, flexible, collaborative, open and secure). Stop telling your prospects how bad they look and prime them with what they can be.

SUMMARY

Wow! It turns out that there are many ways to alienate prospects. As I mentioned, these crimes may be more subtle than featuring crimes, but they can be much more destructive. Failure to help people across the Bridge is one thing; behavior that blocks them from ever approaching the Bridge is quite another. Eliminating alienation crimes can be difficult. Ask a peer to help you by watching out for the key phrases and situations that I have described.

Before we move on to the next type of crimes, let's take a minute and think about the most dangerous environment for alienation crimes: The Web! It's very easy to commit an alienation crime during a web demonstration and never even realize that you did it! On the web it can be very difficult to see and judge the reaction of the audience. Combine this with your desire to establish yourself as an expert with an audience that you don't know, and you have the perfect environment to commit an alienation crime. Have a peer sit in on your next web demo to make sure this isn't happening.

GROUP #3 - CHAMELEON CRIMES!

We're trying to be as clear as possible in demonstrating the capabilities and benefits of our software. The prospect is trying to clearly understand how our software works and how it will assist in what they're trying to accomplish. Considering our goals are well aligned, there should be no problem, right? Wrong!

So if we're all looking for the same thing, why do our efforts so often spiral into confusion and frustration? For an answer, consider the Chameleon: Chameleons are small lizards very adept at changing to match their environment. They don't attempt to alter their environment, they change their colors and patterns to blend into that environment. There's a lesson to learn in their behavior.

We can avoid confusion and frustration by adapting, as much as possible, to our prospect's environment. We can learn and leverage their data, their terminology, and the characteristics of their business.

THE WIDGET SYNDROME

Widgets are items no one sells or uses yet we feel compelled to use them in our demonstrations. They have no meaning. No one can relate to them. (For you technical demonstrators, I am not referring to the type of web code that can be inserted in web pages.)

I have a considerable amount of experience selling software to industrial distributors. Their business model focuses on selling a variety of products including tools, abrasives (sandpaper), cutting products, etc. Prior to a demonstration, I enter products in the database identical to what my prospect sells. Some prospects make this a requirement, as they should. For years, I successfully competed with another software firm who insisted on selling *widgets* during their demonstration. In their opinion, a product was a product. But when a prospect considered it important to see *their* products, my competitor rarely made the short list. (Can you guess who suggested to the prospect that it should be an important issue?) My competitor had great software, but failed to build a Demonstration Bridge to their prospects.

This Widget Syndrome problem is not confined to just ERP systems and business data. I've seen the problem in all kinds of demonstrations and presentations. You can see examples in business intelligence demonstrations, integration presentations, even technical infrastructure presentations. I once saw a presentation of Service Oriented Architecture (SOA) capabilities where the services were labeled 'Service 1', 'Service 2', 'Service 3', etc. The presentation, as you might expect, was boring and ineffective because those labels were meaningless to the prospect.

Spend time during your Discovery getting examples of products, account descriptions, customers, servers, services… whatever applies to your prospect and the solution that you're presenting. "Oh, come on," you say, "that is such an old fashioned ploy. My sophisticated buyers will see right through this trick." Actually, they'll be impressed you made the effort to get closer to them. As corny as it may seem, the prospect will respect you for your efforts and, more important, be in a better position to relate to your product and services simply because the data is familiar to them.

Here's an interesting observation I've made over the years: when I insert my prospect's data into the demonstration, they'll occasionally interrupt me by pointing out an error I've made. They'll say something like, "Well, I see what you're trying to accomplish here with the Wet-Dry Vacuum Cleaner, but that's not exactly how we work with that product." There was a time when this would make me panic. Thoughts would race through my head like, "Oh no, I'm dead meat now. He's going to throw an objection at me that I won't be able to answer." In actuality, this is a sign he's with you! The prospect understands what you're presenting. He's crossing the Bridge. He's simply paused for a moment to get some clarification. Usually, he's only pointing out a very subtle difference. I *always* stop in my tracks and ask a few clarification questions. I then show him how he can use my software to sell the Wet-Dry Vacuum Cleaner exactly the way he wants. You and your prospect have just taken another step across the Bridge, side by side.

You may be thinking, "What happens if I can't address the subtle difference? Doesn't that blow my feature out of the water?" No. You politely nod your understanding and explain there may be a difference that needs to be addressed. You *always* write down the difference in front of him. This assures the prospect:

- You understand.

- You're taking an interest in their business, problem or situation.

- You're professional.

- You'll follow-up in the future.

The Widget Syndrome is not just about demonstration data. Remember what I said about widgets at the beginning of this crime? *"They have no meaning. No one can relate to them."* The same thing is true any time the presenter fails to bring the prospect's situation into the *conversation*. If you show international capabilities to a prospect that operates in only one country, you're committing the Widget Syndrome crime. If you cite increases in profit as a benefit to a non-profit organization, you're talking "widgets" to them. If you demonstrate complex fleet operations to a company with two trucks, it's just another example of the "Widget Syndrome" crime!

Make your demonstration as personal and close to the prospect as possible. Try to transform them from presentations into meaningful, relevant conversations. Don't fall into the lazy habit of always showing the same information or citing the same examples to every prospect. Never demonstrate data that's sterile and generic. Your prospects are all different and all have unique needs. Customize your demonstration, including examples and benefit statements, to fit their situation. They'll be much more likely to identify with you and your software.

TECHNOBABBLE

Software professionals are the masters of technobabble. We speak in meaningless company and technical jargon. Those of us in the software industry don't realize how much confusing jargon we throw at a prospect. Every industry has it, but none more so than the computer and software industry. If you think it impresses your prospect to spew this industry *garbage,* you're sorely mistaken.

Assume you're about to spend the morning presenting your integration solution, using the interface between order entry and inventory systems as an example. In the room are the executive vice president of operations, the director of information systems, the chief financial officer, and the vice president of sales. You open your day with, "Our presentation today will start with a company overview. Then we'll demonstrate the ESB from our SOA suite and show you how it will address your integration needs. Finally, we'll look at how our BPEL support interacts with the XML data in the document exchange to provide data-aware BPM orchestration." As you spew this out, you're thinking, "This is great! I'm going to nail this one because none of my competitors can talk like this." Meanwhile, your prospect is thinking, "I wonder if this is going to take all day. I need to remember to pick up the kids right at 5:00 or the daycare will fine me."

You're assuming the executive vice president for operations is paying close attention to you. In reality, he's thinking, "What's a BPEL? I've heard of SOA but what is BPM orchestration? What does this do for us again?" Do you think this person is going to stop you and ask for clarification in front of all the people who report to him? Of course he won't. He's not going to risk the embarrassment of not knowing what all these terms mean. More important, why would you ever want the opening of a presentation to contain information that leaves your audience guessing? Your opening needs to be clear, concise and powerful. It must be attention grabbing and pique their interest. (In a later chapter we'll spend more time on your opening and how the message should be dramatically different than the one described above.)

It's easy to make the mistake of thinking *everyone* knows the meaning of acronyms like BPEL, SOA, and BPM. But it's not just acronyms that get us in trouble. We use words like 'orchestration' and 'activity streams' with the assumption that everyone will understand the meaning of those words in our context. Should you risk it? No way! Skip the technology and marketing jargon and speak in the prospect's language. Prospects can relate to and understand their language, but *not* your jargon. Their company, industry or personal "speak" may contain jargon, but it's *their* jargon. Using their lingo, especially early in the demo, will help you connect with your prospect. Using your jargon will alienate them.

Don't assume that technobabble is limited to the IT department and technical software. I recently came across an example from the world of business intelligence, and this example was aimed right at the business executive! The demonstrator was showing how various dashboards could be used either on the desktop or on a smart phone or similar device. Their exact words were, "we can deliver this capability on premise or with mobility devices." What??? I lost track of what the demonstrator said next, as I was trying to picture a business manager saying, "Gee, I sure wish I could get those sales numbers on premise."

I challenge you to figure out how often you desensitize your audience by using technobabble. Here's a suggestion: videotape yourself in a demonstration and spend time documenting all the jargon, acronyms, words and phrases. For each one, come up with a term that better represents what a typical audience member would say, and is easier to understand. I guarantee your prospect will relate to your conversation long after you've left their parking lot. Include in this exercise the way you describe your support and implementation staff positions. Your prospect needs to feel as if your staff will become part of their organization and not a group of technical outsiders. A common mistake demonstrators make is to describe their own people using acronyms. For example, a system consultant is an SC, or a software integration person in an SI. Avoid referring to people in your organization by any-thing other than his or her proper title. Your prospects can relate to your team members' full titles, but once you make those titles an acronym, the audience will view your team members as outsiders. A technique I use to introduce the people behind my product is to prepare a short resume about each of them that includes their job experience, something on a more personal level (interests, hobbies, etc.) and a digital picture. This makes your team real people and not techno-crats who could never relate to the prospect's needs.

Of course, if you're going to eliminate your proprietary ter-minology, you'll need something to put in its place. Some-times, a simple non-technical replacement will suffice. But if you really want that prospect to come across the Bridge with you, go all the way. Be brave and bold. Take the initiative. During the Discovery, write down every possible prospect specific acronym, phrase and industry-specific saying you hear. Question them on their meaning. Don't be concerned they may be thinking, "What a bozo, he should know what '¼" copper 90s' are." Your questioning will simply help you later. As they describe what all this mumbo-jumbo means, write it down and later commit it to memory. Think about how you can use it in a demonstration. Let me clue you in on some-thing; using this technique will vault you past 95 percent of your competition!

During a demonstration, you could use one of the pros-pect's terms or acronyms incorrectly. If so, your prospect might correct you. Don't panic. This is great stuff! You have their attention. They're actually listening to you and your message. They know you spent the time to learn their business. And if your competitor didn't, this fact will become *very* obvious to your prospect. Provided you learn from your mistakes, you'll actually gain their respect rather than lose it!

Here are some examples of using a prospect's jargon:

- When demonstrating to a plumbing distributor, talk about "¼" copper 90s," not bicycles.

- When talking about network and server architectures, use their data center location names and their server names.

- When talking to a heart surgeon, talk about a "CPT procedure code" describing open-heart surgery, not a "general office visit charge."

- When demonstrating to a restaurant chain, talk about one of their "stores," not one of their "restaurant locations."

- When talking about integration, use the names of their applications, not generic systems.

In addition to the Discovery Process (and good old experience!), the following are some great sources for this information:

- The prospect's website.

- Their marketing materials, product information, catalogs, etc.

- Your customers who are similar to your prospect.

- Your implementation people.

- Trade association literature.

- Seasoned sales or sales-support people.

One *crucial* way of creating a difference between you and your competition is to replace technobabble, 'insider' corporate labels, and generic terms with terminology that's specific and meaningful to your prospect. Learn your prospect's ways of communicating. Learn their acronyms. Learn what they call their shortcuts, products, entities, etc. The more you learn and use this information in your demonstration, the more you'll be perceived as an expert. Once this happens, you'll be an ally. They'll trust you. You'll be elevated to a level your competitor isn't likely to attain. You're successfully leading your prospect across the Bridge to your system.

SUMMARY

There are variations of the Chameleon crimes I have listed here, but they all go back to one simple truth: If you do a great job of understanding and adapting your demonstration to the prospect's environment, you'll dramatically improve your chances of winning the deal. But there is an added bonus: Your demonstrations will go faster, there will be fewer questions, and you can even help shorten the sales cycle by adapting to the prospect, instead of asking them to adapt to you. It turns out that Chameleons are pretty smart little lizards!

GROUP #4 - BLIND CRIMES

In writing this book, I tried to think of everything that results in a successful demonstration, and everything that throws a demonstration off track. As the various chapters of the book started to come together, it became clear a well-planned, properly organized demonstration made functionality and benefits clear and concise, while a poorly organized demonstration resulted in a lack of clarity; a certain fuzziness in the prospect's mind. Simply put, they could not 'see' the benefits that you were attempting to convey. That is how these crimes became 'blind' crimes.

THE BLIND LEADING THE BLIND

Assume you are giving your demonstration and things are rolling along. You've gained the executive's trust because you've built a case for the value of your software during your presentation. The executive has stayed in the room for more than 30 minutes. You've got momentum. Then someone from the audience asks you a question, but you don't have an immediate answer. Consequently, you jump to a screen you *think* contains the answer but it doesn't. The executive says, "Mary, don't worry about it. I believe you when you say you can do this. I don't really need to see it right now." Wow! What a great endorsement, and from the executive no less! However, you won't be denied, saying, "Hang on, I think I can find an answer to that. It will just take a second for me to find it." The search begins. You start popping up screen after screen. Menu after menu. Inquiry after inquiry. Five minutes later the executive has left the room. Someone reiterates, "Mary, really, don't worry about it. Perhaps you can take it down as a follow-up item and get back to us on it." To this you reply, "Oh, I know the information is here somewhere. Hang on for just a moment." More screens and, finally, you give up. Your momentum is destroyed, the president is gone, and you just eroded some of your credibility. You find yourself slugging it out again in an attempt to gain back their enthusiasm. The path across the Bridge has become cluttered with confusion.

Here's the rule of thumb I use in this situation: if I can't find the information in three clicks or less, I write down the question in my demonstration notes. I let them know I'll research the situation and get back to them. Then I move on.

To illustrate this point, think of a time when a friend told you about a great movie she saw. She starts by describing a great scene. This gets you interested. The conversation goes something like, "And right when the lion is about to jump on…Oh, who's that guy? Wait, it's on the tip of my tongue. I think its Mark something-or-other. No, the actor's name is Mel something. Yes. No. I know it's…oh, it's right on the tip of my tongue." Doesn't it drive you crazy when you're on the receiving end of this type of conversation? Likewise, it's incredibly disruptive in a demonstration when you flash through screen after screen after screen searching for an answer.

The only exception to this rule is a prospect that, for some unknown reason, insists on an immediate answer. If that's your situation, you'll have to perform some research. Here are some suggestions:

1. After three clicks, always ask for permission to write down the request and provide an answer later. If that doesn't work,

2. Freeze the projector screen or cover the lens while you search for the answer. If after a couple minutes you still can't find the answer,

3. Ask permission to have one of your teammates research the issue while you continue the demo. They can sit in the back of the room and perform their research without disrupting the demonstration. At a logical breaking point, have your teammate *circle back* and provide the answer.

Don't meander through the software in search of answers to tough questions. It will break your momentum and continuity. Either write down the question so you can follow-up with them later or have a team member research the question while you march forward.

THE HAMSTER WHEEL

Visualize a hamster (rodent) in a cage with a little metal wheel in it. Once the hamster gets on the wheel, he runs in place, going absolutely nowhere. They'll do this for hours for no apparent reason. Have you ever felt that way in a demonstration? It's as if all you're doing is *reacting* to your prospect's questions, requests and objections, rather than showing salient features that will help them in their business. If so, you weren't selling your product. You were simply running on the wheel.

This crime can happen anytime you lose control of your demonstration. Loss of control is a frightening situation for a software demonstrator. It means your prospect is taking you where *they* want to go, and that's probably anywhere *but* across the Bridge. Once you lose control, the only thing your prospects will take away from your demonstration is the satisfaction of knowing you answered a lot of their questions. When this happens, you'll find yourself in the middle of a pack of competitors fighting for your professional life!

Avoiding the Hamster Wheel is simple. Maintain control of your prospect. Lead them where they *need* to go. It's fine (in fact crucial) to answer their questions. However, you *must* keep them on track and under control. The best way to maintain control is to bridge-demonstrate. Relate your software to their business, their vocabulary, their challenges, and their goals. The Discovery is your best opportunity to learn the information you'll need to maintain this control. Without enough information, you run the risk of running in circles with your "hamster" competitors!

If you do end up in the wheel, you need to get out. How? One way is to use the "Why don't I take one more question" technique. You hear politicians do this at press conferences all the time. It's how they maintain control of their press conference. A second way to get out of the wheel is to let go of the mouse and get away from the keyboard. Physically move away and walk over to your white board or flipchart and start writing down their questions. Once you write them down, you can discuss when you'll be addressing their questions in your agenda or, if you will be able to address them at all.

One final rule when it comes to the Hamster Wheel. If the decision maker puts you in the wheel, run on it with a smile on your face. I once worked for a CFO who would constantly interrupt salespeople and their presentations. One of those salespeople made the mistake of telling her that he'd get to her questions later. She promptly showed him to the exit!

I included two different crimes in this classification, but there is a special relationship between them. The first crime, *The Blind Leading the Blind*, will push you into the second crime, *The Hamster Wheel*, almost every time.

SUMMARY

Of course, you can also find yourself on *The Hamster Wheel* directly, without first committing the other crime! In fact, I've seen some presenters jump on *The Hamster Wheel* willingly, as if they like running in circles, never getting anywhere.

The *Blind* crimes are especially frustrating to presenters. It seems that you're jumping from one feature to another, scrambling to answer questions and clarify points, and always, always running out of time! At the end of the day you're exhausted and unclear on what has been accomplished. Here's something you may not have thought of: The prospect has the exact same feeling at the end of the day – exhaustion and a feeling of lack of accomplishment. You can help yourself and the prospect by planning the demonstration in a logical manner, presenting information in an organized fashion, and not letting the prospect take control of the demonstration.

PRESENTING CRIMES

Over the years I've learned a lot about presenting. When I look over the crimes listed in this section, I cringe thinking about how many times I have committed these crimes. Perhaps you can learn from my experiences.

"Presenting" crimes are those general crimes that can occur no matter what you're demonstrating or presenting. They can be committed by salespeople, pre-sales, implementation teams, and executives. They can occur at any point during a presentation or demonstration. But they all share one common characteristic: They damage the connection between you and your audience, and in doing so, they make that critical Bridge crossing more difficult.

PRESENTATION CRUTCH

For those of us old enough to remember the early days of sales presentations, we were glad to see the demise of the salesperson with a stack of transparencies in one hand and an overhead projector gripped firmly by its neck in the other hand. At last we were freed from the tyranny of being forced to sit in a darkened room for an hour staring at a mind-numbing series of slides filled with too many words and not enough meaning.

Now we have PowerPoint, Lotus Symphony, Apple Keynote, Prezi, Sliderocket and more! Combined with the right projector, we can now sit in a bright room for an hour staring at a mind-numbing series of slides filled with too many words and not enough meaning. What an improvement! We even have a name for this new, improved format: "Death by Powerpoint."

Many pre-sales and sales people use presentation slides as a crutch and most prospects don't appreciate it in the least. Prospects want to see a software demonstration from a real person who can lead them across the Bridge from their old system to a new, highly productive one. They've spent a lot of money to sit through your presentation and they want *steak,* not just *sizzle.* Gone are the days of making a visual point by using a white-board or flipchart but, so too are highly interactive, focused demonstrations of the software that fits their needs. They've been replaced by *canned* slide presentations. Well, if that's what you've been doing, I'm here in front of you to ask you to rethink this kind of presentation.

The diagnosis of a poor presentation reveals three primary symptoms:
- Lack of a primary message.

- Incorrect perspective – yours versus the clients.

- Too much clutter which defocuses the prospect.

There's nothing wrong with an organized, focused slide presentation. I use them in every demonstration. However, they should *never:*
- Be more than 30 minutes long.

- Contain more than 15 slides.

- Have more than six bullet-points on a slide.

- Have an overabundance of bullet point slides.

- Use an overabundance of cute graphics and animations.

On the other hand, if you're going to use slides in your presentation, you should *always*:
- Build the presentation from the message outward. What is the key point you are trying to convey with each slide.

- Make sure the content on the slide ... pect's perspective not just yours. Us esses, discovery information, etc.

- Use graphics that are professional and pertinent. Use high quality, legally licensed photos versus unprofessional clipart.

- Launch into your software at several points throughout the presentation. This helps keep the presentation interesting and varied.

- Include video clips and screen captures in your presentation. Just make sure they fit the topic at hand.

- Mix your medium by using a flipchart or whiteboard to illustrate points and engage the audience.

- Check with your prospect during your Discovery to make sure they aren't anti-PowerPoint. If they are, present your material using notes, whiteboards or tablets.

Lengthy slide presentations have a tendency to lure you into teaching your prospect about your software instead of effectively demonstrating how it will improve their situation. It's very common to spill out the raw capabilities of your software in a slide presentation without focusing on benefits that specifically apply to this prospect. Obvious you say? I challenge you to look at your existing library of presentations and review the date they were last changed.

Assume you're demonstrating some contact management software to a credit and collections clerk. The software application is specifically designed to assist the credit department in the laborious task of collecting money from customers faster and more efficiently. Below is a bullet list of features you could see in a typical slide presentation used in this type demonstration.

Credit & Collections
➢ Fully Telephony Enabled
➢ Tracks Collection History
➢ Integration with Standard Desktop Tools
➢ Accounts Receivable Aging Dashboard

Let's examine some dialogue that might support the above slide. "Our accounts receivable collections system integrates with your telephone system so you can auto-dial your customer. It can also track the collections history on them. Your collections staff can write a letter to the customer and the system will auto-address it. Finally, you have visibility to accounts receivable aging at any time." Is there any particular reason this salesperson thinks his prospect can't read? Do you think they'll be able to hold the prospect's attention? Five slides into this presentation, everyone in the audience will be wondering whether they'll have time to pick up their dry cleaning during the lunch break.

Here's a better dialogue. "Steve, your new software can auto-dial for your collections people. In addition, it has the capability of tracking the entire collections history on that customer. But we didn't stop there. Your collections staff will now be able to automatically address and send a collections letter to your customer. Finally, while they're in the process of talking to the customer on the telephone, they can view that customer's accounts receivable aging information. Does this sound interesting to you?" At least this dialogue is more conversational. But it still lacks persuasion. Showing slides with this dialogue will hold the audience's attention for longer than five slides, but not much longer. They'll be thinking about their dry cleaning on the *tenth* slide! What's still missing? Benefits! Take a look at the dialogue again and ask "*So What?*" after each bullet point.

"Steve, your new software can auto-dial for your collections people." *So What?*

"In addition, it has the capability of tracking the entire collections history on that customer." *So What?*

"But we didn't stop there. Your collections staff will now be able to automatically address and send a collections letter to your customer." *So What?*

"Finally, while they're in the process of talking to the customer on the telephone, they can view that customer's accounts receivable aging information." *So What?*

Does this sound interesting to you? *NO!* Don't kid yourself. While your prospect may not be saying it out loud, they're thinking it. What are your cues this is happening?

- Irrelevant questions.

- Objections to your points.

- Multiple requests for clarification.

- A nice long yawn!

Now, let's reorganize both the words and the dialogue.

Your Future Credit & Collections
- ➤ Improve Efficiency of Your People
- ➤ Identify History of Past Problems
- ➤ Influence Customer to Pay Sooner
- ➤ Information at Hand for Improved
  Customer Communications

The presenter addresses the slide with, "Wouldn't it be great if your staff had the ability to increase the number of calls they make in one day? Your new software can assist you in improving the efficiency of your staff by automatically dialing the customer with a simple double-click. Our other customers have found their staffs are more effective in collecting money if they know the history of collections calls prior to contacting the customer. Your new software will also give you that capability by showing every collections call and the outcome of the call. Influencing a customer to pay can sometimes come in the form of gentle but direct pressure. One option you'll now have is the ability for your system to immediately address and email or text a custom collections letter or message to your customer while they're still on the phone with you! Talk about getting their attention! Finally, talking intelligently with the customer about the status of their account is critical. You can't afford to look foolish or unknowledgeable to the customer about the status of their account. For this reason, you will have up-to-the-second account information thus improving your customer service. Can you see how these tools would help you collect more money, faster?"

Is it wordier? Slightly. But it needs to be. People can relate to conversation and real life scenarios. It helps them cross the

Bridge. Once they relate to the information you're present-ing, they also remember it. Insert *"So What?"* in your next dia-logue. Its hard work, isn't it? Of course, you'll want to know ahead of time if these points are beneficial to your prospect. (You'll have learned this in your company Discovery.) One of the benefits of presentation tools is you can quickly and eas-ily customize a presentation to fit the needs of each prospect. Take advantage of this capability, but make sure you maintain control. If you can't, I'd suggest going back to transparencies!

THE CORPORATE JUNKIE

There's one point in a demonstration when almost eve-ryone uses a presentation tool. It's the dreaded *Company Overview*. You know this presentation; it's the one that no one likes but everyone does. It brags about your company's pres-ence, their storied history, their financial stability, an acquisi-tion timeline, and their position in the market. There's often a quote or chart from an industry analyst showing how well regarded your company is (by analysts, at least), and there's always that one slide that I call "logoland". You know the slide; 30 or so customer logos jammed onto one screen, perhaps grouped by industry. Prospects dread the 15-30 minutes spent on this "look at me" presentation.

"But wait", you say. "We have to make sure the prospect knows how strong and experienced we are." True enough. But I would ask you to go through the same exercise described above. As you look at each corporate positioning slide, ask yourself, "So What?" In doing so, make sure you have the pros-pect's perspective at the front of your mind. Here's an exam-ple: Your prospect is a U.S. company with one manufacturing plant in Mexico. So you display corporate slide showing that you have offices in 54 countries around the world, with customers in over 100 countries. The slide also shows the incredible growth rate you're seeing in Asia. "So What?" Another example: Your prospect is a large insurance company. Your corporate industry slide highlights how revenue and customers are broken out in the seven different industries you address (including insurance), and your "logoland" slide has a proportional representation from each of those seven. Again, put yourself in the prospect's frame of mind and ask, "So What?" I'm betting that one or two solid customer case studies in insurance, combined with a demonstration of your expertise in the insurance industry, would do more to put your prospect at ease and start them moving across the Bridge.

It's not that all of the facts, figures, and customer references are bad. But they're not useful unless presented from the prospect's perspective. The corporate information from marketing is a rich source of raw materials for your presentation. But the final presentation must *always* be appropriate to this specific prospect and constructed to speak from this prospect's perspective.

There's one additional advantage to all of the presentation review and customization. Once you have clarified the messages, eliminated the slides that are not relevant from the prospect's perspective, and de-cluttered your presentation, you'll find you can deliver the whole corporate presentation in much less time. And trust me, that's exactly what prospects are looking for.

You should also consider postponing the corporate presentation to later in the demonstration. This is especially true if the prospect already knows your company. Start your demonstration with something more compelling and interesting. Provide them with your value proposition, summarize the goals of the demonstration by incorporating what you learned in Discovery, demonstrate the end of the story first; the hottest, most relevant, most differentiating portions of the software.

NOT AGAIN

Have you ever performed a demonstration and realized you're consistently making the same mistake? For example, while demonstrating some general ledger software, a prospect asked me, "Bob, can you please show me what an on-screen ledger card looks like?" I replied, "Sure, let me go to our inquiry screen. I'll enter a general ledger account number, click this button and show you the ledger entries for this account." Unfortunately, there was not any data associated with this account, so no information displayed on the screen. I continued with, "Well, this account doesn't seem to have any data. Let's look at a different example." I entered a different account and still no data. "Well, if you can imagine there's data on the screen…"

Three demonstrations later, another prospect asked me the *exact* same question. Because I never bothered to set up the data after the first disastrous demonstration, I found myself once again saying, "Picture this…" I repeated this mistake for a full year before I finally took the time to find an account with data that allowed me to effectively present the benefits of our general ledger inquiry screen.

This crime seems so obvious it's almost embarrassing to write about! Take the time to list the top ten mistakes you make on a repetitive basis. Next to each mistake put a deadline for correcting the mistake. There's no excuse for not correcting repetitive mistakes.

HOUR GLASS HYPNOSIS

We have all been there. As the computer begins processing, the hourglass or the wheel appears on the screen and we all just stare at it, trying to will the thing to go away and for the software to return with the results. If you're the presenter at the front of the room, it can sometimes seem like hours. It can seem like hours to the audience as well! You know what they are thinking: *"If it is this slow with one user, what will it be like when we if 150 users running at once?"* OK, we all know that's not how it will work, but it's how people think. I once had a friend that explained it this way: "My laptop is running slow because it's running on batteries so of course it's running a little slower." It was great watching the audience as they processed this information. First came the little nod of acceptance, then the quizzical sideways glance, and finally the small smile as they realized he was joking.

All joking aside, we need a way to deal with the dreaded hour glass, both when it is expected and when it is not. Let's start with the easy one, those situations where you know the software will take some time to process information. Since you know where these spots are, so have your words ready. Explain what's happening. List a few benefits of what they have just seen. Have some questions at the ready that will support the value of what you're showing. You might, for example, ask them how they get the same information today. Or what tools they're using for the same capabilities. With a little rehearsal you can mask those short delays, eliminating the discomfort for both you and the audience.

If the delay is unacceptably long, have a results screen already populated, either in the software or as a screen shot. Yes, you'll need to tell the prospect that you're showing them pre-processed results, but that's OK. They primarily want to know what they can do with the software, not just how it performs in an artificial situation on a laptop at the front of a room.

Unexpected hourglass situations require a little different handling. The very best situation is to have a teammate that can cover for you while you figure out what's going on and get the demonstration back on track. Most of us aren't very good at doing two things at once, particularly under pressure. Have your teammate take over the conversation by talking about benefits, asking questions, and generally covering the subject you would normally be showing. In the meantime, you can fix or go around the problem. But always remember this: ***Don't show your work!*** Disconnect or otherwise block the projector so the audience will stay focused on your teammate, not the screen. If you're by yourself, it might be a good time to either call a break or go to your back-up slides and information. You did prepare back-up capabilities, didn't you? Whatever you do, don't just be hypnotized staring at the hourglass, and don't leave the screen up for everyone else to be hypnotized as well.

THE CATCH-PHRASE AS A CRUTCH

I admit, this one is more of a misdemeanor than a felony. Just about everyone I know (including myself) has a tendency to latch on to phrases and gestures. Typically, these "catch-phrases" are handed down from a respected mentor, and they become a regular part of your demonstration vocabulary. Other times, they're simply bad speech habits. Whatever the case, they'll annoy your audience.

Here's an example. I have a tremendous amount of respect and admiration for Guy Lammle, one of the founders of

NxTrend Technology. Guy was really good at coming up with *his own* catch-phrases to illustrate important points. Many of the phrases blend his business savvy with the grass roots approach to life he learned growing up in Nebraska. Because so many people respect Guy (and the fact that he's the boss!), it wasn't uncommon to hear others using a "Guy phrase." A number of years ago, Guy began using the phrase "the reality is." In context the phrase would sound something like, "A lot of people think we're simply a software company, but *the reality is,* we're also a service company." Suddenly, every salesperson and manager in the company was using the catch-phrase "the reality is" at every opportunity in his or her presentations. It became a corporate trademark that quickly wore itself out. Imagine being a prospect and receiving five presentations from different managers in the company and each one includes the phrase "and the reality is" multiple times. Believe me, overused catch-phrases are distracting and annoying.

Another example relates to a top salesperson that I know who uses the catch-phrase "et cetera, et cetera" when describing multiple software features. For example, he'll be showing the prospects how they can price a product in the order entry system and he'll say something like, "And in this field, you can price the item to the customer using a list price less a discount, a target margin, et cetera, et cetera." What does this mean? Why not finish the point with the other price methods that apply to the customer's needs? Once this catch-phrase is used for the third or fourth time, *it* becomes the focal point rather than the beneficial features of your product. That's why catch-phrases are dangerous.

Other catch-phrases and gestures to avoid:
- A paradigm shift.

- Process re-engineering.

- Collaboration.

- No problem.

- As a matter of fact.

- To be honest.

- Cool!

- Ahhhhh.

- You know.

- "Um" as filler.

- Pencil tapping.

- Clicking a pen in and out.

- Jingling change in your pocket (empty your pockets before you begin).

- Flicking the laser pointer on and off.

- Any type of slang or personal word pattern that becomes distracting.

Most people with catch-phrases never realize they're using them. Seek help from your selling teammates to eliminate them from your vocabulary. Ask your colleagues to point out when you overuse a phrase or gesture. If appropriate, provide your teammates with the same feedback. You'll be amazed at the ones you've latched on to without even realizing it!

Without becoming paranoid about them, avoid catch-phrases, repetitive slang and annoying habits. It will make you a better demonstrator.

SUMMARY

Presenting crimes come in many different varieties. Of those listed above, the Presentation Crutch is certainly the most serious. In fact, most presenters would win more deals, please more prospects, and have more fun if they just spent some quality time with their slides. Take the first step and revamp your slide deck(s) to cut out all the irrelevant information, replace words with images, and simplify your messages. Then spend a little time before each demonstration to customize the slides to properly reflect the prospect's interests and concerns.

TEAM CRIMES

Some crimes are so special that it takes a whole team to commit them! If you're like me, you often find yourself in situations where you're demonstrating with several colleagues. And while you appreciate their support and assistance, it can be a little unnerving. Team demonstrating takes practice and coordination. You can't put eleven people on a soccer field and automatically expect them to play well, even if they're all professionals. It takes a coach, a game plan, and practice. And yet we throw a team into a demonstration that's critical to closing a deal with little more preparation than a hurried conversation on the way to the prospect's office.

The crimes detailed below are easy to prevent. A little bit of teamwork, some basic ground rules, and perhaps a touch of practice here and there will solve the problem. As an added bonus, the ride back to the airport together after the demonstration will be much more relaxed.

WHY DON'T YOU SHOW THEM…?!

I remember a large opportunity that I had that necessitated multiple experts from our company to perform the demo. I was in the audience with the prospect while one of my team members was demonstrating some business intelligence executive dashboards. I noticed that he didn't show one of the dashboards that alerted the executive of a low margin situation. We always showed that screen. I think you know what happened next. I raised my hand and asked him "say Niel, aren't you going to show them the low margin warning screen? I think they would really like to see that." Niel raised his eyes to me followed by his chin. He then smiled, walked out straight towards me and said "That's a great idea Bob, why don't you show that to them!" Everyone in the room laughed and I was truly embarrassed. He then quickly said "Actually, I don't have the data configured to show that today but perhaps we can show that in a follow up session?" The prospect agreed and we moved on. After the demo Niel and I talked. I said "please don't ever do that to me again" to which he replied "No problem as long as you never do that to me again!" Needless to say, I learned my lesson. Committing the "Why don't you show them…" crime is a gamble you or your teammates will surely lose. There are simply too many variables demonstrating complex solutions to take that chance.

PILING ON

In American football, you'll occasionally see a penalty for unnecessary roughness. Being tackled by one person is OK, in fact it's how the game is expected to be played. And, yes, occasionally it takes a couple of defenders to tackle the player with the ball. But continuing to have players jump on top of the growing pile of men is referred to as piling on and is against the rules. Think of the poor person at the bottom of that pile!

It only makes sense that piling on is against the rules in American football. Similarly, it should be against the rules in sales calls, presentations and demonstrations as well. Piling on can happen at any point in the demonstration, but it usually happens in response to a question. Someone in the audience asks a question because they are confused by what they just saw demonstrated. The presenter, the one at the front of the room, tackles the question and attempts to answer it. But that's not enough for all of the other team members. Just to make sure that the question is thoroughly answered, every other member of the team has to jump on it as well as each person adds their opinion and critical fact. Just imagine being the poor person at the bottom of the pile – the person that asked the question! If you're lucky, they're simply overwhelmed. More likely, they're confused and wondering just why the whole team was so defensive about a simple question.

The rules are simple: The person at the front of the room has the responsibility of answering the question. They may answer it, defer it, or ask for assistance with it. Depending on the ground rules you established before the demonstration, they may ask for help verbally or non-verbally. If you're not the person at the front of the room, your job is easy – don't jump in unless the presenter asks you to.

In Chapter 9, Team Demonstrating we'll go into more depth on how to work great as a team. If team crimes are a constant problem with your team and you have an event coming up, go to our website NOW (www.2WinGlobal.com) and download an article titled "Stand Up, Sit Down, Don't Fight, Fight, Fight!" You can e-mail this article to everyone on your team for a quick-fix for common team crimes.

CHAPTER SUMMARY

Wow, what a list! While the number of crimes may seem overwhelming, it won't be long before you recognize them in progress and instinctively take corrective action. If you concentrate on performing a thorough Discovery of your prospect, many of the crimes will eliminate themselves. You'll eliminate even more by simply slowing yourself down and asking lots of questions during the demonstration. Focus on making a mental bridge between your Discovery information and your software features. This will put you one step closer to a winning demonstration. Prioritize the crimes you commit most frequently and work on correcting those.

Respected professionals like doctors, lawyers and accountants are required to participate in continuing education every year. Every professional sport has a training camp where players practice fundamental skills before the season begins. Teams and individuals practice throughout a season to ensure their fundamentals remain sharp. Why expect anything less from our profession? Commit yourself to continuing education and practice. Constantly drill yourself on demo crimes. Look for outside help and expertise to improve your demonstration techniques and processes. It's only through a constant personal commitment to continuing education that you will remain crime-free.

If you have identified a new demo crime, I'd love to hear about it (bobr@2WinGlobal.com). And please, include the story behind the crime being committed!

CHAPTER 5
The Discovery Process

PURPOSE

In the first four chapters, I've referred to the "Discovery Process." Now it's time for us to examine this very important topic in detail. To illustrate the importance of this step in your demonstration, think about refinishing a fine piece of furniture such as your grandmother's dining room hutch. You begin by moving the piece of furniture into your workshop. The refinishing process itself starts with the application of a varnish stripper, a small area at a time. This is an incredibly laborious process that takes hours to complete. The old finish is carefully removed with steel wool. You'd never use a scraper or power tool because they could gouge or scratch the surface of the wood. After weeks of work, you're now ready to smooth the surface with fine sandpaper. At long last, you can clean up the hutch and begin carefully applying a stain and finish. It's at this point you get really excited! The fruits of your labor are finally being displayed to you one section at a time. After weeks of preparation, your application of a finish takes only 30 minutes! When you're finished, you're proud of your work. If your grandmother were there to appraise the finished product, she'd be your greatest admirer.

The Discovery Process (or Discovery for short) is much like the preparation work you perform in refinishing that piece of furniture. It's only through careful *preparation* that your demonstration will have a smooth, polished look and feel. Shortcuts in the beginning will produce an uneven, incomplete and unprofessional demo.

A properly executed Discovery will almost guarantee for you:

- The opportunity to create allies for your demonstration.

- Information about the attendees' personal backgrounds.

- Valuable information about their business jargon, customers, vendors, employees and data to use for the demo.

- A way to begin establishing trust with your prospect before the demonstration ever begins.

What's the difference between a Discovery Process and a pre-demonstration interview? The name implies the difference: *Process*. A good Discovery is more than just a casual interview. It follows a three-step process that we will cover in this chapter. But both have the same goal: To build relationships with your prospect and learn as much as possible so you can reflect that knowledge in your demonstrations and presentations.

Granted, it's not practical for all software demonstrations to begin with a full-blown Discovery. For example, you wouldn't perform a Discovery process if:

- You sell in a retail environment and a prospect walks-up to you requesting a demonstration of Apple iTunes.

- You're an inside or base-account salesperson responsible for selling additional software to a nationwide customer base. It is still important to gather as much information as practical, but a full Discovery for small upgrades is cost prohibitive.

- You are at a trade show and someone walks into your booth and requests a demonstration.

- The price of your software doesn't justify the time and expense for a full Discovery. Do not, however, use this as a justification for not learning what you can about your prospect.

However, if you're selling a comprehensive piece of software used throughout an organization, a thorough Discovery is crucial. You must gain access to the departments and individuals involved in this massive change. It's important to meet with as many of the demonstration attendees as possible *preferably at their offices*.

If your primarily demonstrate on the web or in markets that restrict contact with the prospect many of the concepts you are about to read still apply but, in condensed form.

STEP ONE: PRE-DISCOVERY

As with your grandmother's hutch, the hard work starts long before the main event. Pre-Discovery work is everything you need to do to ensure successful interviews.

Regardless of how you first become engaged in an opportunity, it is your responsibility to ensure that you have the information needed to make the demonstration successful. That's why I suggest an internal 'engagement interview': A number of questions that you use consistently with whoever invited you into the opportunity. The sample engagement interview form below can be used as a starting point, but you will want to develop a standard set of questions that is relevant to your selling environment. When you do, be sure that these points are always covered in your questions:

- Why is the prospect interested in the solutions that you have been asked to present? What problems are they trying to solve or what opportunities are they trying to exploit?

- Within the prospect, which individuals should you focus on, both during Discovery and during any presentations or demonstrations? Who is the champion and who is the detractor?

- Where are we in the sales process? If your interaction with the prospect is successful, what will be the next step?

- What is our overriding message for this prospect? What financial values are we trying to find or validate, and what shape will our eventual value proposition take?

When you first start asking these questions of your own people, you will likely meet resistance. The account manager may say something like, "Don't worry, just show up and do your usual demo." But be persistent. If you ask your questions consistently you will start getting the answers that will make you a more valuable team member both during Discovery and demonstrations.

Your Pre-Discovery work is not over when you have the above answers. In fact, it is just starting. With a better idea of *why* you are involved, you can now turn your attention to the prospect themselves. In other words, you can do research. I like to do three types of research: Industry, Prospect, and Opportunity. When I was selling to wholesale-distributors, I made it a point to understand that industry, but I also worked to understand the niche in the industry occupied by my prospect. I worked to understand terminology, issues, and metrics unique to the industry. If your solution applies to many industries, spend a little internet time to learn what you can about how the industry operates and what it measures. If your solution is more industry specific, you will, over time, learn the details of the industry in greater depth.

Those of you who demonstrate a technical, middle-ware solution might be wondering why it is important to understand how a company measures itself. With the increased need to cost justify capital and expense expenditures, you need to understand how your technical solution can contribute to their organizational goals.

We talked earlier about what you can learn about your competitors just by searching websites. The same is true for your prospect. You can learn about key players, organizational performance and outlook, organizational and geographic structure, vendors, partners, and major customers. In short, you can enter Discovery interviews fully prepared. That preparation shows a commitment and passion that prospects will notice.

With your engagement questions answered and your research completed, it is time to formulate interview strategies, including the following:

- Identifying a sponsor to help you with interview schedules and methods. Often, the account manager or salesperson will have already identified the sponsor or champion. In fact, you should find out this information as a part of your engagement interview.

- Building a Discovery strategy that includes who to interview, how to conduct interviews (in person or by phone?), and key issues and value points that you must find or validate.

- Building a Discovery question set. Smart interviewers develop a set of open-ended questions that serve very specific purposes in an interview. Some questions are designed to uncover broken processes. Others are designed to help you understand key metrics and value points. Still others are designed to guide conversations towards a more strategic or more tactical discussion.

- Building a strategy for overcoming Discovery objections. I'll cover these objections in more detail towards the end of this chapter. The point here is to make sure that you anticipate and have answers for the objections that you are most likely to hear in this particular opportunity.

STEP TWO: DISCOVERY INTERVIEWS

Now that you've done the initial work to get your Discovery set up, what do you do when it is time for the actual interviews? The number one thing to remember is you're there to *gather information* that will enable you to deliver a powerful, compelling demonstration. The key to a successful Discovery is employing three *basic communication skills*: ask lots of questions, listen intently and write down your notes.

Since you'll be spending time with your prospect, you will definitely be presented with a number of selling opportunities. Obviously, you want to make the most of any selling opportunity you have, but use common sense. You've set the expectation that the Discovery is a time for you to learn about them. Don't blow your credibility by overtly selling.

Although you've established an agenda for your visit, be flexible. Respect the time commitments that you've made, but keep your eyes and ears open. I'm continually surprised by how I uncover some of the most valuable information from sources that I didn't even know existed before I started.

As a final point to consider in conducting your interviews, remember that you are there to understand three aspects of every process or capability:

1. Current: How is a job currently done? What gaps or problems currently exist? What systems are utilized to help automate or simplify the current method of working?

2. Desired: What changes would the interviewee like to see in this particular area? Don't assume that your solution will be the answer, probe to find out the answer that the interviewee most favors.

3. Impact: As we have already discussed, change is hard. So there should always be a reward for change. If you can get down to true metrics (time saved, errors eliminated, manual steps automated) then you can offer up that reward in the form of benefits during the demo.

Let me give you a short example of the importance of this current/desired/impact approach. A number of years ago I demonstrated an order management system to a mid-sized prospect that was not fully automated. I asked the current and desired questions but, not the impact question. During the demo, I made a big point of showing how, once completed, all orders would automatically be billed and electronic or paper invoices would be produced. I even emphasized the benefits of eliminating steps and reducing errors. I was feeling pretty good when I saw a hand go up. The question asked was this: "What about Ben?" I was stumped. I had no idea what they were talking about. To make a long story short, it turns out that Ben was the person that checked every price on every line item on every order before the order was billed and closed. Had I asked my impact question during my Discovery interview, I would have had a good answer for Ben. As it was, I had to stumble and backtrack until we determined what Ben would do going forward!

Now let's look at an actual interview. We'll assume that you have a good interview strategy; you have prepared the proper questions and are prepared to take proper notes using the current/desired/impact consideration. You have walked into the interviewee's office or reached them on the phone. Now what?

First, it's important to properly introduce yourself upon meeting each individual you'll be interviewing. Here's the introduction I normally use as I move through the organization. "Bill, Bob Riefstahl. It's a pleasure to meet you! Bill, I would like to briefly introduce myself. Again, my name is Bob Riefstahl and I'm Regional Sales Manager for FutureF Software." (I always like to provide my name twice because most people simply can't remember the pronunciation, which is why I also hand them a business card.) My introduction continues, "Bill, I've asked to meet with you today so I can learn about the job you perform, the processes you go through and the likes and dislikes you have about your current software. I can promise you this: I won't be selling anything to you today. I'm simply here to learn. Briefly, I've been with FutureF for eight years and have always been focused solely on your industry."

To lower their guard, I stress that I'm "not selling today." This usually helps me get more information from them later. Naturally, some people don't believe this statement; so don't start talking about your company or products. Focus instead on asking questions about the person as an individual and the job at hand. I also tell them a little about myself. When they know I've been with my company doing the same job for eight years, it adds to my credibility. If you've only been with your company for six months, this statement will be less beneficial. Instead, talk about how long you've been involved in their industry, the software industry, etc. There's nothing wrong with adding a personal note to your introduction as well. I enjoy letting my audience know I'm married and have two boys. This invites them to see me as an individual rather than just a software salesperson.

Some people advocate small talk. Use some discretion and common sense when engaging in small talk. Discussing your plane trip in a negative light is a cliché to avoid. I prefer discussing something I notice in their office or lobby. If I see golf plaques, statues and pictures everywhere, it's safe to assume they enjoy golf. Since I play golf and if it seems appropriate, I go ahead and ask them about golf. If they begin the meeting by being short and curt with their answers or seem impatient, I drop the small talk completely. They're giving strong cues they're not in the mood to chat.

As you begin building trust and rapport with your interviewee, it is time to move forward into information gathering. We have already discussed the current/desired/impact formula, but I like to get a little more specific in what I'm looking for. My questions and my approach to each interview will be based on a combination of our sales approach and position as well as the role and expectations of the interviewee. It is all based on a simple quadrant that helps me focus on the information that will be of most value:

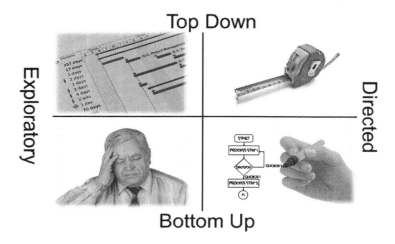

- **Exploratory to Directed:** Depending on your product and the nature of the opportunity, you might be performing a true exploratory Discovery; probing for problem areas, working to understand the spectrum of business problems and their impact, and working to truly understand what the prospect would like to see changed. This works great when selling large ERP-style systems in a competitive replacement opportunity. It is also well suited to a longer sales cycle with, presumably, a high anticipated value. But it is not always the right approach. Often you need to direct your Discovery towards a very specific set of problem areas with an anticipated solution and value that matches your offerings. This is particularly true with add-on products, specific point solutions, and any environment with a short sales cycle or low revenue potential. In the case of a directed Discovery, you are less interested in *finding* solutions and value and more interested in *validating* the sales team's assumption of solution and value.

- Top Down to Bottom Up: Every opportunity starts from a given perspective. In some cases, that perspective is top down – based on management looking to improve overall performance either organization wide or in a particular area. Management measures by numbers and goals, not by processes and tasks. In other cases, the perspective is bottom up – recognition of serious problems in processes, capabilities, or systems. These opportunities are recognizable more by the problems discussed than the impact of those problems. In either case, you will want to understand current, desired, and impact; but your approach will likely be different. When working top down, you will want to first understand the measures by which the organization is judged, the current metrics associated with these measures, and the goals for improvement. Then you can look for the changes that help in obtaining those goals. In a bottom up opportunity, you will start by understanding the processes and problems, then work your way up to determine the impact improvements in these areas can deliver. This distinction also helps you in determining the questions you ask of different people: In general, upper management and executives will be more interested in discussing value, while line management and staff will be more interested in discussing processes.

In addition to the actual information gathered, you should always be looking for three critical bits of information from every interviewee:

1. **Buying-Motivation** – What's the number one thing they want to get from the change?

2. **Personality Mapping** – How can you expect them to act and respond during demonstrations and presentations?

3. **Unique Market Position** – What sales or service offerings differentiate your prospect in their marketplace?

1. Buying-motivation - I'm sure you're thinking, "Buying-motivation? Isn't that a rather obvious thing to find out? After all, I'm a professional and certainly savvy enough to ask this question." I realize that you understand, appreciate and embrace the concept of speaking to the *ultimate decision-maker* to learn their buying-motivation. However, the dynamics of a software demonstration also make it important to learn the buying-motivation of the *non-decision-makers*.

Non-decision-makers are the other people involved in the evaluation and decision process. These people are sometimes referred to as coaches, influencers, recommenders, evaluators or blockers. They could also be a spouse, child or a brother-in-law! The point is simple: these individuals will make up most of your demonstration audience. Although they won't make the ultimate decision, they're key to the *decision process*. For that reason, you need a sense of everybody's buying-motivations.

With a comprehensive software product, the Discovery is the best way to uncover buying-motivations. While interviewing each individual slated to attend the demonstration, ask them, "If this was your sole decision to make, and you were the only person affected by the decision, what would you look for in a new software system?" The answers you receive will become the foundation of how you will present different benefit statements to different individuals in your demo.

Rarely do I ask buying-motivation questions until I've had an opportunity to spend some quality time with each person. Typically, I've already asked questions and learned a great deal about them as individuals, their job functions, the processes they perform and what they like and don't like about their existing software. By this point, I've established some degree of credibility and trust. That's when I ask the buying-motivation question ("If this was your sole decision…"). Since I've taken the time to fact-find and build credibility before asking the question, I generally have a sense for the answer that they give me. However, I always find their responses interesting. Some are surprising. On occasion, I'll get a totally unexpected answer.

For example, during one Discovery, I remember spending 45 minutes with a purchasing agent. I learned all about his personality, his job and his likes and dislikes about their system. When I asked him the buying-motivation question, his response was, "I wouldn't change a thing if it were my decision. Sure, I think we could improve a few things in our software, but I really think this software search is a waste of time." My only thought at that moment was, "Wow, I'm sure glad I learned this *before* the start of the demonstration!" As I continued my interview, I learned:

- Although he was not the decision-maker, he could make my life miserable during and after the demonstration.

- He could cause enough trouble to totally collapse the selection process.

- He was going to be argumentative.

- So, I prepared myself accordingly, both for the demonstration itself and for the time following the demo. In the end, my preparation paid off. He became one of our strongest advocates. You know why? We were the only company that:

- Spent time learning what he needed.

- Showed him how he could use the software to do his job.

- Followed-up after the demo with materials that were relevant to him ("white papers" about our purchasing process and reference letters from customers whose purchasing department had been improved).

After interviewing everybody, I find it helpful to categorize all the buying-motivation responses. I do this in the left pages of my Discovery Log; Rusty uses his Interview Profile. I use the following groups when I do this exercise:

a) Micro-job-functionality.

b) Strategic.

c) Political.

d) "Anything is Better Than What We have Now."

e) No-change.

f) No-response.

a) Micro-Job-Functionality – Individuals who respond in this way usually want to eliminate a daily job function. Examples might include the following:

- I want to eliminate having to take information from three reports and key them into a spreadsheet.

- I don't want to press the return key sixteen times just to begin taking an order.

- I want to have *one* inquiry that gives me all the information about a product.

These responses are almost always from non-decision-makers. Even so, if people who respond in this way are included in the demonstration, their participation will have an impact on your overall score. This is true even if they're not formally identified as member of the selection team. Their presence and ability to raise objections creates influencing factors. If you ignore this fact, you're in for a long and ugly demonstration! Treat these individuals (and all non-decision-makers) with care and respect.

Micro-job-functionality folks are particularly valuable because they provide specific information for building your demonstration. They'll give you real, everyday problems. They're a great source for samples of data, business forms and process flows. Verify your understanding of the information they provide every step of the way. This will help you anticipate questions and problems. Verification will also help to build trust and credibility and assist you later when you ask your buying-motivation question. With all this information, you'll be able to demonstrate solutions, not just software. If you can get this group moving in one direction, they'll walk right across the Bridge for you.

There is something to watch out for with the micro-job-functionality group. During your interview, they will usually tell you their problems. Then, they'll want to know, *right now*, if your software can do anything about them. "Bob, can your software fix this problem?" It's imperative that you fend off as many of these questions as possible. I've found that if you answer too many questions during the Discovery, your demonstration is anti-climatic. Worse yet, some of these people will come to the demonstration with the sole purpose of finding holes in your software because they think what you told them during the Discovery was too good to be true. Save your aces for the big event!

If you're asked a "can your software solve" question, give them an evasive answer. For example, "Jean, I have some ideas in this area, but I'd prefer presenting them to you during the demonstration. Since you'll be the ultimate judge, I know you'll want to make sure the software can solve that problem. The best way for me to help you with your decision is by providing you a proper demonstration of our software. Is that okay with you?" Most of the time, they're comfortable with this kind of response and will appreciate your honesty (and the small dose of flattery!). Your forthright attitude will help you build trust and credibility.

A micro-job-functionality response to your buying-motivation question requires patience. Get more information. Dig, dig, dig. Avoid answering their direct questions and let their interest build. In addition to providing valuable information, these individuals can help you generate excitement and enthusiasm both leading up to and during the demonstration.

b) Strategic – This response usually comes from a senior manager or leader in the company. Their response will reflect that they are looking at the *big picture*. Strategic responses are usually in the form of a financial payback for the new software. Typical strategic responses include:

- I want the new system to reduce our transaction costs by 20 percent.

- We need the new software to help us figure out a way to add three percent to our margin.

- The new software needs to reduce errors across the company.

People with strategic responses are almost always on the selection team. They understand the interdepartmental operations of the company. They're experienced enough to look beyond a "really cool software feature" that's a perfect solution to their problems. More important, they understand the financial goals of the company. They like to evaluate software based on overall value. They often have preconceived ideas of where these financial improvements can be derived. Unfortunately they rarely volunteer that information to you. It almost becomes a mystery game. For that reason, it's critical you learn as much as possible about their buying-motivation. Interestingly, they don't want to divulge that information for fear that you'll show it to them! Seems ridiculous, but it's true. In their minds, if they volunteer this information and you show them exactly what they're looking for, you now hold all the leverage for the sale. They hate being in this position, so they hide behind their response.

Earlier, I alluded to the television show "Columbo." I find the Columbo investigative technique works when I have somebody (typically an executive) who's giving me generic responses to my buying-motivation questions.

For example, let's say I get the response, "I want to increase our margins with the new software product." In "Columbo-fashion," I begin digging. Here are some of the questions I ask:

- Can you give me some examples of ways you think software could increase your selling margins?

- Have you experienced software products that offer features to help you increase your margins? Can you describe them for me?

- Do you have any industry associates who have been able to increase their margins through the use of their software product? Who are they? What software do they use?

This strategic responder has provided you with a mystery to solve. Don't make the mistake of assuming you know how to solve his margin issue. You need to find out what *he* has in mind. Use this information to shape your demonstration. Include specific examples that fit the executive's goal of increasing margins. Demonstrate methods he can relate to. With this accomplished, you'll find the executive much more willing to cross the Bridge.

Here are a couple tips that relate to executives in general:

1.   A properly timed interview with the executives is important. Whenever practical, I prefer interviewing them *last*. They'll appreciate the amount of time you're investing to learn as much as possible about their company. This helps build their trust during your demonstration.

2.   In addition to asking the buying-motivation question, I like to share with them a synopsis of what I learned

in my Discovery. During the sharing process, it's important to remain reserved and not disclose too much information. I do share some of the comments made by his staff regarding buying-motivations to verify the validity of these comments.

Staff opinions sometimes don't coincide with those of management. This phenomenon creates an interesting dilemma. Let me share the story of a hard lesson I learned working with a Tennessee company several years ago. During my Discovery, I was scheduled to interview a number of executives, middle managers and front-line personnel. I started with the executive vice president and ultimate decision-maker (executive). He answered my buying-motivation question with something like, "I really need the new software to help us increase our sales." Since I knew of many ways to show this in a demonstration, I figured I had what I needed, so I moved on.

During my interviews with the sales manager (middle management), he answered the buying-motivation question with, "I need our salespeople to improve their performance. I believe a good software package will eliminate a number of unnecessary steps and give them more time to spend on the phone with customers."

Next up were the salespeople (staff). They told me they really needed the ability to override the price of certain items because almost all their customers want to negotiate price. So, they needed the capability to re-price items. The authorization step their existing system enforced was slowing them down.

At the end of the day I added up my facts. They were as follows:

- The salespeople needed to override price.

- The sales manger wanted to streamline order entry, ensuring sales efficiency and positively impacting sales.

- The executive vice president wanted to increase overall sales.

I was armed with some *great* information, or so I thought! The next day I demonstrated my software to the same group of people. During the order entry segment of the demonstration, I went to a line item, positioned myself on the price field and began explaining all the ways they could manipulate the price of an item while the customer is on the phone. "You can enter a discount amount, perform cost-plus pricing, target-margin pricing or simply type over the existing price with whatever price you need to make the sale!" (Addressing the buying-motivation of the salespeople.) "At the end of the sale, provided the overall margin is within a corporate set tolerance, the order is automatically approved. Your sales manager no longer has to approve every order. Can you imagine the efficiencies you can derive from this feature alone?" (Addressing the buying-motivation of the sales manager.) "This capability will certainly help you increase your sales because your salespeople are now free to speak to more customers per hour translating into increasing sales." (Addressing the buying-motivation of the executive vice president.) "What do you think?"

At this point, the salespeople were giving each other "high-fives." The sales manager was staring at the executive vice president who slowly turned to me and said, "Bob, this is exactly what I want to avoid in our new system. You missed the whole point. Increasing our sales at the cost of profits isn't exactly my goal. I can't believe you have *any* customers allowing this kind of lunacy. Can you turn that feature off?"

For the next 30 minutes I attempted to climb out of the hole I had inadvertently dug for myself. This happened because I made two crucial errors during my Discovery:

1.   I didn't dig for enough information during interviews with my strategically motivated buyers (the executive vice president and the sales manager). With more questioning, I'd have learned the salespeople were always overriding the price because their current software could not support a customer adjustable pricing method. My software would eliminate 99 percent of their need to negotiate prices. Had I focused on setting up prices rather than changing them during order entry, I'd have hit a home run! I *assumed* a logical connection between price override capabilities and greater efficiency. Had I learned more about *their* needs in this area during my Discovery, I would've formulated a better plan.

2. The order in which I interviewed people was backwards. If I had interviewed the executive vice president last, I would've completely avoided the pricing controversy.

c) Political – This type of response to the buying-motivation question is usually given because the individual wants to make the *right* response. They want to align themselves with somebody else in the organization. (Typically, a political response is a mirror image of the buying-motivation of their boss.) Matching this other person's response is their primary objective. If you're not interviewing upper management until later in the day, it can be difficult to spot this type of response. Political responses are dangerous because you're prevented from learning what this person really wants and expects from the software.

For example, let's say you're interviewing a sales manager and she responds to the buying-motivation question with, "As you may have heard from our executive team, we need a software package that'll allow the company to increase shareholder value over the next three years." Hum? Do you know many sales managers who think in terms of shareholder value? I don't. The ones I know are interested in more sales, increased margins, less errors and better information. However, because this person is political, they want to make sure they look good in the eyes of her boss. In order to maneuver around her initial response, try asking probing questions like, "I understand and appreciate the need to increase shareholder value. Many of our customers feel the same way. But allow me to drop down to a little lower altitude for a moment. What do you think the new software needs to do in order to make your personal job easier?"

When dealing with political individuals:

- Get it down to a personal level. Ask a few more questions. This is the only way you'll learn what they really have in mind for a new system.

- Ask your buying-motivation question when you're alone with them. By shielding them from outside pressures, you'll have a better chance of getting around their political response.

- Ask them whom they report to and then ask them if their manager feels the same way they do. If their answer is "yes," you know who is driving their political response. If they answer "no," ask them who else in the company feels the same way they do. This will flush out their alignment.

d) "Anything is Better Than What We have Now" – Be cautious if you get this type of response to your buying-motivation question. Why be cautious? The person is stating up-front he'll show you no loyalty or preference over your competitors. If yours is the only software product they're looking at (a perfect world), you're safe. However, if there are competitors involved (the world you deal with every day), you need to push for a more specific response.

Think of being in a shopping mall and you're extremely hungry. I'm talking *dizzy* hungry. You need and want food quickly, so you hustle over to the food court. In front of your eyes are eight restaurants offering hamburgers, pizza, tacos and five other delightful choices. In your condition, any food will do. You decide to get tacos, and you feel satisfied after eating four. But you'd have been happier two hours later if you had made a healthy choice. Satisfying your pain was your concern, not the nutritional value of the food.

By accepting an "anything is better than what we have now" response during your Discovery, you run the risk of being one of the "other" restaurants in the food court. If, however, you press for more information and learn what this individual is in the *mood* for, you can deliver it in the demonstration. The best way to accomplish this is to spend time with them in their day-to-day job. Learn how they do their work one task at a time. For each task, ask them how they'd like to see it improved. You'll gather a wealth of information that will help you demonstrate how your software will improve their job. Before you know it, they'll be craving what *you* have to offer!

e) No-Change – "I'll tell you right now, if it were my vote, I would keep the existing system and maybe enhance it to better meet our needs." This response usually comes from individuals who are concerned the new system will either severely disrupt their job (and life) or replace them completely. Interestingly, these people can sometimes turn out to be your best advocates! They're unquestionably the toughest group of people to lead across the Bridge. Think of them as "mules" that need plenty of coaxing, prodding and pushing to get them to take that first step. But once they're moving, they can haul a tremendous amount of stuff!

No-change responders tend to be some of the hardest and most loyal workers in a company. Because of their deep loyalty, management appreciates them. They usually have been in the organization for years and won't be replaced until they retire. Information services managers often fall into this group.

To gain the loyalty of a "no-changer," you need to spend a great deal of time earning his or her respect. Do *not* attempt to raid their world with an onslaught of software functionality. This will only make them more stubborn. Focus on listening rather than talking. My Discovery experiences have been that no-changers will volunteer information that helps you probe deeper into their needs. Be very careful not to leave an impression you're trying to *set them up* in the demonstration. Give them a caring ear and they'll pour their hearts out to you.

I remember a prospect I had in Meridian, Mississippi. They were evaluating our software to automate their 70-branch operation. At the time of the Discovery, all their branches operated independently. There were no business rules enforced, and the only computer capability that existed in each location was a PC. These were simple PCs that utilized an ancient operating system and were strictly used by a secretary for billing purposes. The company was considering a centralized, high-performance mainframe environment with a separate workstation for almost every employee. Suddenly, a ten-person branch location would have ten workstations (and users) instead of a single PC. Needless to say, our first (and biggest) challenge was convincing these people who could not even type, much less operate a computer system, that this project was feasible.

The corporate office sent me to the Meridian branch to meet with Charlie. He was the branch manager and though he'd been with the company over 20 years, he'd never touched a computer. In fact, he absolutely *hated* computers. Management's objective in sending me to meet Charlie was to expose me to the formidable task of convincing him this project would be good for his branch operation. They determined that if I could convince Charlie the system was worthwhile, I could convince anyone in the company!

I received a tour of the facilities from my MIS sponsor and interviewed some of the staff. For the most part, the employees recognized a centralized system would be a tremendous improvement "as long as it didn't require them to adhere to any new disciplines" (hint, hint). As you can imagine, the concepts of "to a centralized system" and "procedural disciplines" go hand-in-hand!

After the tour, my sponsor led me to Charlie's office. (I felt like a lamb being led to slaughter!) Charlie calmly shut the door and for the next 90 minutes, lectured me about how computers were destroying business. He hated them and, while he wouldn't sabotage the project, he wanted to make sure:

- We didn't turn his branch upside down with this "damn computer."

- He didn't want it to require any discipline, rules or effort on his part.

- I knew his would be the *last* branch to come up on the new system.

As expected, Charlie's response to my buying-motivation questions was, "If it were my vote, I wouldn't change a thing around here."

During Charlie's 90-minute tirade, I kept very quiet, remained attentive and simply listened to what he was saying. There was no point trying to convince him he was wrong about the new system. When the timing was right, I changed the subject from a discussion about computers and software to *his business operation*. I asked Charlie lots of questions like:

- What do you think makes your branch so successful?

- What causes your customers the most frustration?

- Charlie, what customer issues frustrate your employees?

- What would help you work with your headquarters?

Charlie poured his heart out to me. It quickly became evident a centralized system would help Charlie's people a bunch. The men at the sales counter had no knowledge of what the other locations had in inventory without picking up the telephone and calling. Our software solved that problem. Using the current system, if a customer was placed on credit hold, the order wouldn't be entered in the system until the credit problem was resolved. They'd give the customer the merchandise and then remember (hopefully) to process the order in the computer after the customer had been taken off credit hold. Our software provided both control and flexibility for this process. The list went on and on.

During the interview, I *never* suggested or disclosed the capabilities of our software and how it could solve Charlie's problems. I was saving that for the demonstration. This was the time to listen, not sell. While doing a Discovery, always remember the age-old saying "You were given two ears and one mouth for good reason!"

As you can imagine, the demonstration was a smashing success. Charlie's participation throughout the demo was very cooperative, reserved and conservative. He eventually became one of our best advocates. To this day, his MIS people joke about Charlie because he's the first to scream if his location goes down!

f) No-Response – This is the silent-but-deadly response. These folks differ from no-changers in that they'll actually harbor information from you. For one reason or another, they simply don't want to share information. You can expect a buying-motivation response like, "Nothing comes to mind." Closed body language (arms folded in front of the chest) also signals you're dealing with a "no-responder." They'll also try to create an environment where your meeting is often interrupted. For example, during your interview they'll leave the door to their office open, inviting their staff and co-workers to pop in. They'll answer every phone call and after hanging up, proclaim how busy they are. Sound familiar?

When you encounter no-responders, expect them to be a thorn in your side during your demonstration. There could be a variety of reasons why they're miffed:

- Although they're attending the demonstration, they may not have been asked to be on the "selection committee."

- Perhaps they didn't agree with the final choices for the demonstration.

- They may be unhappy with their job or with management.

- They simply have a negative personality.

It's not your job to figure out the source of their irritation or solve their problems. You simply want and need specific information for your demonstration and that's how you can make them your ally. If you make a no-responder your ally, your competitors are in for *one tough time!* That's because no-responders tend to be very loyal and opinionated. When you gain their loyalty, your competition is left out of the game.

If you run into a no-responder, I suggest using a fast-in-fast-out routine. They don't want you to waste a lot of their time. So, at the beginning of the interview, reinforce that you only intend to take a few minutes of their valuable time. If possible, get your sponsor to help you identify these people before you arrive so you can plan your questions accordingly. If they take you by surprise, immediately shift into high gear. Move right to your buying-motivation questions (their top three likes, dislikes and suggestions for improvement). It's okay to request further information if you have a direct reason for asking the question. But don't expect a "getting to know you" session. This is strictly business. Gather the information you need for the demonstration and leave. At the conclusion of your Discovery, meet with your sponsor to see if you can learn more about no-responders. Ask something like, "Gee, Mary and Joe seemed really busy. What can you tell me about them?" If they were particularly uncooperative, your sponsor may be embarrassed and will tell you all you want to know and more.

Be direct and 100 percent business with the person who simply doesn't want to be involved in the interview or doesn't want to volunteer any information. If you can, learn who fits this profile ahead of time through your sponsor. Plan on asking quick, direct-response, business related questions. Minimize the amount of their time you take.

2. Personality Mapping - Understanding your prospect's buying-motivations enables you to prepare *what* you need to demonstrate. Determining what I refer to as "demonstration-personality" will help you anticipate *how* an individual is likely to participate and conduct themselves during your demonstration. As you'd expect, your Discovery is the best time to figure this out. You'll also be better prepared to answer objections if you've done some personality mapping.

Although a great deal of information is available on how to answer objections, a demonstration demands its own set of rules. What works for one personality trait doesn't work for another. Also, competitive advantage can be gained by combining an individual's buying-motivation with their demonstration-personality. Use this knowledge to properly pace your prospect as you lead them across the Bridge.

Here are the personality classifications I look for during a Discovery. As with buying-motivation, note these in your Discovery Log or Interview Profile.

a) **Lay-in-the-Weeds.**

b) **Visionaries.**

c) **Panacea.**

d) **Doomsayers.**

e) **Worker-bees.**

a) Lay-in-the-Weeds – From a personality perspective, lay-in-the-weeds individuals enjoy springing a trap on people. At an opportune moment, they love to pounce on your misfortune.

Bass are a type of freshwater fish that provide an excellent analogy. Bass like to hide under logs, ridges and in weeds. They're also notorious for backing themselves into a shallow weed bed and waiting for some poor, unsuspecting victim to swim by. At just the right moment, they spring into action and devour their prey whole! Lay-in-the-weeds individuals act in much the same way. They'll sit in the demonstration and wait for just the right moment to ask you a question that typically has more than one right answer. If your response contradicts what they believe to be correct, they'll devour you!

Once I interviewed a purchasing manager who was reluctant to answer my questions. "Bill, how do you forecast today?" Bill replied, "Many different ways. What ways do you support?" Warning! Warning! This told me during the demonstration he was going to be adversarial. I knew I had a lay-in-the-weeds personality on my hands. Sure enough, during the demonstration he asked the question, "Are those all of your methods of forecasting?" Since we offered a number of other forecasting methods, I answered, "No, we have several additional methods." After finishing, he asked the question again, "Do you have any other forecasting methods?" I had exhausted direct methods of forecasting, so I responded with "No." Well, he jumped all over that. "These simplistic forecasting methods won't work for us!"

Bill became relentless in his effort to discredit my software. Luckily, he ended up alienating all his peers and we won the business anyway. But, I should've spent more time in the Discovery learning *Bill's* forecasting methods. This might have helped me prevent this situation altogether. I might have begun that section of the demonstration by comparing our forecasting methods with his methods. I also could have admitted that our two methods didn't agree 100 percent. At the very least, I'd have taken the sting out of Bill's remarks.

If through your Discovery you determine you'll have a lay-in-the-weeds personality in the room, proceed very cautiously during the demonstration. Remember the "Don't Answer That" demo crime from Chapter 4? It's critical that you avoid this crime when dealing with lay-in-the-weeds folks. Respond to their questions with your own clarification questions. Draw out their *real* questions and you can avoid all types of problems during the demonstration.

b) Visionaries – As you'd expect, these are people who look beyond what they're currently using and into the future. They know where they want to go and they're realistic about getting there. They're a *dream* in a demonstration. If you gain their confidence and buy-in, they'll often become leaders during the demonstration and will help you sell. Visionaries are usually the first to take a step across the Bridge and the first to reach the other side.

Visionaries can be identified in the Discovery interview by several characteristics:

- They're change-oriented. They subscribe to the school of "if it's not broke, break it because we might improve it." They know their company is in need of improvement, and they're willing to accept the pain associated with change in order to be better. But be aware, they're not *pure* risk-takers. Rather, they take calculated risks. If you prove worthy of their confidence, they'll endorse you.

- They're often students of industry experts. During your Discovery interview, glance around their office. Try to notice industry-related books on their shelves. This makes for excellent introductory conversations. If prompted, they'll discuss the contents of the books. If your software happens to adhere to the approaches found in these books, you just scored a touchdown! (Naturally you'll want to make sure they believe in the principals in the book before you go for the score.) Prepare yourself to mention their books (if appropriate) during your demonstration.

- They're very open in interviews. They do the talking when you ask an open-ended question. They're not overly concerned with protecting their company's sacred cows.

- If you've established credibility, they'll ask you for your "opinion." Until that happens, keep your opinions very short and reserved. Remember that you're there to learn, not sell or teach. You must save excitement and solutions to their issues for the demonstration. However, if you have an issue or concern (i.e. questionable feature), visionaries are the ones you should use to test the waters.

While interviewing Sergio, a visionary CFO for a very large company in New York, he described the need for a more flexible and graphic method of performing queries of their database. Like most large enterprise-wide software applications, we implemented our software on top of a powerful relational database. One advantage of doing this is the query tools you can put in the hands of end-users to extract information from the database. Conversely, one *problem* with a relational database is the tools you can put in the hands of an end-user! If there are too many people using these tools, or they are inexperienced, performance can slow to a crawl. That's especially true with software that does heavy transaction processing (like ours did). Transaction-style databases aren't designed to accommodate unlimited, on-demand reporting, regardless of the computer's power. With this concern in mind, I asked myself, "Could this be a CFO who wants to and knows how to query a database?" While looking around the room, I noticed Sergio had multiple books on PC-based query products. Sergio went on to say, "We really need a system that'll allow us to accomplish these types of queries on our desktop. Can your software do that?"

Caution flags went up right away. If I answer this question wrong it could shake the confidence he had been building in me. Sure, we could *theoretically* allow every end-user access to this type of tool, but that would sacrifice performance. However, because Sergio had been very open in our conversations and he was not concerned with sacred cows around the company, I decided to test the waters. "Sergio, tell me a little about whose hands you would put this query tool in." Sergio responded, "Oh, only a few of us who know what we're doing. As it stands right now, our MIS department has all the data locked-up because there are no good tools available. Every time we need something special, they have to write a custom report for us." I had my answer. Sergio was responsible and knowledgeable with a relational database. He knew who should and should not have access to these query tools. So, I gave him the answer he was looking for, "Well, you'll be pleased to know the type of query tools you like are available for advanced users like yourself. As you already know, these tools in the wrong hands can be dangerous. Only a few people should have this type of access to the data. I'll make a note to make sure and show you how these work during the demonstration."

Two things were accomplished with my response:

1. Without me having to show him anything, Sergio was now convinced our solution was the right package. He'd be excited when he saw the tools in the demonstration and would sell right alongside me!

2. I set a trap for any competitor who later suggested to Sergio that it's OK to allow *anyone* access to the database.

When dealing with visionaries, it's important to get a sense for the company's overall personality. Contrary to what many people think, visionaries aren't always in a position of authority or power. From your perspective, it's unfortunate when this occurs. Visionaries who aren't in the power circle are often discounted. Typically, this happens in organizations that adopt technology late or are experiencing slow fiscal growth. Aligning with a visionary when the overall company has a more conservative personality may *feel* good, but it can often prove to be a strategic error. In these situations, go for an alignment further up in the corporate organizational chart.

A visionary in a position of authority will be your greatest asset. Unfortunately, your competition will realize this fact as well. This makes bridge-demonstrating that much more important. The goal is to get the visionary on your Bridge before the competitor. The earlier you do that, the better the odds of others in the organization following the visionary. Yours will become the software and company against which all others are measured.

Visionaries are excellent allies in a demonstration, as long as they're in a position of authority or power. If you bridge-demonstrate to them, they'll quickly and effortlessly move across the Bridge to your software.

c) Panacea –These people can usually be identified very early in the interview because they're highly critical of their existing system and express unrealistic expectations for the new software. Contrary to what you might think, they're extremely dangerous! They say things like, "Our software is terrible. For example, our bill-paying system sucks! I read an article that said our software should handle our bill-paying procedures without *any* of my involvement." We all know a statement like that is very unrealistic. Panacea-types think the new software is going to solve all their problems. While it's true they're enthusiastic about installing new software, they can do far-reaching damage in the demonstration if you can't meet their expectations.

With these folks it's important you rein in their expectations and bring them *gently* back to earth. Better this happen during the Discovery than have them come to the demonstration with unrealistic expectations. Let your competitors foster false expectations. The *best* thing that can happen to you is for your competitor to lead a panacea-type into believing their dream bill-paying feature is possible, then have it prove unrealistic during the demonstration! Your competitor's mistake seriously damages their credibility while it aligns you with this individual. Let them fall on their swords. Telling a panacea-type "no" establishes credibility. This response may not be what they want to hear, but they'll appreciate the time to recover from the fall before the demonstration.

When a panacea-type asks me about their dream feature, my preference is to let the air out of the balloon *slowly*. I like to say something like, "Mark, someday that'll be a great feature. Where did you read about this?" Mark probably won't remember. Panacea-types have always "read something" but rarely remember where. I continue, "Mark, I don't want to give you any unrealistic expectations. You'll still need to review your bills with our software. However, I'm confident our software will streamline your current bill-paying procedures. I'll make sure to show you how in the demo." Basically, I let Mark down while also throwing him a bone to bring him back up a little. This helps him recover but still sets the right expectation. Notice I didn't tell him what features we had to help him with his bill-paying procedures. Remember that this isn't the time to sell. I want to leave a teaser and move on.

Panacea-types can still give you trouble during the demonstration. (All the more reason to identify them during the Discovery.) They tend to get emotional and have strong positive and negative reactions. In fact, during the demo, it's critical you remain focused and use the Tell-Show-Tell technique discussed in Chapter 3, *Important Demonstration Concepts* (*tell* them the feature they're about to see, *show* them the feature and then *tell* them what they just saw). If you vary too much from this approach, panacea-types will become a real problem. Don't expand too far beyond your original thought or you'll wander into a quicksand of problems.

Make an ally out of panacea-types during your Discovery. This is not to say you should agree with everything they say. With them, reality is usually okay as long as you believe in their cause. They like to consider themselves experts in the company when it comes to selecting the latest in technology. Help them *feel* like an expert. In addition, you want them to sense you're there to further enhance their expertise. Panacea-types love having their expertise enhanced! Also, if you have the good fortune of a *killer* feature in your software, they're the perfect people to educate. They'll use it against your competitor time-and-time again.

Panacea-types come in all levels of an organization. Beware of the panacea-owner or CEO. They're the hardest to control. They want the software to perform some type of "gymnastics" like they read about in *Fortune* magazine. If they're hard-drivers, panacea–CEO's won't want to hear about realities. They want you to tell them *it can be done.* (Unfortunately, they'll probably request this as a special condition of the contract as well!)

For example, I performed a Discovery for a company in Houston where the president was a complete panacea know-it-all. He talked incessantly about his knowledge of how a new system should work. After ten minutes of this, I was ready to run for the door. After 90 minutes, I was searching around his office for something on which to hang myself. What made matters worse; he was your classic *95-yard spiker*. That is to say, he was famous for taking the football down to the 5-yard line and spiking it! (Stopping just short of the goal.) I finally decided to quit challenging his ideas. Instead, I began building on them by forcing myself to get enthusiastic about his ideas and getting him to tell me more about how he would imple-ment them. When his ideas were completely unrealistic, I asked some innocent questions, which helped him realize their impracticality. This allowed us to move on to the next subject.

All this aided me in gaining his confidence. I was a *believer* in his cause and he loved it. He even shared with me my competitor's offering and what they were telling him. In those few areas where I had a solid solution to his panacea-view of the world, we really bonded. Finally, I got him excited by offering solutions in several areas he hadn't even considered. Now he had even more ideas than when we started! You're probably thinking, "But you said not to give away the excitement of the upcoming demonstration during your Discovery interviews." You're right, but sometimes it's necessary to make an exception in order to win over panacea-types. And be assured, I held back a few choice features for the demo itself.

Panacea-buyers are a bit like nitroglycerin; they're very useful, but dangerous if not handled with caution. If you don't handle them properly, they'll blow-up on you. If handled correctly, panacea-types will blow-up your competition!

d) Doomsayers - These are the prospects who think that there is no solution to their problems, and the only thing new technology will do is ruin their world. If only the world would quit changing, they could maintain control and be successful. They want nothing to do with new software. The natural tendency with doomsayers is to conclude interviews with them as quickly as possible. However, cutting short their interview is a mistake.

It's easy to think their personalities are impregnable, but they almost always have a vulnerable spot. Be patient and ask many open-ended questions. Once you locate their soft spot, you have an advantage. When you address their need in the demonstration, you'll enlist the doomsayer into your camp *and* everyone around him who has been trying for years to make him smile.

To find their soft spot, your job is to be a detective. Surround the person with lots of probing questions especially as it relates to his job:

- What do you like to do first thing in the morning?

- If you only had five minutes left in the day, what would you try to accomplish?

- What are the three most frustrating aspects of your existing system?"

Continue asking questions until you determine his needs. But don't declare victory too early. It's easy to be fooled into thinking you've got what you need. For example, if you ask him the three most frustrating aspects of his job and he provides an answer, you follow-up with, "If we could offer a solution to 'frustration x' would it be of interest to you?" All too often, the answer will be, "No, because the real problem is 'frustration y.'" Dead end. Keep digging until you find his true soft spot. Once you find it, make a note in your Discovery Log and then make sure you address it in the demonstration.

e) Worker-Bees – These are the front-line people. They're usually open and honest with no hidden agendas or political motives. They're loyal employees who are willing to help you in any way possible. Worker-bees typically have a great deal of experience and longevity with the company and are one of your best sources of information during a Discovery.

- They know their existing system and environment.

- They're capable of showing you how things work in the current system.

- They'll describe what it is they like and dislike about it.

Worker-bees tend to view life *tactically* versus *strategically*. They're focused on their existing job. Worker-bees seldom have a clear vision of where they want to go. They'll probably be among your earliest candidates to cross the Bridge during the demonstration. Handling them means making sure you demonstrate improvements to their jobs. Connect with them by showing your software using *real life* situations and processes with *their* data. To assist you in this effort, get screen prints, data and examples of documents during your worker-bee interviews. It is most important to leave with a clear understanding of their needs, aggravations and processes in order to properly demonstrate to them.

Worker-bees carry the respect of their managers and peers. They're considered company experts. Other people in the room will watch their reactions to your demo. Worker-bees get excited during demonstrations and almost always show it. These are the people who make statements like "cool!" or "that's exactly what we need." They don't hide their emotions. You know right where they stand. If you score, you'll know it. If you miss the mark, you'll know that too. But at least you'll know!

Worker-bees are a very important group. They're the on-ramp to the Bridge. Use them as a barometer for your demonstration. Gauge your relative success or failure during the day based on their reactions. Tap into their perspectives. They'll help you focus your efforts during your demo. Satisfy them by properly preparing, and you'll be far ahead of your competition.

3. Unique Market Position - One of the real gems to be uncovered during a Discovery is knowledge of a company's Unique Market Position. By this, I'm referring to:

- Their unique contribution to the marketplace.

- What differentiates them from their competition?

Don't be fooled by big, broad value statements like, "We're better than our competition because we offer better service." Other disguises include "our people" or "our attitude." If you get these responses, you'll need to do some mining to determine your prospect's true Unique Market Position. Ask questions. Find out what wins them business. What makes them better than their competitors? Why do they keep their jobs after an election? Dig into specific programs, promotions, marketing techniques or service options they offer. Keep in mind their Unique Market Position is what they *perceive* to be their reason for success.

Middle managers (sales, operations, accounting, etc.) usually know the company's Unique Market Position. However, they're generally reluctant to disclose it. They're afraid you'll share it with their competition! So, be careful when gathering this information. Even more important, be discreet once you have it. This becomes particularly challenging if some of their top competitors are using your software. If you have trouble determining the Unique Market Position from the middle mangers, go to their direct reports. Typically, they're much more open with this information.

Once you uncover their Unique Market Position, figure out a way to demonstrate how your software can support and improve it. Pick out features that will contribute to what they are trying to accomplish. If necessary, discuss a modification to your software. Do not attempt to skirt this key issue. That would be a mistake.

During a Discovery in San Francisco, I had interviewed 11 people throughout a day. They sold commodity items (the same items as all of their competitors) so determining their Unique Market Position was critical. No one could give me an answer to my "what makes you unique" question until I met the 12th person in the warehouse. He happened to be one of their delivery drivers. When I asked him what made the company unique his response was, "That's easy! Let me show you the back of my truck." He proceeded to give me a tour of his truck and 50-foot trailer. Inside his trailer he had a computer system, credit card machine and a complete stock of materials. He would drive to an electric power plant and sell the maintenance crew repair tools and products from the back of his rig. Turned out their competitors used the old-fashioned telephone ordering method.

With this information in hand I created a special section in my agenda that addressed this Unique Market Position. In fact, I built a demonstration theme around their Unique Market Position. I demonstrated an end-to-end process flow for replenishing the trucks and selling products out of the truck.

After being awarded the business, I was told that none of my competitors knew to address this critical aspect of their business. I asked my new customer the question, "Why didn't any of the competitors go to the effort of demonstrating process flows for this obviously important area of your business?" Their response was "Well, they never bothered to ask us about it." Shoot, if I hadn't dug ten miles deep in my Discovery, I wouldn't have known about it either!

The best theme I can think of for any demonstration is one that wraps around a company's Unique Market Position. The result can be a very powerful and long-lasting message. Because demonstration themes are the best way to help your prospect remember your demonstration, it may be the most valuable use of this information.

STEP 3: POST DISCOVERY

So you properly prepared yourself for Discovery, you have conducted a number of great interviews, either in person or over the phone, and you have gathered up valuable information that can be used in later presentations and demonstrations. Now what?

Here is an example on what *not* to do: I was in Houston working with a prospect on a new system that automated the scheduling and dispatch efforts for a large service organization. John, the salesrep, and I were trying to get the prospect to put automated devices in all their trucks. These devices were tied in to a centralized schedule and dispatch system that completely eliminated the need for the dispatcher to use radios or cell phones to figure out where each truck was and who could best respond to a repair call.

John and I had worked together on a number of similar opportunities, and we had fallen into a pattern of Discovery where we would split the work. One of us would concentrate on the field service part of the business and the other on the office workers. In this case, I had spent some time with the service people and John had focused on the office. We had the benefits down cold, we understood management's focus on service quality, and we could demonstrate service scenarios that closely matched their business. The demonstration was going great, right up to the point where I asked the dispatcher for confirmation on how much time she could save by not having to raise service people on radios. That's when things fell apart.

In our rush to the demonstration, John and I had never compared Discovery notes. We had each interviewed a number of people, but had never sat down together to map out what we had learned. Unbeknowst to me, John had learned that the dispatcher had serious doubts about changing systems. According to John's notes, she enjoyed the time bantering on the radio and saw no need to change. If John and I had a good system for documenting our findings and communicating our conclusions, I might have avoided the ten minute rant that occurred when I opened the floor to the dispatcher. But without a better communication method, we didn't stand a chance. And we didn't get the deal.

You'll be gathering a lot of information during your Discovery, and you need to come up with a technique for recording and sharing that information. Really, we're just talking simple note taking. However, if you're not prepared and organized both before and after your interviews, you run the risk of forgetting what you learn, not incorporating it into your demonstration, and failing to communicate key information to other team members. As it did with John and I, that can seriously impact your ability to close the business.

I like to split the information I document and share into two areas: Information about the work, and information about the people. The former tells me what to show and how to show it. The latter tells me the right approach to everyone that I will be working with.

INFORMATION ABOUT THE WORK

It's likely your software has hundreds of features, functions and reports. It's impractical, inadvisable and downright undesirable to show all these features in a demonstration. You'd be committing the ultimate "Data Dump" crime if you did this to your prospect. Instead, ask yourself, "What specific features do I need to demonstrate to help lead my prospect across the Bridge?" To answer this question, you need to examine the prospect's business process flows or job functions and determine which of your features best apply to these process flows.

If you have knowledge of your prospect's industry you're probably already familiar with many of their process flows. For example, I have a pretty good knowledge of distribution. So, without visiting any particular distributor, I know that one process flow starts with the purchase of inventory and ends with the payment of an invoice. I also know this purchase-to-pay flow typically looks something like this:

1. Determine existing inventory levels of products on the shelf.

2. Calculate the proper purchase quantity for each item in inventory based on a forecasting formula.

3. Issue a purchase order to the vendor.

4. Receive and inspect the materials from the vendor when it arrives.

5. Fill backorders for customers waiting for the received materials.

6. Put the remaining materials away.

7. Receive the vendor's invoice.

8. Match the vendor's invoice with both the packing list of received material and the original purchase order to make sure there are no pricing or quantity errors.

9. Schedule payment of vendor invoices based on cash-flow analysis and due dates.

10. Print and mail checks to the vendor.

Did I list all these steps so you can learn how a distributor purchases and pays for inventory? No. What I want you to notice is how *many* decision points there are in this one process flow. Each decision point gives me the *opportunity* to show the prospect how our software can address one of their potential needs. If I understand their process flows, and how they can change for the better, I can prepare a very powerful demonstration. Can you see how this information helps me lead them across the Bridge?

Obviously, a distributor has many other processes in their business. The industries you service whether it is manufacturing, government, financial markets or others will have their own unique process flows. So the question is, what level of detail do you need to understand with regard to these process flows? You need to know the tasks associated with each major process flow. A comprehensive list of steps, like the purchase-to-pay example above, will suffice.

Another possibility is to flowchart each process. Although this level of detail isn't required, it can leave a very positive impression with your prospect. Some of your prospects have probably tackled the massive task of flowcharting their processes. If that's the case, ask if you can use these flowcharts to help you prepare for the demonstration. I'd be willing to guess if they've invested the effort in creating process flowcharts, they'll be pleased to provide you with the information. Here are a couple situations where I think it's important, in fact necessary, for you to obtain or develop process flowcharts:

- *When it's important to convince your customer you know their business processes exactly.* This is often the case when you have a general product but you're competing against a specialty product that's specifically designed for your prospect's industry. In this situation, flowcharting will help prove to the prospect you understand their business as well as your niche competitor.

- *When you're having difficulty understanding their business.* If you can't get a grasp on how they conduct business, you may find it useful to visually flowchart the processes prior to the demonstration. If you go to this effort, use flowcharts to your selling advantage. Make them an example of your professionalism and desire to become a partner with your prospect.

- *If you're new to the company/industry in training.* Flowcharting will assist you in developing a solid understanding of your chosen line of business, paying you dividends far into the future.

Even as a veteran, it's important to document process flows for your target industries. Although each prospect is unique, there'll be obvious similarities between businesses in the same industry. If you lack the knowledge to accomplish this, contact the manager of implementations for your company. Ask to be introduced to some person on her staff who can assist you. Existing customers are another good source for this information, especially if they are in the same industry. Ask if you can spend a day with them observing their people and asking questions. Explain your goal to learn more about their business and industry. If they haven't documented their process flows, offer to share this information with them when you're done. They'll almost always assist you.

As a last resort, don't be afraid to admit your inexperience to your prospect. Ask if you can return after the Discovery to spend more time with their staff to learn their processes firsthand. I once did this with a prospect in Atlanta. In addition to being new to our software, my knowledge of their industry was limited and our company had no training materials to assist me. To make matters worse, our software was fairly new to the industry. After spending two days on-site with my prospect, I wrote a 20-page report documenting and flowcharting their process flows and explaining how our software would offer them improvement. Although the report took a lot of my time and research to produce, after reading it, the president of the company was extremely impressed with my knowledge of their business and industry. In the end, we won the deal, even though I knew very little about their business when I first walked in the door!

After gaining a solid understanding of your prospect's business processes, the next focus of your Discovery is to identify what software features you need to show (or not show), during your demonstration. It'll be important to prioritize these features based on the needs and interests you uncover during your Discovery interviews. I like to use one of the following five categories (and corresponding codes) to group my software features that relate to my prospect's needs and interests:

a) **Meet Minimum (MM)**

b) **Meet Minimum Plus (M+)**

c) **Exceed Existing (E)**

d) **Drastically Exceed Existing (E+)**

e) **Doesn't Matter (DM)**

Earlier, we talked about developing some type of log to record the information you gather during your Discovery. When you start talking process flows with your interviewees, make sure your log is out and your pencil is sharp. If you recall, I use a spiral notebook because it offers me a lot of flexibility. However, matching features to process flows is one instance where I recommend using a tool, something like the Feature Survey Form shown below. The sheer volume of features you probably have in your software makes this necessary. This tool makes it both productive and effective to match software features with process flows. Use your company's marketing and technical specification literature to generate a master list of features in your software. Then place them alongside the business processes you identify and confirm them during your Discovery interviews. Using category codes makes your note taking easier. All this will help you produce a demonstration roadmap that moves your prospect across the Bridge efficiently.

Prospect (From Profile) Salesrep (From Profile)	Date:	Additional Comments MM = Meet Minimum M+ = Meet Min Plus E = Exceed E+ - Drastically Exceed DM = Doesn't Matter P = Problem R = Research

Accounts Payable

Name:
Selection Team: yes / no
Top Issue:

Centralized AP yes / no		EFT (820) yes / no
Floorplan / Consignment yes / no		Auto Match Invoices yes / no
EDI (note documents) yes / no		Laser Checks yes / no

Accounts Receivable

Name:
Selection Team: yes / no
Top Issue:

Centralized AR yes / no		C.O.D.S. yes / no
Floorplan / Finance Co yes / no		Split Check Postings yes / no
EDI (note documents) yes / no		Lock Box Postings yes / no

Credit & Collections

Name:
Selection Team: yes / no
Top Issue:

Centralized CC yes / no		Pre-Liems yes / no
Contact Managment System yes / no		Credit Limits yes / no
Multiple Credit Managers yes / no		Job Control Limits yes / no

Phone Sales / Customer Service

Name:
Selection Team: yes / no
Top Issue:

Contact Managment System yes / no		Electronic Catalog yes / no
Real time entry / availability yes / no		Issue own PO's yes / no
Marketing Campaigns Calls yes / no		Heavy Non Stocks yes / no

Warehouse

Name:
Selection Team: yes / no
Top Issue:

Bin Locations yes / no		Will Call Area yes / no
Bar Coding / RF yes / no		Assembly Area yes / no
Service & Repair Shop yes / no		Consigned Inventory yes / no

a) Meet Minimum (MM) – During your Discovery, make sure you verify the critical tasks their existing software performs. Provided a task supports a sound business process, you'll need to demonstrate this capability with your software. I call these **MM** features. As a reminder to demonstrate this capability with your software, code your Feature Survey Form and notes with **MM** whenever you uncover one of these features.

Occasionally your software may need to be modified to address one of these features. Don't panic. Just note the modification needed next to your **MM** code and be prepared to discuss how you'll accomplish this during the demonstration.

b) Meet Minimum Plus (M+) – These features are typically noted in a request for proposal (RFP). To your prospect, the features that fall into this category justify the purchase of new software. If it were not for these desired features, they'd keep their existing software. It's important to distinguish the **M+** features from the **MM** features. Separating the two will help you understand what they do today versus what they want to do in the future. This is powerful information for leading them across the Bridge.

c) Exceed Existing (E) – These are features in your software that will improve your prospect's existing processes but *they're not aware they exist*. These features will usually surprise your prospect. They may have heard about these capabilities but have never seen them demonstrated nor do they have a good idea of how they apply to their business.

If you're not careful, **E** features can put you on dangerous ground. During your Discovery, make sure to verify these features with your prospect. Test their applicability with one of your *visionary* interviewees. Though not quite as mature as your software's **MM** and **M+** features, **E** features are readily available. **E** features are "in transition" because they haven't yet gained widespread acceptance within your customer base. When that happens, they'll become **M+** and eventually **MM** features.

Let's look at the following example. The ability to sell products over the Internet was considered *cutting edge* in 1996 (see **E+** below). In 1997, Internet business transactions were not widely used in business, but were being considered in most software purchases where the Internet offered a potential medium for the sale of product. In other words, this feature moved to an **E** category. By 1999, Internet business transactions were fairly commonplace and had become an **M+** or **MM** feature for most prospects.

If your prospect shows absolutely no interest in your **E** features, don't dwell on them. (Remember the demo crime "I Love This Part of Our Software.") If they show some minimal interest in these features, I like to discuss them under a special "honorable mention" section of the agenda. That way my prospect gains an appreciation for how my application can grow with them if their business needs change, but I don't overwhelm them with features that are not directly applicable to them.

d) Drastically Exceed Minimum (E+) – These are your classic *killer* features. **E+** features usually require a radical rethinking of how a current process is accomplished. For example, for years sales analysis was performed against the main database of an enterprise-wide system. Almost overnight, the software industry woke up to the concept of "data warehousing." In this environment, sales analysis data was downloaded from the main system to a completely separate PC server. This dramatically improved the accessibility and manipulation capabilities needed for sales analysis. Even though the software I represented at the time offered outstanding data warehousing capabilities, not all of our prospects considered it a top priority. For those who identified this as a key issue, I highlighted it in my demonstration. For all others, I used less (if any) fanfare.

As with **E** features, be careful introducing **E+** features. "Does this feature apply to this prospect?" That's the question you have to ask. If it's not a "must-have" for them, de-emphasize it.

e) Doesn't Matter (DM) – Recognizing what *not* to demonstrate is as important as determining what to demonstrate. Let's say your software has a really *hot* production scheduling capability for manufacturers, however, your prospect is a distributor who only does some light assembly work and has absolutely no interest in production scheduling. What should you do? Note it as a **DM** feature on your Feature Survey Form and leave it out of your demonstration. The **DM** is your reminder a feature is simply not important to this prospect, so there's no point wasting their time.

Remember our discussion about process flows? The proper combination of process flows and software features is critical preparation material for your demonstration. Use the Feature Survey Form to cross-reference the prospect's process flows with your software's feature list. The features you note alongside a business process will be like a pilot's checklist prior to take off. Use the codes described above and leave plenty of room for notes. This information provides you the primary construction material for your Demonstration Bridge.

It's rare that a software product fits a prospect 100 percent. You may find you'll need to make some modifications, workarounds or accept deficiencies. If this potential is uncovered during the Discovery, make sure to research the problem area and discuss it *prior* to the demonstration.

This is a tough one for most demonstrators, because you're looking for weaknesses in your software. Most of us would rather avoid disclosing these weaknesses and ignore them. After all, every time you uncover a potential problem with software-fit, you jeopardize your ability to sell the account. Right? Wrong! The only mistake you can make is having your competition find out about it first. The sooner you identify problems, the better. This information, when addressed properly, will actually put you ahead of your competition. Rather than a non-fit situation surprising you in the middle of the demonstration, you'll have time to think it through and plan a work-around or modification. You'll look completely prepared and professional. Remember our earlier discussion about anxiety? What's the primary cause of anxiety? Fear of the unknown. For software demonstrators, potential software-fit problems can be a big unknown. Recognizing the problem exists and having time to define and develop a resolution plan will remove much of this fear and anxiety from your demonstration.

I had just such a situation while working with a prospect in Des Moines, Iowa. When I performed the Discovery, I learned about an important piece of functionality the prospect needed but wasn't available in my software. Before the demonstration, I spent time researching other possibilities. When the subject came up during the demonstration, I was prepared with a PowerPoint example that listed three options I'd come up with. Two of the options were workarounds. The third was a modification. Although none of the three options were a perfect match, I appeared prepared and professional. They finally told me, "Bob, you clearly understand the problem and are close to a solution. Let's move on and we can get back together on this at a later date for finishing touches." I learned later that both my competitors failed miserably in this area. They attempted to talk them out of this needed functionality that existed in the prospect's current system. Simply put, I beat my competition because I was better prepared.

As you do your Discovery, document problems right alongside features on your Feature Survey Form. Use a code of *P* to denote a possible problem. Spend time learning all you can about this problematic functionality. If possible, talk to more than one person at the company about the issue. Take lots of notes. After the Discovery, discuss the problem with your sales and implementation colleagues. They may have run into a similar situation. Also, call some of your customers who are in the prospect's industry. If they have the same problem, learn how they deal with it. In any case, present a solution (even if only in theory) during the demonstration.

A related situation you might run into during your Discovery is a prospect that describes a cool feature you've never heard of before. Although these situations don't necessarily pose a problem, they do require the same type of research on your part. I like to share this information with my development staff. They spend lots of time dealing with "problems," so they love to apply their creative juices to new features. Perhaps they can help you turn your prospect's "I heard about" feature into something you can either demonstrate or discuss during your presentation. When completing your Feature Survey Form, code these with an *R* for research. Again, good notes are necessary to properly research and present a viable solution.

Seek out problems. As difficult as they are to face, it's always better to know about them *before* the demonstration. Use in-depth questioning during the Discovery to flush them out. Even though you prefer to ignore them, identifying problems early will set you apart from your competition. That's your challenge.

INFORMATION ABOUT THE PEOPLE

We have already talked about personality types and buying motivations. These are two most critical pieces of information that you need to capture and communicate to team members. Remember our dispatcher that liked talking on the radio and did not want to give it up? Well, it turns out that *her* primary buying motivation was paperwork: She did not like having to fill in all the paperwork associated with scheduling and closing a service order. Had that been well documented and communicated properly, we could have steered the discussion in that direction and brought her across the bridge.

As we have already discussed, not every buying motivation will be strategic. Certainly our dispatcher's motivation was not strategic, it was tactical and personal. But that is really the point: Rarely do people come across our bridge for corporate strategic reasons. If they did, Discovery would not be so important. Every person we interview will have a buying motivation, and if we understand and communicate those motivations around the team, then we stand a better chance of crafting and conducting a demonstration that will connect with our audience members.

In reality, our radio-loving dispatcher was also a bit of a doom sayer. She had been using the same system for years, and was pretty well convinced that any change would be a mistake. You will see that a lot in a doom sayer; they love complaining about the problems in their current methods, but they see still more problems in any suggested change. If John and I had properly discussed our findings prior to the demonstration, I would never go to this person to ask her for confirmation of a benefit. Doom sayers never see the benefit that you would like them see. Clearly communicating personality types between team members is critical. You never want one of your team members to get into a bad situation with an audience member that could have been avoided simply through a bit of communication beforehand.

Our poor experience in this one deal convinced John and I that we needed to come up with a better approach. So we defined a 'Profile' worksheet that we both used to communicate information about the people. We kept it simple and straightforward, but it helped us in avoiding the type of gaffes that happen from a lack of communication. You can see an example of this worksheet below.

Discovery Interviewee Profile Form

Name: _____

DISCOVERY 2 *WIN!*

If it were up to you...

1) If it were your decision to make, what are the main reasons you'd suggest your organization change software?
2) If the software change only affected your department, why would you pick a new package?
3) Outside of personnel issues, what are the most frustrating things you deal with in your software today?

Top 3:

Unique Market Position:

Data Examples:

Forms	
Screen Prints	
Reports	

Talk-the-Talk Terms

Discovery Interviewee Profile Form

Influences:

Technology Oriented?   Yes   No

Visual Cues:

Reference:

Bring:

Other:

PT: W   D   L
                    V   P

Operational Benefits:

Value Benefits:

OVERCOMING DISCOVERY OBJECTIONS

As we have discussed, successful Discovery efforts start with an identified sponsor. This individual, who should be one of the prospect's upper level managers, will help you arrange interviews and, if Discovery is on site, will host you during your visit. Typically, they're the project leader or head of the software selection committee. Be aware this person is going to have one primary concern about the Discovery: the possibility of you monopolizing their time. It's a valid concern on their part. You must convince them you simply need to be introduced to your first interviewee and you'll take it from there. Because you will face this situation frequently, be prepared with a well-rehearsed response. For example, "Andy, I know what you must be thinking. You have 101 things to get done with your *regular* job, so the last thing you want is to lead me by the hand for the next couple hours. Since I have the names of the all the individuals I need to meet with, all I really need is for you to get me started with the first person on the list. They can direct me to the next person when we're done. I think this will allow me to make efficient use of your, and quite frankly, your staff's time. I'm sure I'll have some questions over the course of my interviews, so I'll check in with you regularly throughout the day." This approach usually opens the door to assistance.

Occasionally, you'll run into resistance from your sponsor regarding the *need* for a Discovery at all. They might say something like, "Hey, why do we need to spend a day doing that? Everything you need for your demonstration is in the RFP." When presented with this objection, it's your job to convince your sponsor of the *value* in performing a Discovery prior to your demonstration. When faced with this objection, I recommend you support the value of:

1. Their RFP.
2. Their people.
3. Your time.
4. The time to be spent in the demonstration.

Here's a response you might in answering this objection. "Jim, you're right. Your RFP does have a great deal of the information I need to perform the demonstration. In fact, I could walk in today and begin a demonstration of our software based on what I know from the RFP. I appreciate the time and expense you've invested in it. However, sometimes there can be interpretation issues with an RFP. You mean one thing but I interpret it a different way. Having the chance to visit your office and meet your people will insure that doesn't happen. I also understand and appreciate the value of your people's time. My time is valuable as well. However, the most critical time for all of us is when we are all in a room together for the demonstration. I really need to learn how your company does business from the people who manage and perform the everyday tasks. With this information, I can focus my demonstration so it's truly valuable to you and them. My guess is, by the end of the demonstration, you'll appreciate this approach. In fact, Steve Anderson at 25th Century Building felt the same way before their demonstration. He actually thanked me after the demo for having done my homework and for being so thorough."

Hopefully, Jim will let you in the door at this point. If not, the next objection you'll probably encounter will be the "level playing field" response. "Bob, that's all well and good, but none of the other vendors were allowed to perform a Discovery prior to their demonstrations. It simply wouldn't be fair if I allowed you this luxury but not them." I'd come back with, "Jim, you're right. It wouldn't be fair if I had privileged information and the competitors did not. Here's what I'm willing to do. After I've completed my interviews, I'll write a report of my findings and e-mail it to you. From there, you can forward it to my competitors. In this way, we will all have the same information." (Of course, you'll probably leave a few key details out of the report.)

If that doesn't work, don't give up. Ask permission to set up telephone interviews with the people attending the demonstration. These are clearly less valuable than face-to-face contact. But telephone or web interviews are better than nothing!

All other objections from Jim will normally revolve around the time commitment necessary to accomplish the Discovery. Again, this is where you need to assure him you won't monopolize his or anyone else's time. Also, reinforce the fact that the value of an informed and thorough demonstration will more than offset his or his staff's time investment.

Once your prospect has granted you permission to visit, start preparing for your interviews. I highly recommend sending a suggested agenda for the Discovery to your sponsor well in advance of your visit or interview calls. Purposefully omit names on the agenda. Allow them to think about the agenda for a few days. Then contact your sponsor and have her identify the names of the individuals he recommends you interview. After getting the names, visit with your sponsor about the people you'll be interviewing. There will usually be one or two people who will be a challenge. Knowing this up front will assist you in preparing for your Discovery.

There's one exception you should make with regard to leaving names off your preliminary Discovery agenda. Make sure you specifically state that you plan on meeting the appropriate executive for the organization. . Put in black and white you intend to spend a few minutes with him or her. It's important to meet the executive(s) most closely associated with the opportunity during the Discovery (if possible) to learn their buying-motivations firsthand.

ADDITIONAL DISCOVERY RECOMMENDATIONS

We've covered the key aspects of the Discovery. However, before we move on, let's examine a couple miscellaneous points.

Business Surroundings - When doing a Discovery on site, I make sure to mentally map my surroundings. You can learn a great deal about the owner and key executives of a business by noting cars in the parking lot, building exterior, lobby, telephone system, filing cabinets, offices and desks. All of this information provides clues as to the personality of your ultimate buyer(s).

I remember visiting a prospect outside of Philadelphia. The parking lot had a BMW 7-Series parked right next to the front door of a very old building. All of the other cars in the parking lot were basic American models. As I walked in the door, the lobby was secured. It was furnished with old carpet, chairs and a couple of wall plaques honoring their sales achievements. The most recent plaque was six years old. The phone system wasn't much better than two tin cans on a string. Once I got past the lobby, I observed only gunmetal gray desks and ancient file cabinets scattered everywhere. With the exception of the CFO's windowless 8' x 8' office, everyone was in a bullpen.

While discussing the project budget, the MIS manager told me it didn't matter how much money was required. They were going to buy the right system this time. I asked what happened last time and he told me they had settled for an inexpensive system. At that moment, I knew I didn't belong in this account. When compared to our competitors, my software was expensive and impressive. I also knew from past experience that old spending habits are hard to break! The owner would never go for our price tag.

Did I heed the visual cues I was getting (and my instincts)? No. In need of business, I continued pursing the client. Of course, I finished the Discovery without meeting the owner. I moved forward with the demonstration and it was compelling. The users loved it! Again, the owner was not available to attend. Upon my return to negotiate the contract, I finally met the owner. He made it clear in the first five minutes there was no way he was about to spend the money I had in the proposal. I looked for support from the members of the selection team who were in the room, but they became lambs. Within an hour I left their facilities with nothing to show but hours of wasted time! The Discovery I performed weeks before had given me all the information I needed. I just failed to accept the business surroundings clues.

The offices of your Discovery interviewees also provide valuable visual clues. For example, during a prospect Discovery in Los Angeles, most of the department managers were cordial, with neat and organized offices. They were very helpful and full of information. They wanted a new system and recognized the benefits it could provide. The CFO was another story. On and around his desk he had *green bar* reports stacked as high as his head. He collected money off of these reports "the old-fashioned way" and wanted nothing to do with changing his existing routine. Had I performed this interview on the telephone, I never would've seen these visual clues. Without the clues, I'd have demonstrated our advanced on-line collections tools and completely alienated the CFO in the process. Instead, I brought samples of traditional collections reports and showed him how the new system could allow him to stick with "proven techniques for collections." He was thrilled and we eventually earned their business.

Look for visual clues during your Discovery. Note them in your Discovery Log. They can tell you a great deal about the company, the ownership and the people who will attend your demonstration. Clues can be an invaluable resource for preparing your demo and may help you win the deal.

Name Dropping - As we have discussed, it's mandatory you research your prospect (via the Web, Dunn & Bradstreet, Hoovers, etc.) as part of your Pre-Discovery activities. Talk to your existing customers that are in a similar business to learn more about them. If you know a consultant who's familiar with the prospect, ask if they'd be willing to share some information with you.

From all these sources, find out the companies your prospect does and does not respect. The last thing you want to do in the demonstration or during small talk is to proudly drop a customer's name only to learn your prospect has little or no respect for them. On the other hand, you can set a great trap by dropping the name of one of their hated competitors who is running *your* competitor's software! This aligns your competitor with their archenemy and can sometimes eliminate them from contention.

During your Discovery interviews, plan on dropping the names of your customers who are your prospect's friendly competitors. This is good practice for the demonstration. Better to make a name-dropping mistake with a single person during a Discovery interview rather than in front of the entire demonstration audience. Also, whenever possible, do your name-drop testing with line personnel, not the managers who will attend at the demonstration. This will help you appear informed and less contrived with the real decision-makers during the demonstration.

If you haven't been with your company a long time, you may find it difficult to know which customer names to discuss. Look on your sales resource site for case studies, reference letters, quotes, etc. If that fails, broadcast an email to your colleagues (sales, support, implementation, etc.) requesting all customers that fit the profile of your prospect. Follow-up with the co-workers that reply to learn more about the customers and contacts they recommend. There's nothing more embarrassing than dropping the name of a customer who you know nothing about, is a poor reference or is not recognizable to your prospect. Another effective way to find out names of complementary customers is by simply asking the people you interview during your Discovery. They'll often tell you exactly whom they benchmark themselves against. This is powerful information for your demonstration.

Name-dropping is a good technique to use during both your Discovery and the demonstration to lead the prospect across the Bridge. As you recall, this is part of "Talk the Talk." They'll feel comfortable with the names you mention which will draw them closer to you. Don't forget this important aspect of your demonstration. Again, the best way to properly prepare for name-dropping is by conducting a Discovery.

Demonstration Room - If you'll be demonstrating at the prospect's place of business, try to do at least one Discovery interview on site. While there, take a few minutes to investigate the demonstration facilities. If you need an internet connection, make sure the room is equipped accordingly. Test the connection, don't depend on someone's assurances. If you need a screen, white-board or flip chart, make sure they are available in the room. Now is your chance to examine the environment where you'll be delivering your message. Chapter 8, *Your Demonstration Setting,* will discuss the demonstration room environment and layout in greater depth.

I recall an on site Discovery in Pittsburgh where every person I interviewed was constantly interrupted during the time we spent together. It was extremely frustrating. They were very busy that day. I went forward with my demonstration in their conference room the next morning. The demonstration was no different. It was scheduled to start at 8:30 a.m. I finally got everyone in the room at 9:15. However, I never had the same people in the room for more than 15 minutes because throughout the day people were being called out of the room. A month later I learned I was eliminated as a contender. When I asked them for a reason, they told me my software appeared difficult to follow and didn't seem to flow very well. No wonder! I also learned my competitor had convinced them to hold the demo at an off-site location. My misfortune became my competitor's advantage.

It's critical to control your environment during your demonstration. Schedule the demonstration in a location that minimizes interruptions whenever possible. You may need to convince your prospect an off-site location for the demonstration is to their benefit. Use your Discovery time to determine if this is necessary. A frequent objection will be, "I can't afford for all my people to be away from the office the entire demonstration. Sell the magnitude of *their* decision and how it is in their best interest to make the most of that day. Offer to cover the cost of the room and lunch as an incentive.

Business Forms – If you sell your software in the business world you can count on your prospect using business forms in either printed or electronic format. Forms are treasure maps that uncover valuable information about your prospect. There are two types of business forms to seek out and copy:

- Internal Forms – These are only used inside the organization. Businesses typically use these forms because they have complicated process flows that cause errors; a real target for you demo.

- External Forms – Examples include invoices, checks, customer statements, purchase order forms, etc.

Make sure the sample business forms you collect *include* data. An actual customer invoice is considerably more valuable to you than a blank version.

CHAPTER SUMMARY

A thorough Discovery of your prospect isn't a luxury item. It's mandatory! The process alone will help prevent more than half of your demo crimes. The information you learn will focus your demonstration on *exactly* what your prospect wants and needs to see in your software. You might use the information you learn to walk away from the prospect because you know your software doesn't fit their needs. Knowing that, at least you won't waste any more time on them! Be organized in your approach. Take comprehensive notes. Learn all you can about their buying-motivations, personalities and Unique Market Position. Use this information to create a demonstration your competitors can't touch.

CHAPTER 6

Checklists...Preparing For The Demo

Professional pilots use a checklist before *every* flight. Though they fly thousands of hours per year, they *never* take off without going over their checklist. You'd think they would have it committed to memory. Actually, they do. So why do they continue to use it? One simple slip-up can cost the lives of everyone on the plane. Why take the chance?

Demonstrating software is a far cry from the life or death situation of a pilot. Even so, can you think of one reason why you shouldn't be equally professional about the items you bring to a demonstration? If you had five minutes to walk out the door with everything you needed to perform an effective and powerful demonstration, would you forget something? Being organized is being professional. Think of the time you'd save and the anxiety you'd avoid if you had everything you needed for your demo identified and ready to go (a spare bulb for the projector, an extra extension cord, etc.). Below is the checklist of critical items I use for my demonstrations. Develop something similar to assist yourself. Then review it prior to *every* demonstration.

Demonstration Checklist

Proof Sources:
- ❑ Magazine or Trade Articles
- ❑ Index of Reference Letters
- ❑ Company Reference Books
- ❑ White Papers
- ❑ Quarterly News Letters
- ❑ Research Papers
- ❑ Handouts as Required
- ❑ 3rd Party Endorsements
- ❑ Corporate Org Chart
- ❑ Corporate HQ Picture
- ❑ Promotional Video
- ❑ Cost Justification Worksheet

Software Preparation:
- ❑ Practice Opening
- ❑ Agenda
- ❑ PPT Customizations
- ❑ Demo Script
- ❑ Discovery Document
- ❑ Contact Mgmt Activities
- ❑ Prospect Data Examples

Presentation Materials:
- ❑ Sample Reports
- ❑ Integration Standards
- ❑ Documentation Example
- ❑ Discovery Process Manual
- ❑ Videos w/ Workbooks
- ❑ Implementation Plan
- ❑ Training Class Schedule
- ❑ Web Instruction Examples
- ❑ PowerPoint™ Index
- ❑ Source Code Examples

Equipment:
- ❑ Laptop
- ❑ Projector
- ❑ Gaffer Tape
- ❑ Flip Chart
- ❑ Markers & Eraser
- ❑ Screen
- ❑ Extension Cord
- ❑ Video Extension Cord
- ❑ Power Strip
- ❑ Network Cable
- ❑ Laptop Speaker (Videos)
- ❑ Sound Cable (Videos)

Prospect Information:
- ❑ Contact Mgmt Printout
- ❑ RFI/RFP
- ❑ Directions
- ❑ Attendee Checklist (see attached)

Physical Facility:
- ❑ Room Layout
- ❑ Network Connectivity
- ❑ Web Access Information
- ❑ Passwords
- ❑ Demo Script
- ❑ Speaker Phone
- ❑ Lighting System

Courtesy Items:
- ❑ Drinks
- ❑ Ice/Cooler
- ❑ Food a.m. & Lunch
- ❑ Room Preparation

I have a slightly different version of this checklist that I use for web presentations. With the web, it is important that you have both your physical and technical environment in proper order. For example, I make sure that all unnecessary features of my laptop are turned off prior to the demonstration. This prevents possible distractions and avoids any potentially embarrassing situations while I am sharing my desktop.

Web Demonstration Checklist

Proof Sources to Share:
Loaded in web tool, provided as download, or web links
- Magazine or Trade Articles
- Index of Reference Letters
- White Papers
- Quarterly News Letters
- Research Papers
- 3rd Party Endorsements
- Case Studies
- Promotional Video

Software Preparation:
- Practice Opening
- Agenda
- PPT Customizations
- Demo Script
- Discovery Document
- Contact Mgmt. Activities
- Prospect Data Examples

Presentation Preparation:
- Desktop Icons Hidden
- Browser Widgets Hidden
- eMail Shut Down
- Instant Messaging Shut Down
- All Notifications Off
- All Slides Pre-Loaded
- Webcam Tested
- Audio Tested
- Desktop Sharing Tested

- Application Sharing Tested
- Web Training Link Loaded

Equipment:
- Laptop
- Primary Connection
- Backup Connection
- External Web Camera
- External Mouse
- External Keyboard
- Headset for Phone
- Headset for PC (VoIP)
- 'Monitor' (Person or PC)
- Laptop/Keyboard Stand

Prospect Information:
Printed and accessible to you during the demo
- Contact Mgmt. Printout
- RFI/RFP
- Attendee Checklist (see attached)
- Interaction Checklist

Prospect Technology:
Shared with prospect well before the demonstration
- Meeting Notifications Sent
- Technical Requirements Documented
- Technical Support Documented
- Web Access Tested
- Audio Access Tested

Checklists can go beyond what you physically bring to the demonstration. Also use them to organize who's attending the demo and their primary interests. It helps me prepare for my audience if I know the title, primary responsibility and top three interests of every attendee. The following Demonstration Attendee Checklist is another form I use. I've found sending my demonstration sponsor this form helps make it easier for them to gather the information I need. Again, you're welcome to use this template or you might want to design your own.

DEMONSTRATION ATTENDEE CHECKLIST

Session _____

Attendee _____ Title_____

Primary Responsibility _____

Attendee's Top 3 Interests In Demonstration (What do they want covered?)

1. _____
2. _____
3. _____

Session _____

Attendee _____ Title_____

Primary Responsibility _____

Attendee's Top 3 Interests In Demonstration (What do they want covered?)

1. _____
2. _____
3. _____

Session _____

Attendee _____ Title_____

Primary Responsibility _____

Attendee's Top 3 Interests In Demonstration (What do they want covered?)

1. _____
2. _____
3. _____

I like to begin reviewing completed versions of this form a week or so before a demonstration. It helps me organize information critical to my success. For example, if one of the people attending the demo is an AP clerk and is primarily interested in how we reprint checks, I know to be prepared to show them lots of detail. On the other hand, if the CFO wants to know what tools are available for cash planning, he's going to be after a bigger picture. The night before the demo, I take another look at the Attendee's Checklist to make sure I've memorized everybody's name and I'm prepared to address his or her unique interests. When they walk in the room the next day, I'm ready for them! What great information to help deliver a winning demonstration.

Friends accuse me of being obsessed with checklists. Guilty as charged. Here's a funny "checklist" story. During the latter stages of writing the first edition of this book, I provided a copy of the manuscript to one of my colleagues, Ted Bellamy. I asked him to review it and provide me feedback. Several weeks later, Ted asked me to assist him with a demonstration to one of his prospects. While driving from the airport to their office I asked Ted what he thought of my book. He gave me the obligatory "Oh, it's great. Really good ideas." "Yah, yah, Ted," I said, "Tell me what you *really* think." So, Ted shared a couple of honest comments, one of which was, "I think you go a little overboard on the checklist thing." OK, point well taken. Ten minutes later, we arrived at the prospect's office and started setting up for the demonstration that was to begin in about an hour. Suddenly, Ted came running up to me in a bit of a panic. "The connection in the room we're using won't let us get to our servers. The closest connection is in a room down the hall. I checked with Jason (our demonstration sponsor) and he said they don't have a cable that long. They also don't have open wireless. We're in trouble!" Lucky for Ted, I had brought a long cable with me. It was one of the items on my demonstration checklist!

CHAPTER SUMMARY

After having read two very lengthy chapters (*The Demo Crime Files!* and *The Discovery Process*), you're probably thinking, "What? Is that it?" Yes, that's it. Checklists aren't complicated, they're just *extremely* important, which is why I insisted on having one whole (albeit short) chapter devoted to that single topic. All the preparation in the world and mastery of every demonstration technique won't mean a thing if you don't have what you need to actually deliver your demo! And it's so simple to avoid making that mistake. Use a checklist.

CHAPTER 7
Demonstration Fundamentals

A baseball purist can spend days explaining the fine points of the game. The fact is, baseball is a complicated game. If there are players on first and second base and the batter gets a double in the right field gap, the second baseman positions himself for the relay, the pitcher backs up home, the shortstop moves to second and the catcher prepares to block home plate! *However*, amidst the complexity, baseball is a game of three very simple fundamentals. You hit the ball, throw the ball and catch the ball. If a team can't excel at these three fundamentals, all of the strategy in the world won't win a ballgame.

Like baseball, demonstrating is a complex business. But also like baseball, fundamentals are the key to success. Demonstration fundamentals include things like efficient time management, powerful openings, compelling Value Propositions and constant analysis of key signals from your prospect. Without these fundamentals, a near perfect strategy won't win the day.

GOING FIRST OR LAST

If you are involved in a competitive deal, should you demonstrate first, last or in the middle? It's an age-old question. Most people have an opinion. If they don't, they want *the* answer. I believe every case has to be judged separately.

Assume the prospect has narrowed their selection to three vendors. Consider the following:

- Going first allows you to establish the benchmark for all other competitors that follow. If you know your competition, you can also set traps for them.

- Going last gives you an advantage because it will be easier for the prospect to remember your demonstration.

- Going second is the worst position. You aren't able to set traps and you won't be remembered!

I find a significant determining factor of going first or last is how well the evaluators work together in a group. If I'm demonstrating to a group in a very structured environment, and that selection team does not work well together (as evidenced by many conflicting opinions in Discovery), I prefer to go last. Selection teams need to learn how to work together in a demonstration. Before your prospect's selection team has learned to be good demonstration participants, significant time is wasted while they argue procedural questions amongst themselves. Under these circumstances, there's a greater chance your software will appear complicated, even if you're employing quality demonstration techniques. Any advantage gained from setting traps for you competitors will be offset by the lack of control.

If I'm working with a group that works well together and I'm able to set the agenda, I prefer going first. Also, with a smaller audience, the group dynamics are less complex. I can remain highly focused and impact-oriented even if my audience is inexperienced. Because it's easier to control my audience, I set lots of "make sure any software package..." traps for my competitors.

Your place in the demonstration order does have an impact. But placement is no substitute for thorough preparation and sound delivery techniques.

CURRENT EVENTS

Discussing current events prior to and during the demonstration is invaluable. Rather than unrelated small talk, I'm referring to events in their business or industry. Current events worth discussing include information and articles about:

- Their industry's direction.

- Their company.

- People within their company.

- Their suppliers.

- Their primary customers.

- *Your* customers who are similar to them.

- Information you can legally and ethically provide on their competitors (they'll love this!).

Notice anything missing from the list? You! Never mix talk about you, your company, your management or your travels to their locale. Don't worry. There'll be an appropriate time and place to discuss all these topics. Just keep in mind, when it comes to current events, your prospect wants to hear and talk about things of value and interest to *them*.

One approach is to think in terms of their office geography. Topics like the weather and your trip are well outside of their parking lot. Information you know about their industry brings you to their lobby. Finally, by talking about their company, employees, products, customers and suppliers, you're invited inside.

Discussing current events that directly impact your prospect's business or them personally will be much more effective than unrelated small talk.

TIME MANAGEMENT

Managing your time during the day is important. When you're unable to stick to the agenda, you probably lack control of your demonstration. There are many ways to lose control:

- If you start the demonstration late, you'll feel like you're playing catch-up the rest of the day.

- If you allow open-ended breaks, expect problems.

- If you put together a "loose" agenda (no specific topic area start and stop times), you'll lose control.

- It's of utmost importance to keep track of your time and manage it carefully throughout the demonstration or presentation.

Time management starts with proper preparation. You've performed a prospect Discovery. You understand their needs. Focus on them. Let's say you know your prospect uses cost-plus pricing and you've confirmed with management that they have no interest in changing this practice. Don't waste time demonstrating the sixteen other ways to determine a customer's price. Save valuable time by keeping your demonstration focused on their verified needs and interests.

START TIMES

In 90 percent of my on-site demonstrations, the prospects arrive late for the start of the demo. With web demonstrations the number may be even higher. This is particularly true of demos that start first thing in the morning. There are lots of reasons:

- Someone invariably arrives late because of traffic. On the web there is always someone that has connection problems.

- People usually want to check their e-mail and voicemail first thing in the morning and before every meeting

- Once everyone finally congregates, they'll want to chat.

- If you've planned a Monday morning demonstration, someone might forget about the demonstration over the weekend.

- Monday mornings require time to talk about what happened over the weekend (sports, activities, etc.).

The bottom line: these are all time wasters! Here are a few suggestions to help you avoid these frustrations:

1. Avoid Monday morning demos if possible.

2. Publish a start-time for a *Monday* morning demonstration 30 minutes before you actually need to begin.

3. Publish a start-time for *Tuesday through Friday* demonstrations at least 15 minutes before you need to begin.

4. On web demonstrations, always send out the appointment reminder for 15 minutes prior to your actual start time, and make sure the web meeting and phone connection are up and running 15 minutes before the start to encourage people to connect early.

BREAKS

"Okay, we're at a logical stopping point. Why don't we take a break for a few minutes?" Sound familiar? And what time did the demonstration reconvene? Ten minutes later? Probably more like 30 minutes! Being vague about the length of breaks is a bad idea. Some would argue you're being courteous and respectful of their time. After all, they have a business to run and need time during the break to take care of things. I disagree. The business at hand (evaluating your software) is what's important! If you're not specific with your break times, you send the message that your time, presentation and solution aren't important.

Breaks need to be clearly defined, precise and strictly adhered to. A better way to announce a break would go something like, "Okay, we're at a logical breaking point. The time I have is 2:33. Let's take a 12-minute break? I'll begin again at 2:45 sharp." At exactly 2:45, begin presenting (assuming at least one person is back in the room!). If you begin promptly, I guarantee you're audience will quickly find their way back into the room. If for some reason that doesn't happen, find your demonstration sponsor and let them know it's time to begin. Ask for his or her assistance in rounding people up.

Later in the day, when everybody is getting tired, I like to have some fun with tardy prospects. I suggest instituting a fine for returning late from a break. A drawing at the end of the day determines who gets the money collected from "fines." I appoint someone in the room to keep the clock. Then I ask for volunteers to be the "tardiness judge." I'm always amazed at the enthusiasm generated by this game. Most people *like* to be on time and it drives them nuts when they have to wait for stragglers. Punctual people will have their hand in the air hoping to be a judge or keep the clock!

Here are a few other tips to help you maintain control of your breaks:

- Keep them short, never longer than 15 minutes.

- Make them an odd, precise time, rather than ten or 15 minute increments.

- Prior to the break, tell them what feature or capability you're going to cover when they get back from break. Make sure the feature you pick is very important to them.

Breaks in web demos are particularly difficult to manage. Once you have lost them, there is little hope for getting them back. And, in fact, you may never know if they came back or not! My best advice on web demo breaks is to avoid them: Schedule your web demos for 90 minutes or less. If you need more time, schedule a second session, preferably for a different day. It is almost impossible to keep somebody focused on a remote demo session for any longer, and once they are gone they will quickly move on to the tasks that they *wanted* to be doing during those 90 minutes!

INTRODUCTIONS

Yourself - Your prospect wants to know who you are. They want to know how long you've been with your company, what your qualifications are for giving this demonstration, your experience level and a little bit of personal information about you. In the first two minutes they want to size you up; determine if they like and respect you. The prospect is going to be very selfish during these two minutes. They want to know anything and everything that's beneficial to them. If you're demonstrating with a team, the same holds true for your other team members. I advocate having the team leader introduce himself or herself first so the stage is set for the other team members.

Here's an example of an introduction I use. "Good morning! My name is Bob Riefstahl, and I'm the Regional Sales Representative responsible for serving you during your evaluation. I'll be conducting the majority of the demonstration. I'm joined today by my colleague Bill Anderson who is a sales-support representative. Bill will introduce himself shortly. I've been with FutureF four years. For three of those four years, I've been a member of the Chairmen's Club for excellence in sales and service. Prior to FutureF, I worked in your industry as a general manager of a manufacturing plant. I'm married and the father of two boys and live in Colorado Springs, Colorado. I'm honored to be invited into your company and look forward to spending the day with you!"

Let's examine this introduction for a moment and analyze its content.

"Good morning. My name is Bob Riefstahl, and I'm the Regional Sales Representative responsible for servicing you during your evaluation."

In this section of the introduction, I have enthusiastically greeted the audience. I pronounced my name (I have a rather difficult name and find people appreciate learning how to pronounce it). They know my position in the company and my primary duties as they relate to them.

- "I'm joined today by my colleague Bill Anderson who is a sales-support representative. Bill will introduce himself shortly."

  I briefly introduced Bill and explained his role but made it clear he will introduce himself. Remember, you're front-and-center and right now they want to hear about you, not another team member.

- "I've been with FutureF four years. For three of those four years, I've been a member of the Chairmen's Club for distinctive sales and service."

  They now know I've been with the company for some time and have been successful. People like dealing with successful people. If you've received awards or have earned special degrees, go ahead and briefly mention them. They want to hear why you're good enough to command their attention.

- "Prior to FutureF I worked in your industry as a general manager of a manufacturing plant."

  The prospect has already guessed I'm at least 40 years old, so they want to know what I did prior to coming to FutureF four years ago. They want to know if I've been in a related business and if that experience is valuable to them. If you've been with your company less than five years, it's especially important to tell them about your previous job. However, you typically don't want to go back more than two jobs. They don't want to hear your entire career history, and if it sounds like you're a job-hopper, they surely won't be impressed.

One exception to this rule is if you had a job in their industry. People like to hear you've been on their side of the table. If four companies ago you had a job relevant to their business, skip a couple of jobs and speak to that experience.

- "I'm married and the father of two boys and live in Colorado Springs, Colorado."

    Prospects like to know a little about the *fabric* of the person presenting to them. They want to know you're a real human being, not a robot or technoid. I'm not advocating giving them your family history. Just tell them some little tidbit about yourself on a personal level. It could be a personal interest such as "I am an avid golfer" or "I enjoy the outdoors." This gives them a feel for you as a person. Naturally, if the decision-maker and you share some interest, share that information! For example, if the CEO is an avid NASCAR racing fan and you are too, mention this to the audience. It helps make a connection and build common ground.

- "I'm honored to be invited into your company and look forward to spending the day with you!"

    Honored is a powerful word. Use it, but don't abuse it. Most people take this word very seriously, especially if they served in the military. You're making a powerful statement if you choose to use the word "honored." Mean it. Be sincere and enthusiastic when you deliver this statement. It will stick in their minds.

An introduction is really just another example of an Elevator Pitch. If you want to deliver your introduction effectively and in a convincing, sincere and enthusiastic manner, you have to write it down and memorize it. Then place yourself in front of a mirror and practice it over and over until your delivery is natural and seamless. Here's another suggestion: change it slightly for each prospect. Shape it. Mold it. This will help keep your introduction fresh and focused on your prospect. Your audience will judge you in the first two minutes of your presentation, so invest the time to leave a positive impression.

Your Team - Now that you've introduced yourself, it's time to turn the ball over to your teammates (if you're not demonstrating alone). Their introduction should follow yours in structure. If you're in charge of this demo, it's your responsibility to make sure they're prepared. I'm not talking about a quick run through in the hallway or bathroom five minutes before the demonstration begins. You and your teammates should script and practice your introductions in your office. Make introductions a part of your regular training and practice regimen.

Your Prospect - It's now your prospect's turn. You've already set the stage for the structure of the introduction. This takes a little pressure off of them. Some prospects will follow you verbatim. Most will not. At a minimum, ask each member of the audience to share their title, primary responsibility and what they hope to learn during the demonstration. Because you completed the Demonstration Attendee Checklist as part of your Discovery, you probably already know this information. However, there might be a few surprises during the introductions.

- It's not uncommon to have last minute additions to the prospect's selection team (new hires, promotions, etc.).

- Somebody could have been unavailable when you made your Discovery visit.

- Certain personality types attending your demo have *planned* to give you a different response.

- Others are not as sinister, but may have picked up a new idea from another demonstration.

- You could also have a clever competitor who's setting some traps for you.

Whatever the situation, it's much better to find out changes during the introductions rather than in the middle of your demonstration!

If you're demonstrating to a group of 15 or less, have a pen and paper ready. I like to copy a technique many waiters use in a restaurant. Prior to the demonstration, diagram the room and seating arrangement. As each person identifies himself or herself, jot down their first name only, title and interests. Just like a waiter has to make sure to match the right food to each person seated at the table, this helps me deliver the features and benefits each person ordered during the Discovery. With a web demonstration, you will want to follow the same technique. Make sure you know who is at your 'virtual table' by recording everyone's name. Don't depend on the software's attendee list as often there will be multiple people in a single room. Your digram may be by city or location, but make sure you have all of the names collected. You will want them later in the demonstration.

CREATING THE RIGHT AGENDA

Each of your demonstrations should have a unique agenda. It's rare that a single agenda will address the needs of even two prospects. If you're using the same agenda repeatedly, it indicates you're not focusing on the individual needs of your prospects. The topics (sections) and order of your agenda may remain relatively consistent, but the time spent in each area of the software should always vary.

Like scripting a good action-adventure movie, your agenda should include an exciting opening. If you have a real *grabber* within your software and your research indicates it's important to the prospect, show it first. Remember that you're looking for high-impact. Therefore, do not under any circumstance water down your exciting feature by committing the "Teaching versus Demonstrating" demo crime (Chapter 4). Start the demonstration out with a big bang! You want a "Wow, how did you do that?" reaction from your prospect. Use the opening of the demonstration to get them excited and interested in starting their journey across the Bridge. Your agenda opening is designed to electrify your prospect. The goal is to persuade them to set aside their fear of change (crossing the Bridge) and focus on the *result* (your software on the other side of the Bridge).

After they react to your opening, it's time to move into the plot of your action-adventure film. The main plot should consist of the building blocks of your software as they relate to your prospect. Whether your demonstration is one hour or four days, the main body of your demonstration needs to focus on the buying-motivations you uncovered during your Discovery. Don't confuse this with a license to bore your prospect with master files, dull entry screens and option screens. Concentrate on their process flows. Make sure this is reflected in your agenda. They're considering a change from their existing system to yours for this reason. Now's the time to give them the reasons to make that change.

If possible, begin the main body of the demonstration by tackling the prospect's *biggest challenge*. For example, if you sell a manufacturing system and your prospect's biggest problem has to do with shop-floor scheduling, your agenda should address that issue right up front. Here's an illustration. A few years back I was demonstrating to a plumbing distributor. The only thing they were truly passionate about was order entry. It was a one-day demonstration and there was a great deal of material to cover. We started the day at 8:00 a.m. I totally frustrated the prospect by waiting until 1:00 p.m. before we started talking about the order entry portion of my software. What would normally have been a compelling part of my demonstration became a war! I learned my lesson from that demonstration. Now, after my big opening, I always proceed directly to my prospect's primary interest. By immediately applying the techniques discussed in this book to this key issue, I find my audience is much more attentive and trusting during the remainder of the demo.

Choosing the first section of your demo should be easy. It will be the prospect's most significant pain uncovered during your Discovery. Where you go from this point needs to be a balance between your prospect's needs and interests, and how your software is organized. You don't want to just blast through all the topics you uncovered during the Discovery. You need to blend this information with the natural segmentation of your software. Think of the construction of an entire neighborhood of custom homes. Each home in the new neighborhood is built in sections. You break ground (the exciting beginning), perform foundation, framing and rough plumbing/electrical (main section of the demo) and finally finish the home (exciting ending). Yet, each home is unique because the owners selected features and options that were right for them. Similarly, each demonstration agenda needs to uniquely address the needs of your prospect within the organizational boundaries of your software.

Just as your overall demonstration needs three main parts (an opening, main body and closing), each "topic section" needs to be similarly segmented. At a minimum, each section needs to have an interesting opening and a compelling close. Assume you're demonstrating an accounting system that has seven main functional areas: accounts receivable, accounts payable, general ledger, payroll, human resources and fixed-assets. So, for example, fixed-assets should be a section in the main body of your demonstration. And, like the demonstration itself, this subsection of the agenda needs an opening, main body and closing.

If you're like me, you're wondering, "How in the world do you make fixed-asset accounting interesting and compelling?" Although this may not be an exciting topic to you or me, if there are people in your demonstration who struggle day in and day out with fixed-assets, you can be sure it's exciting to them! During your Discovery, you determined fixed-assets to be an area of concern for your prospect. They told you what they needed the new fixed-asset package to accomplish. You have the information needed to create an interesting (okay, maybe not exciting) opening and closing. Open with a solution to the main reason the prospect is interested in a new fixed-asset software package. Close by showing them your most exciting and relevant fixed-asset feature. Depending on the time available, cover other features and capabilities of interest in between your opening and close. Your Bridge is now being constructed one section at a time. The only thing missing is some motivation for your prospect to take steps across this section of the Bridge and to feel comfortable continuing the journey. That's when your passion and sincerity come into play. Show conservative confidence in your software, company and innate ability to address their specific needs. Before moving on to the next section of the Bridge (your agenda), summarize all the needs your software addresses in this area.

Prior to closing your demonstration, make sure the decision-maker and those who will influence the software decision are all present. This will influence your agenda because the "big feature" or capability that you hold for the end must be of specific interest to the decision-maker. Use this technique to "bait" the decision-maker, improving the chance that they will be present for your big finish. Just like the opening, your demonstration conclusion should be powerful and compelling.

To summarize, your agenda needs to be dynamic and very carefully planned, incorporating the following elements:

1. An exciting opening.

2. An initial topic addressing the primary need of your prospect.

3. Main body of relevant topics (buying-motivations).

4. A compelling conclusion.

5. Customized for each prospect.

THE PROPER OPENING TO YOUR DEMONSTRATION

Because the opening to your demonstration is so critical, let's spend a little more time examining it. First, be on the lookout for "technobabble" in your opening. Bad openings are usually plagued by technobabble. Let's begin by reviewing the technobabble-laden opening we looked at in Chapter 4, *The Demo Crime Files!*

"Our demonstration today will consist of a company overview, a demonstration of how our O.E. module will address the needs of your service department, and finally how our S.C. will remotely configure your SaaS implementation to work with your existing SOA environment."

Now let's look at a technobabble-free version of the same opening:

"Your demonstration today has been structured to address the interests and concerns each of you expressed to me when I visited you company a couple weeks ago. By the end of the day, my goal is for you to understand:

1.   How the new system will have a positive impact on customer service.

2.   How your people will quickly and easily take advantage of the features in the new system.

3.   How the new system will leverage the software environment you already have in place and working, and minimize your overall implementation cost."

Let me pause for a moment to encourage you to write down the goals on a flipchart as you review them with your audience. Then leave them displayed the entire day and refer to them periodically throughout your demonstration.

The opening continues with, "Rather than start with a 15 minute/30 slide overview of our company, I thought you would appreciate it if we spent 5 minutes demonstrating to you a solution to what you told us was your most important initiative. From there we will present the agenda you worked with us on and demonstrate precisely how your people will utilize the new order-processing system to improve your service to your customers and improve your efficiency and profitability. We'll then discuss how our implementation team will work with your team to manage a smooth and effective transition from your old system to your new software, eliminating any loss of productivity. Finally, we'll describe how FutureF can minimize your ongoing cost of connecting your other locations by leveraging the equipment and environment you already have installed. In the end, if you agree I've accomplished these goals, I'll ask you to invest one more day and visit a customer who is using our software. During this customer visit, you'll learn first-hand how successful you can be with our product."

In contrast to the first opening, this one offers a number of improvements:

- No use of jargon that puts a pause in the prospect's mind.

- Not committing the "Corporate Junkie" crime. Starting with their most important initiative.

- Agenda was negotiated and created together so they have ownership.

- Attention is focused on your message and not your words.

- Stresses the fact that this is *their* demonstration, customized to address what they said they wanted covered.

- Focuses on business benefits of the various stages of the presentation.

- Provides some stated takeaways or goals they can leave with at the end of the day. This gives them a clear, understandable path of where you're heading and what you expect from them at the end of the day.

An opening needs to consist of the following elements:

1. Make it *personalized.* You can use a similar opening for multiple prospects as long as each one is tweaked to fit the needs of your audience. The opening is conversational in nature and sometimes contains a story about a customer of yours that they respect. It usually incorporates the theme of the demonstration developed specifically for them.

2. Make it interesting and show them what they are interested in first.

3. Create definitive *takeaways.* Takeaways are messages or information you want your audience to "take with them" when they leave your demonstration. They make for a powerful opening.

4. Produce a *call to action.* You're going to ask for something at the end of the demonstration. It doesn't have to be a signed contract or a commitment to buy your product. Your *call to action* needs to be something they will do if you accomplish your goals, whether it's a contract, a visit to one of your customers or a trip to your corporate office.

The best technique for performing a hard-hitting, meaningful opening is to write it down *word-for-word* and then practice it in front of a mirror or video camera. It will pay big dividends even if you are like me and you feel awkward practicing and filming your opening. I wish there was a better way, but there simply isn't.

Your written and memorized opening must be your own words and thoughts; not something you borrowed from somebody else (your manager, a respected senior salesperson).

Your words help deliver your message with passion and sincerity. First impressions are critical in your demonstration, and this is your chance to make a positive one. Don't take for granted your prospect owes you their attention just because they invited you to demonstrate your software. Make a powerful, compelling and sincere first impression. To accomplish this, you need a rock-solid opening.

IDENTIFYING THE DECISION-MAKER

It's critical that you can identify the decision-maker at your demonstration. Sounds pretty obvious, huh? Unfortunately, that's not always the case. If all goes well, you'll have met her during your Discovery. Keep in mind, it's not uncommon for her to be out of the office when you made this visit. However, if your software sale represents a significant investment for the company, you can bet the decision-maker will be available for your demonstration. She might not be there when you get started, but she'll more than likely participate for at least a few minutes to gauge you, your company and your product.

If you didn't meet the decision-maker during your Discovery, request a brief meeting with her before the demonstration starts. That way, if she comes in after the introductions, you'll know what to focus that portion of the demo on. This meeting will also give you a few moments to pick up some personality clues.

When the decision-maker enters the room during your demonstration, be prepared to send some material her way. Do everything you can to *plug* her into the demonstration as quickly as possible. Also, shape your agenda to be flexible so you can cover a topic of keen interest to the decision-maker when she is available.

I remember a demonstration in Portland, Oregon a number of years ago. We had the *hottest* product on the market. Other distributors carrying the same product lines as my prospect were signing up with me left and right. I had a competitor, but they had an inferior product and were experiencing financial problems. This deal was a *lock!*

I showed up for the demonstration without an in-depth understanding of my audience. I hadn't performed a Discovery nor had I requested a list of the demonstration attendees and their areas of interest. I didn't customize the demonstration with their information (data). After all, we owned this market! We were simply in too good of a position to lose this deal. They had told me the decision would be left to the evaluation team, so when the CEO stepped into the demo for a few minutes and then walked out, I wasn't surprised. I assumed he saw things were going positively and was relying on his team to make the proper recommendation to purchase our software. At the conclusion of the demonstration, I asked the participants how they thought it went. They all said it went fine and they'd get back to me with their next step.

After about two weeks I had heard nothing. I called my contact, the MIS manager, and she told me we were in a *distant* second place. I was shocked! I immediately inquired who was in first place and why. She told me it was my inferior, financially strapped competitor. She said their software just fit better. Since I knew that was not the case, I kept digging. Turns out the CEO had heard from their major supplier that our product had some problems. This prompted him to participate in my competitor's entire demonstration. They simply did a better job of keeping his interest!

Obviously, I committed too many crimes to name. But the most critical mistake I made was not having any type of contact with the ultimate decision-maker. I didn't even know what he looked like before he walked into my demonstration! I should have contacted the CEO ahead of time, established a rapport and learned his primary needs and concerns. With that information, I could have rectified the misconception about our problems and demonstrated exactly what he wanted to see when he walked into the room.

ADAPTABLE VALUE PROPOSITION FOR THE EXECUTIVE DECISION MAKER (EDM)

In many organizations, the CEO is the ultimate decision-maker. But for our purposes, I'd like to define the EDM as whoever has unencumbered access and approval of funds. They can sign the check and/or approve the funds. If you're demonstrating your word processing package to a college student who is holding a checkbook, they're an EDM. If you're demonstrating your accounting system to the controller of the company and she's making the decision, approving the purchase and writing the check for your software, for this purchase, she's the EDM.

Chances are, at some point during your demonstration the EDM will ask you *the* question. It could be disguised a bit, but probably will sound something like, "Bob, what do you think makes your software so unique that we should buy it over your competitor's?" Do you remember what you're going to do at this point? Deliver an Adaptable Value Proposition. As we discussed earlier, this is when you throw yourself into an imaginary elevator with this person and hit the tenth floor *express* button. You have until you reach the tenth floor to give the EDM your answer (about 60 seconds).

The reason the value proposition is *adaptable* is because it should change every time you gain more knowledge about how your solution addresses this EDM's strategic initiatives. Early in a sales cycle, you have very limited knowledge about those initiatives. For example, you may only know the metrics someone in this line of business measures themselves by and how your software addresses each of those measurements. However, as you conduct Discovery interviews, you can adapt your value proposition such that it focuses on a key initiative.

If you are in a demo and the EDM asks for your Adaptable Value Proposition answer it by first *staying off the keyboard*. You need to stop whatever you're doing and answer the EDM's question with a carefully prepared and rehearsed response. Your answer might be a couple of your software benefits that connect with the EDM's strategic initiatives. It might also be the way your company takes care of customers if you learned that the EDM is passionate about customer service. Whatever the response, it needs to be carefully worded and delivered without hesitation. It must come across as very specific and fresh, not *canned* or generic.

Each prospect EDM will require a different Adaptable Value Proposition, because each will base his decision on his individual needs. Your Adaptable Value Proposition needs to address those *precise* needs. You're probably wondering how in the world you're going to accomplish this. It's really quite simple. Think about what you've already accomplished.

- During your Discovery, you either interviewed the EDM or learned from others what was important to him.

- You shaped an agenda around the prospect's overall needs and created an exciting opening and closing to your demonstration.

- Take all you know and put it in 60 words or less. As you gain proficiency, this exercise will become second nature!

KEY SIGNALS

Have you ever noticed that during some demonstrations you had a *feeling* about how things were going, whether positive or negative? What helped you formulate that opinion? Were you relying on your experiences from other demonstrations? Was it direct feedback from the prospect? Were you trial-closing?

Experience has taught me there are certain key signals you can look for when gauging your progress during the demonstration. Some indicators let you know things are going well. An obvious indicator would be "Wow, try doing that with our existing software!" Obviously, we all like to hear those. However, indicators are usually less clear. Some overlooked positive signals include:

- The audience stops requiring proof that one of your software features really functions the way you say it does.

- People start helping you answer questions.

- They begin making suppositions as to how to solve a problem that one of their peers introduces in the form of a question or objection.

- You notice they're attempting to solve their own procedural problems rather than requiring you to prove you can handle them with your software.

- The ultimate decision-maker doesn't leave the room. He pays close attention and occasionally participates in discussions.

Don't expect these types of positive indicators at the outset of the demonstration. It takes time to establish credibility for yourself, your company and your software. The credibility gap can vary a great deal from prospect to prospect. It typically takes between 30 and 50 percent of your total demonstration time to establish credibility. If you have a positive reputation in the prospect's industry, it may take you less time to establish credibility could be less. However, if you're not receiving subtle, positive responses from your prospect by the halfway point in your demonstration, you're probably in deep water! If you think this is happening, quickly settle into a mode of soft-selling. For some reason, the prospect doubts you, your company or your product. You *must* build up your credibility in the prospect's mind in order to have a chance at earning their business. In situations like this, I've found relaxing your technique and becoming less aggressive can build credibility.

And now, some indicators that may signal a less than positive demonstration: *NEGATIVE*

- The prospect continually presses you for specific proof during the demonstration that a feature you describe really works.

- The prospect continually argues with you over the foundational aspects of your software. They simply don't agree with the basic fabric of your product.

- You receive no participation from the audience and are faced with continual silence when you attempt to engage them in the demonstration.

- In a group demonstration, you find the group members continually rallying around an objection brought up by one of their peers.

- People leave the room during the middle of the demonstration!

Here's an interesting fact about negative signals: it's easier to deal with a *hostile* audience than a *passive* one. Silence is deadly. At least when the prospect is hostile, you have an idea of how to adjust your approach. With a passive audience, you simply don't know what's wrong. Some people are naturally quiet. Others get quiet because something is wrong. Maybe you said something to offend them. Maybe they don't want to tip their hand. Maybe they don't agree with the things you're saying. Perhaps that is why all of us dislike web demonstrations – there is too much silence! When an audience is silent, you have a real challenge. You need to find and drive interaction points. Humor is one way to break the silence. But be careful when using humor. I find the best way to get a group to loosen up is through self-deprecation. If that doesn't work, I'll *gently* poke fun at them. With most web conferencing software, there are a variety of tools designed to break the silence and drive interaction. Anything to break the ice is appropriate as long as it's not offensive and is done in good taste. With in-person presentations, giving away "prizes" is another fun way to draw out a passive audience. With the web, you might use polls and emoticons. (See the Engaging topic in Chapter 3, *Important Demonstration Concepts*)

Always be aware and in search of key indicators during your demonstration. Pay attention to what the audience is telling you so you can adjust your message and technique accordingly.

CLOSING THE DEMONSTRATION

Our journey is almost complete! You've given a powerful and focused demonstration and are leading your prospect the final few steps across the Bridge. This is the moment of truth, so you close by saying, "Well, that's about it. Thanks for sticking around all day and hearing what I have to say. If you have any questions give me a call and I'll be glad to clarify them for you." Huh? After all the work you've put into preparing and delivering a powerful demonstration, you end with that? Don't laugh. It's amazing how many times I've seen that *exact* closing! I can't stress enough the importance of a strong, emotional and compelling close. Your prospect deserves it. Your team members deserve it. Your company deserves it. *You* deserve it!

Transition into your closing by summarizing the action items you noted throughout the demonstration. This will be easy if you've been writing them down on a flipchart or in your demonstration notes. This is an important step because it reminds your prospect you've been listening and willing to respond to their questions and concerns. Hopefully some of these questions have been answered during the day so they'll feel good about your ability to follow through on this commitment.

A compelling message is the key component of closing *any* demonstration, regardless of length, whether done in person or over the web. My suggestion is to leverage your demonstration theme. Let's go back to the theme we discussed earlier, the one I used for the building material industry. If you recall, it revolved around the Frank Lloyd Write phrase "Form Follows Function," a concept my audience identified with and respected. This theme became the foundation of my powerful and compelling close. Here's how it went. "Form Follows Function. We talked about it a great deal today, and we want you to know as your software supplier, we take this concept seriously. For example, if you go through the trouble of building a custom home, you'll pour yourself into the design of that home. Why? You're building it for a lifetime of living, not just for move-in day. Form follows function, right? When we build software, we do it with the same concept in mind. Our partnership with you, our customer, means that the software we develop will function according to your business needs both today and in the future. Our entire organization is built around this philosophy. At the start of our demonstration, I stated that one of my goals for the day would be to ask you to take the next step with us. (If you recall, I recommended that you write your goals down on a flipchart. Turn to that flipchart page as you make this statement.) That time is now..."

This is my opportunity to leave a lasting impression. I'm going to seize that opportunity. At the end of a long demonstration, I want my prospect to:

1. Leave with a deep, lasting, positive impression.

2. Know I really care about what I am selling.

3. Feel my emotion.

As we discussed earlier, now is the time to ask them for a commitment to the "call to action." Again, this could take the form of a visit to one of your customers, a visit to your corporate office or the contract itself.

AFTER THE DEMONSTRATION

Following your demonstration, you still have work to do. Make it a habit to perform the following tasks upon returning to the office.

Thank you - A hand-written thank you note is a simple thing that will highlight your professionalism and add to your credibility. I'd suggest sending one to:
1. Your demonstration sponsor and the highest ranking individual who attended your demonstration. Make the note short but sincere.

2. The owner of the company thanking them for investing the time of her staff. Again, make it to-the-point and sincere.

3. Assuming your audience was less than 15 people, everyone who attended the demonstration. Just make sure you remember everyone and correctly spell his or her names. Sending thank you notes to more than 15 people becomes unmanageable and error prone.

Follow-up - Take the notes from the demonstration (Demonstration Plan, Discovery Log, etc.) and consolidate them immediately. Time is of the essence. While everything is fresh in your mind, put all the notes into one concise report with a section at the bottom called Action Items. Have it sorted by your teammates so they know exactly what's expected of them. Make sure everyone understands his or her deadlines.

Follow-up with the prospect can be in two forms. I call the first option the "comprehensive approach." This involves sending a prospect-friendly version of the report you created above. A few unique characteristics of this version of the report are:

1. Include direct, concise answers to their questions and action items.

2. Include benefit statements at every opportunity.

3. Solve open issues with the names of customers who had the same issue but solved it with your software.

I refer to the second form of follow-up as the "methodical approach." Rather than supplying your prospect with one report, this approach passes them information one day at a time. You spoon-feed them so your name stays in front of them on a daily basis. I prefer the methodical approach because I always have a reason to contact them. Rather than the demonstration being one big blast, I can spread its *value* out over the remainder of the sales cycle.

If the decision-maker is highly organized or needs a quick response, don't use this approach. Organized individuals don't like a steady stream of correspondence. They prefer one nice, neat and organized summary they can three-hole punch and place neatly in a binder. You'll make good points if you do all this for them. (Making sure the binder has your company's name on it of course!)

How do you know which approach to use? First, plan on using both approaches with any given prospect, depending on the personalities on their selection team. During your Discovery, you can usually spot the "comprehensive response" individuals the moment you walk into their offices. Their desk, bookshelves and pictures are all neat and organized. Because they feel the world works against them, you'll gain points by giving them what they want (one organized report). For all others, steer toward the "methodical approach."

Self-Evaluation - Take time to examine the action items and how you performed. If you know you need to work on a particular area of the software (i.e. the "Not Again" demo crime), make note of it. Stay on top of yourself and improve the areas causing you the most difficulty. No one ever gives a perfect demonstration. Everyone can improve. Be on the lookout if your self-evaluation doesn't reveal much.

That's probably an indication that you're committing the "Stale Demonstrating" demo crime. You just don't realize it yet!

Practice - Practice makes perfect. Trite but true. Here's a story to illustrate the point. In 1991, during the testing of a closed-circuit link between its Washington and New York bureaus, CBS accidentally did a satellite broadcast of a "rehearsal" between anchor Dan Rather and Pentagon correspondent David Martin. When I read about this in the *Los Angeles Times,* I was amazed. Not because of the broadcasting error. What blew me away was that one of the most experienced and seasoned news anchors in the history of broadcasting was *practicing* a big story. If Dan Rather still practice, so can you and I! When it comes to demonstrating software, never assume you're beyond needing to practice.

CHAPTER SUMMARY

The foundation of every sport is a series of fundamentals. In soccer it is dribbling, passing and defensive positioning. In football, it's blocking and tackling. In basketball, it's shooting and dribbling. Before you can be a champion, you have to master the fundamentals. Demonstrating software is no different. If you sidestep the fundamentals that were presented in this chapter, you'll never become a winning demonstrator.

CHAPTER 8
Your Demonstration Setting

People's opinions are shaped by impressions. Think of a town you visited in your past that somehow left you with a bad memory of the place. Maybe the weather was horrible, your car broke down, you were a victim of crime, your hotel was a disaster or you had a huge fight with your spouse. Unless you've returned to the town several other times since the negative experience, you probably still have a bad impression of it today. That's the kind of first impression I had of Atlanta. For some reason, I always seemed to end up there in the winter when it was cold and rainy. Every time I traveled through Atlanta, my flights were delayed. I just didn't like the place. Then, my job transferred me there. That happened to be in the fall, which is a beautiful time of the year to be in Atlanta. In search of a house, I got a chance to visit all the different areas of the city. I discovered that it really was a nice place to live. But that was only because I was forced to spend more time there. It took time to reshape my opinions. If my only contact with Atlanta had continued to be when I was passing through, the initial impressions I had would still shape the way I thought of it to this day.

Chances are pretty good that you will have only *one opportunity* to demonstrate to your prospect. So you can't afford to leave a bad first impression. Make sure the room, equipment, projection, sound, power, lighting, temperature, food and props are up to your professional standards. This is the time and place to pay particular attention to details.

DEMONSTRATION LOCATION

The location of your demo will vary depending on the product you sell and the market you serve. There are occasions where the prospect will come to *your* facility. In many situations, you will be asked to perform the demonstration at *their* office. You may also find yourself demonstrating at a location that is basically *neutral* (a hotel, partner's office, etc.).

Your Facility - With all things equal, I prefer demonstrating in my own facility, for several reasons:

- I have far more control over interruptions versus being at the prospect's location.

- I can predict, and for the most part control, the physical aspects of the demonstration room. Things like lighting, sound quality and appearance of the room.

- I have a dedicated demonstration area, so there's not as much set up and preparation required. But don't get complacent. Although the section titled "Demonstration Room" is primarily intended to address issues when you're away from your office, take the time to apply the same principles to your own demo facility.

Their Facility - With a lot of prospects (typically big ones or when there's comprehensive software involved), you'll be going to their facility to demonstrate. Here's why:

- If they have more than two or three people on their evaluation team, it will probably be less expensive to bring you to them rather than them to you. (Note that this is not bad for you. If you can deliver a powerful demonstration, the more people you have involved, the better.)

- If lots of people will be involved, chances are many of them will only participate in one or two sections of the demo. The prospect can avoid pulling somebody out of their job for a day or two if the demonstration is held at their own facility.

- Your facility may not be large enough to accommodate them.

- Just like you, they want to maintain control. If they feel more in control at their facility, that's where they'll want the demonstration to take place.

Let's stop here to make one thing perfectly clear. There is *no* reason to be fearful of demonstrating at a prospect's facility. If you've been asked to demonstrate at their facility, chances are your competitor has too. You need to make sure you do a better job preparing the demonstration environment than your competitor. This chapter is designed to help you do exactly that. Also, remember it's your mission to bridge-demonstrate. If the customer will be more comfortable at their office and it makes it easier for them to cross the Bridge, then that's what you *want* to do.

Alternate Locations - Sometimes it's better, even necessary, to hold you demonstration at a "neutral" location. Generally, that's because:

- Neither of your facilities has a room big enough to accommodate the number of people who will be participating.

- Though they can accommodate the audience size, the quality of the prospect's facility is just not acceptable. Maybe they want to stick you in some kind of utilitarian room that has horrible lighting, metal folding chairs and junk stacked in the corner. Perhaps you'll be using the wall for your projection screen. These conditions will make it harder for them to cross the Bridge because there's clutter blocking the way! Chances are they realize their facility is inadequate. It's probably just an issue of expense. If you offer to cover the facility costs (including lunch) to hold the demonstration someplace else, they'll go for it.

- The prospect insists on having it at their location, but you're really concerned about interruptions, perhaps because of your experience during the Discovery. A good compromise is to conduct the demonstration in their city or town, but not in their facility. Again, if there is a cost associated with the other facility, you will probably have to cover the expense.

Don't risk a sale on a poor location. Consider these alternatives if you're forced to move your demonstration.

Hotels - Hotels are a useful option. They're probably the most common, albeit expensive, alternative to either of your facilities. However, without proper planning, a hotel can be as bad or worse than the prospect's locale. Ask the same questions and apply the same tests to a hotel that you would to your prospect's location. A good way to control the quality of the hotel's facilities is for you to stay in the hotel the night before the demonstration. That way you can make sure everything is set up and working. Does the room have too much outside light coming through windows? Is there a screen for projection purposes? Do you have access to the internet (if necessary)? Do you have access to a flipchart or white-board? Is it supplied with good quality markers? Is there appropriate power?

Vendors - If you're selling software, you can bet someone has an interest in selling some hardware (servers, PC's, network equipment, etc.) or complementary software (database, office automation, etc.). Take advantage of these situations. For example, if your software runs on a particular brand of hardware, and the manufacturer has a sales office where your prospect is located, consider asking to use their facilities. Generally, they offer excellent conference rooms, projection equipment, screens, telecommunication access and white-boards. However, *never* be complacent about checking out their facilities prior to your demonstration. Make sure you have the best size room for your group and appropriate lighting. Usually the receptionist is prepared to recommend a good deli or restaurant that can cater food and drinks for the demonstration.

When using a vendor's facility apply proper protocol. Some hardware vendors frown on demonstrations using competitive equipment. If this is an issue with your demonstration, be prepared to address it with the vendor when reserving the room. Also, give them an opportunity to either formally or informally address your prospect. Treat the people who are assisting you with respect. After your demonstration, always send a thank you note to the facility coordinator or the salesperson that sponsored your demo. While this may be your vendor, they're doing you a favor. Respect the favor and they'll openly offer to assist you in the future.

Partners - This is a company you work closely with but don't necessarily buy or sell any of their products or services. An example might be an accounting firm that provides implementation assistance for your software. Similar to your vendors, they may have demonstration facilities in close proximity to your prospect.

WEB DEMONSTRATING

Before we leave the topic of demonstration locations, let's look deeper at an increasingly common alternative. Web demonstrations and presentation save time and money for both you and the prospect. The convenience factor often overrides any disadvantage that may exist with not being directly in front of the prospect. This medium offers a practical platform for a demonstration when one or more of the following circumstances exist:

- It's economically prohibitive to travel to the prospect's location.

- You need to do a demonstration on very little notice.

- You need to demonstrate to people in multiple locations at the same time.

- The demonstration is two hours or less.

- You've already performed an on-site demonstration but the prospect needs a follow-up demonstration to clarify a few open issues.

In the world of "do more with less," your time is your most precious resource. Remote demonstrating over the Internet offers you a low cost, time efficient method of presenting to your prospect. Even with all of those benefits, I have found very few demonstration professionals that prefer delivering web demos over live demos. This medium introduces a number of drawbacks to a powerful demonstration:

- You can't see your prospect's reaction to your demonstration. This is a necessary component to the direction and strategy of your demonstration.

- The speed of the Internet isn't always predictable. If the response time on the Internet suddenly becomes slow, it will reflect poorly on your software, even though the slowness has nothing to do with you.

- If you're demonstrating to a group of people, your voice connection is only as good as the prospect's speakerphone.

Many of these shortcomings can be resolved by following these simple suggestions:

- Always test your connection prior to the start of your demonstration to ensure a solid connection and a reasonable response time. My preference is to perform a test one day prior to the demonstration. If that's not practical, plan on testing at least one hour ahead of time.

- Make sure the connection on your end of the demonstration is supported by a high-speed, dedicated link to the Internet. Whenever possible, avoid wireless or shared connections where performance is less predictable. This will ensure reliability and good response time (at least on your end).

- Use a headset for audio. It eliminates background noise, makes your voice clearer, and (if wireless) gives you greater mobility. If you can stand and move during the demo, your energy will stay higher and your presentation will be more engaging.

- Invest in a web cam. Occasional use of a web cam (at the beginning, during questions, when discussing key points) will help in engaging and retaining the attention of your audience.

- Know and practice using the complete capabilities of your web conferencing system. For too long I used our web software as a simple device to share my desktop. But once I started incorporating all of the interaction capabilities of our web platform, my presentations became much more engaging.

- Use the highlighting, emoticon and communications (e.g. chat) features of your web demonstration platform. One of the advantages of web demonstrations is you can often use an electronic highlighter to draw attention to a part of your screen. Doing so is very engaging.

- Steer your prospect away from a wireless or mobile Internet connections. If they don't have a high-speed, dedicated link to the Internet, encourage them to go to a location where it's available. Discourage connections where voice and data are shared on the same network link.

- If your prospect is planning on using a speakerphone, make sure it's high-quality and can handle two-way voice communication (duplex). If their speakerphone is poor quality, loan them a high-quality one. Discourage cell phone connections, they are unreliable and noisy.

- If your link speed supports VOIP, use it rather than a standard telephone connection. With a good digital headset/microphone on both ends, you will sound like you are in the room together.

- If your demonstration needs to extend beyond 90 minutes, schedule multiple sessions. It's too difficult to keep a prospect's attention for longer than two hours over a speakerphone.

- Always stand during a web demonstration. You need your energy to come through your voice and you will be more animated and energized if you stand versus sit.

Under the right circumstances web demonstrating offers a unique opportunity to save both you and your prospect time and money. The practicality of this style of demonstration provides a platform for you to demonstrate to more prospects over a larger geographical area. Just because you're remote demonstrating, don't skip the Discovery Process. Just do your interviews over the telephone. Your demo crime-watch remains in effect. Finally, because you can't see your prospect, work on developing your skills at getting and giving good verbal cues and feedback.

YOUR DEMONSTRATION ROOM

Closely examine the room where you'll hold your demonstration. If you know the demonstration will be held at the prospect's facility and you have a chance to do Discovery on-site, make certain you ask to see the room that will be used. Similarly, if you'll be using a local hotel, pay them a visit. The same holds true for the office of a vendor or partner. Regarding your own demo facility, the assumption is that you're all set. However, as we mentioned earlier, it wouldn't hurt to do a little honest examination of how it could be improved, especially if no changes have been made for a while.

As you would expect, audience size is the primary factor you'll need to consider when you're setting up your demonstration room. This will determine how you address the issues of room size and layout, where the presenter should stand, lighting, room temperature, power requirements, food and refreshments.

Room Size - Make sure the size of the demonstration room fits the size of the audience. A room that comfortably seats 50 people isn't very conducive to an audience of six. It will feel cavernous. In an oversized room, the audience *always* sits behind the first two rows, which places them a long distance from you and the screen. It'll be hard for your prospect to see and hear what you're demonstrating. They have to work harder to understand your message. You have to work harder delivering it. You both become fatigued. It's a vicious circle. Don't put yourself in this situation.

Likewise, make sure the room isn't too small. An executive conference room designed for eight people won't be good for a group of 12 or more. The room gets hot and stuffy because the air conditioning won't be able to compensate for the extra people and equipment in the room. What happens when you sit for hours in a room that is too warm? You fall asleep. It's hard to lead somebody across the Bridge when they're snoring!

Regardless of the actual size, take a few minutes to learn the room yourself. I make it a point to stand for a minute or two in each corner of the room. I want to see the sightlines. I want to understand the area I have to work with at the front. I want to see how the screen and projector look from every angle. And I want to understand how my voice will carry to and from every position.

Location of the Presenter - Here's the rule-of-thumb when figuring out where to stand: place yourself in front and off to one side of your audience. That way, you can see them and they can see the screen.

To facilitate movement and interaction, try to have "center access" to your audience. This won't always be possible, especially in a traditional conference room, but do it when you can. Make every attempt not to block the center aisle with your projection equipment. A center access layout allows you to freely move through your audience and be in close proximity to anybody who is asking a question. This is a helpful technique when fielding questions and addressing objections, no matter the size of your audience. For example, let's say you're demonstrating to a fairly large group, maybe 40 people. Somebody toward the back of the room asks a question. Rather than having to yell at the guy from the front of the room, you can walk down the center to get close to where he's seated. In a normal voice, you're able to ask him to repeat his question, which you then restate for the group. You can then walk back to the front of the room and answer the question for the whole group. Now imagine doing that for a smaller group, say 15 people. Why would you do anything different? You shouldn't. Free movement in the center of the room helps you to engage an audience, no matter the size.

Room Layout - Over the years I've heard lots of debates about the proper room layout for a demonstration. In fact, there are companies that specialize in the design and implementation of presentation rooms. That's great if you're building a new demonstration facility. But most of us are simply trying to make the best of what we have to work with. This is particularly true if you perform demonstrations at the prospect's place of business, a hotel or at a vendor or partner's locale.

One question I hear all the time is, "Should the room be arranged classroom style, conference-room style or in a U-shaped format?" As with everything else we're discussing, audience size is the *primary* consideration (see examples below). However, there are two other considerations when determining room layout:

- Projection equipment and how the lighting, either room light or outside light, impacts the projected image. For example, if the room you're in has a big window on one wall and you're using projection equipment, you probably don't have much flexibility.

- Furniture in the room, and its portability. For example, let's say you're in a room that would be perfect for a classroom style layout. Only one problem; you have a half-ton conference table on one end of the room. You'll be setting up a conference style layout whether you like it or not.

With regard to size, I like to determine room layouts based on the following categories:

1. **One-on-One.**

2. **Two to Six People.**

3. **Seven to 14 People.**

4. **15 to 40 People.**

5. **41 to 100 People.**

6. **101 to 1,000 People.**

1. One-on-One - In this setting, a small conference room with a conference table works best. I prefer to avoid demonstrating in either their private office or mine because of the inevitable interruptions. I think it's a real mistake to bring projection equipment to a one-on-one demonstration. I write from experience. Here's what happened to me when I conducted a demonstration in my company's Dallas regional office. We had just purchased the latest and greatest high-intensity color projection system. At the time, it was an amazing piece of equipment. It supported both computer projection and video. I was bound and determined to impress the prospect with our new equipment. In the end, it was a lack-luster demo. My prospect remained detached throughout the demo, and within two hours I was unplugging the equipment and going *personal* with the demo because I was the only one in the room after my prospect left!

Don't stand in front of your prospect when you're doing a one-on-one demo. This leads to a non-involved, one-way demonstration. Sit next to them with your computer display in front of both of you. I recommend having a white-board or flipchart handy for illustration purposes. Standing up from time to time to write something down keeps you active and your demonstration fresh. In this small, informal setting, prospects often like to stand up and use the whiteboard. Encourage them to do this for the same reasons.

Give a one-on-one demo seated in a small room, without projection or audio-visual equipment. Use a white-board or flipchart for illustration purposes.

2. 2-6 people – As the group grows, audio-visual equipment becomes necessary. Using a projector is more effective than having them hover around your computer display, even when demonstrating to only two people. If you only use your display, and you have people on either side of you, you'll be constantly turning from side-to-side to speak to them. They'll never get a good view of the screen. Everyone will become fatigued.

The room layout in this environment needs to remain personal. I still prefer a conference room with a conference table. If the room is large enough, place the projection equipment on a separate table instead of the conference table. This prevents the projector and image from shaking every time someone bumps the table.

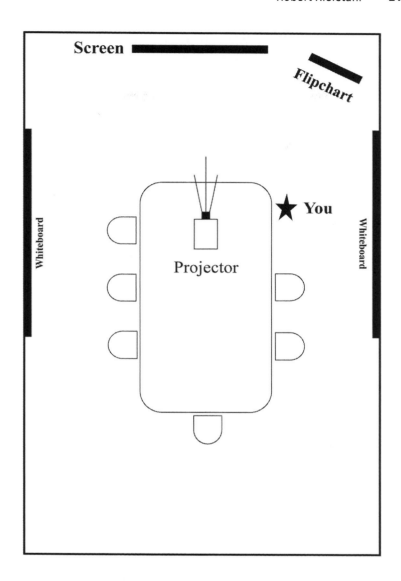

For the 2-6 size group, you'll want a white-board or flipchart for illustration purposes. Some conference rooms have a well-maintained, wall-mounted cabinet opposite the head of the conference table (commonly called a "conference center") that contains a white-board and pull-down projection screen. This is a good solution for *either* screen projection or illustrating your points, *but not both*. It's distracting and inefficient to be constantly raising and lowering the projection screen to illustrate a point on the white-board. For that reason, I recommend placing a flipchart next to the wall-mounted unit. Whatever you do, never project computer screen images on a white-board. This produces a nasty glare-spot that will annoy and distract your prospect all day.

When I'm demonstrating to only two people, I prefer to sit with them while projecting the screen image. However, once the group hits three or more, I stand. It's important to put yourself in a commanding position with a group of three or more. Avoid having everyone sit on one side of the table. This creates an undesirable "me-versus-them" atmosphere.

For this size group (and any larger ones), I never stay in the same place. I'll move around the front of the room during discussions. I squat down in front of the table when I'm trying to make a subtle but key point. If the prospect is making a long and important point, I sit next to one of them during their explanation. Russ Cram, a valued friend and excellent demonstrator, uses an interesting technique. When he gets excited about a key feature and he wants the prospect's attention, he stands on his toes!

With a two to six person demo, a conference room with a conference table is best. Audio-visual equipment is needed, as is a projection screen and a white-board or flipchart.

3. 7-14 people – Putting this many people in a typical conference room is pushing the limit. Even if the conference room table is designed to seat 12, the nature of a demonstration environment will dictate there's probably only room for about seven people.

- The projected image, your colleagues, your equipment and you will occupy some of the space around the table.

- No one can sit at the end of the table where the projector is located because their head will likely block the image.

- No one can sit where you'll be standing.

- You won't want to put anyone in front of the hot projector fan unless you don't mind snoring during your demo!

Once the demonstration hits the seven-person threshold, I like to move to a room that supports a U-shaped layout. A conference-room style will work, but I prefer U-shaped. The primary reason: it enhances interaction with the audience because I'm free to move among them. If a person has a question, I can get to them quickly to make my point rather than having to navigate around a conference table.

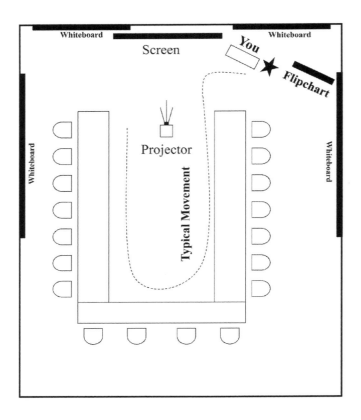

The demands for projection equipment change when your group reaches this size, no matter which layout you choose. You'll need brighter projection equipment, something with at least a 1,200-lumen rating (more on projectors later). If the room has windows, you could run into the "too much ambient light" problem. If that's the case, you will need a projector with around a 1600-lumen rating. You'll also want a minimum screen size of 72" (43" by 57") on which to project the image properly. Again, place the equipment on a special table or cart. Because the room will be larger, bring two long extension cords; one for electricity, the other for the video connection. Also, bring a laser pointer. This supporting equipment will help you manage the larger room setting.

In either of these settings, I stand during the vast majority of the demonstration. Where I stand depends somewhat on my projection capabilities. If my equipment can display the image on both the projection screen and my computer display, I like to stand near the display. This allows me to face my audience and view what they are seeing (on my computer display). If this duel-display is not possible, I like to stand to the side so I can clearly see the projected image without turning my back on the audience. This necessitates adequate length interface and power cords.

With this size audience, you might want to use a podium. Podiums come in many different forms, including fold-up portable podiums. A floor-standing podium that's movable is desirable, but not always available. As long as you have room on the conference table, a tabletop podium is a suitable replacement. When one is not available, I use the case I carried my equipment in (a trick I learned long ago). If you're really organized, you can bring a small tablecloth to cover the case. This makes it look more professional.

Don't worry about a microphone with this size group. I like to use my un-amplified voice with as large a group as possible. When you electronically project your voice, you lose a personal approach.

With a group of seven to 14, you'll need audio-visual equipment, a white-board or flipchart, proper length cords, and a podium. Microphones and sound amplification is not required.

4. 15-40 people – With this many people, there's a good chance you'll be beyond the ability to arrange the room in a U-shape. Even if the room is large enough to support 25 people in a U-shape arrangement, the attendees in the back of the room will have trouble seeing the screen. This will necessitate a classroom-style seating arrangement. This configuration brings the audience closer to the front of the room where they can better see the screen.

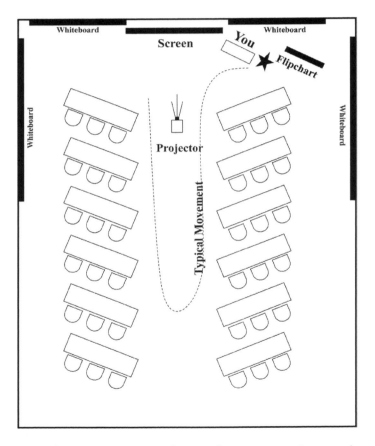

In this setting, a podium of some sort is mandatory. Standing during the entire demonstration is also required because the people in the back of the room can neither see nor hear you if you're seated. Standing also allows you to move around the room to keep both you and your audience fresh. In a larger group, it's easier for the audience to "zone-out" staring at a projection screen. Your movement injects life into your demonstration and prevents this from happening.

This size group is still manageable with your speaking voice. To help keep things on a personal level, I don't recommend any type of voice amplification.

Your screen projection capabilities might require an upgrade when compared to a group of seven to 14. Consider moving to a 2500-lumen or higher projector. Your room will likely require a larger screen and will have more ambient light, make a higher output projector a necessity. In a larger room such as this, make sure that you understand your ability to control the lighting, both natural and artificial, before you start your presentation. If your demonstration includes any multimedia elements (video clips, sound bites, etc.), you'll need speakers, either stand-alone units or ones that are built into the projector.

A group this size requires room layout planning. A U-shaped layout might work, but you'll likely need a classroom style layout. You'll also require some equipment upgrades (projection, speakers, and podium).

5. 41-100 People –First, you're going to need voice amplification. I recommend a wireless, lapel microphone (lavaliere). Because you're going to need a larger screen and a brighter image, your projection equipment needs to be professional quality. For that reason, a projector with a 3000-lumen rating or more is required. In a group this size, any multimedia presentation will need to be powered by real speakers, not the ones on your projector. Seating in this environment should either be classroom or theater style.

With a group this large, it's helpful to have someone else run the keyboard for you. This enables you to freely move through the audience in an engaging fashion. If you use somebody else on the keyboard, it's *imperative* that you practice the entire presentation together. They need to anticipate when to change screens based on what you say. It's OK to say, "Next screen please" a couple times, but you don't want to do that on every screen transition.

Your demonstration is likely to be relatively short, lasting anywhere from 20 to 90 minutes. A shorter demonstration dictates a higher level of excitement, movement and tempo. Make the presentation fun and captivating. To engage a group this large, ask a question, pause for a moment, and then *answer it for them*. People nodding will be your best indicator that you have engaged them. Tell lots of stories your audience can relate to. If you enjoy the moment, so will your audience.

A group this size can be intimidating. Put any "equipment anxieties" to rest by seeking professional assistance. If you don't have an internal audio-visual department, hire an outside firm to assist you. A little extra expense beats having to recover in front of a large audience.

6. 100-1,000 People – This may sound enormous, but the overall demonstration techniques are the same. However, there is a big difference in the equipment you will need. Demand a professional setup for house sound, multimedia and projection equipment. Up until now, you were probably presenting from the floor. Now you're sure to be on a stage. Expect a spotlight on you. Your demonstration may also be filmed.

Preparation and practice on the stage is crucial. I always make it a point to get everything set up and tested long before the demonstration. (You should try to do this whether you're demonstrating to one person or a group of 1,000.) *All* equipment should be tested prior to your presentation. You simply can't afford the smallest mistake in front of a group this large. Check the sound for feedback and the projection for brightness. Don't get stuck behind a podium with a fixed microphone. Make sure you have access to a wireless, lavaliere microphone. Most important, check your computer for speed and reliability. If I'm required to leave my equipment for any reason prior to the demonstration, I leave a hand-written sign on the keyboard warning, "You Touch, You Die!" Think "Murphy's Law" (if anything can go wrong, it will).

Here's a story I love to tell. A couple of great friends of mine (who shall remain nameless) were launching some cutting-edge products in front of over 1,500 people at a large conference. The plan was for the two of them to simulate long distance system communication by "dueling" from opposite ends of the stage. They used the theme song "Dueling Banjos" (from the movie *Deliverance)* as their backdrop. The audience loved the theme and humor as they began the demonstration. Just as they were about to exchange a *live* electronic transaction over the Internet (all being displayed on huge screens of course!), something went awry. Their Internet connection simply *died.* No matter what they did, they received no response from the network server. While one was left on stage to stall for time, the other one ducked behind the stage curtain to find out what had happened. Once it was determined that this particular demo was going nowhere, they regained their composure and moved on to the next new product launch. Standing in front of 1,500 customers, this was the most humbling and embarrassing moment in their professional careers. We later learned that just moments before the demonstration began, a hotel worker accidentally pulled the power cord for the network hub. To this day, these two friends always put a "DO NOT TOUCH!" sign on every power cord they use, even for their alarm clock at home!

Do whatever you can to avoid *bleeding edge* products when demonstrating to this many people. Stay at a high level. Be flashy with your demo, but only show pertinent functionality. The risk in this size group is too high to take chances. You're better off making your business points through verbal and presentation communication (such as PowerPoint™) as opposed to live software demonstrations.

A demo to a group this size is almost never more than one hour in length. Rehearse and time your demonstration multiple times (I like to do four run-throughs). Completely script the demonstration and have it at the podium during your presentation. A script will keep you focused and provides a backup in the event you lose your place during the demonstration.

Timing is important since it's likely a group this large has another presenter following you on the stage. Here are some tips to help you with timing:
- Expect delivery time of your presentation to *shrink* by about ten percent when you're in front of a large

group. Your adrenaline rush and lack of interruptions will push you along. Use the extra time for questions and answers.

- Hide a digital clock on the podium.

- Time your script, and then place time markers in it with large, bold letters. Make the timing marks ten minutes apart. For the last ten minutes, place markers every two minutes. Below is an example of a script outline with time markers.

- Plant a signal person in the audience. Have them prompt you when five minutes is remaining in your allotted time.

12:05	End Introductions
12:15	Software Demonstration
12:25	Return to Slide Presentation
12:35	Return To Software Demo
12:40	Begin Summary
12:42	Complete Summary
12:44	Questions & Answer

The right kind of movement is important with a group this size. Move across the stage, but not into the audience unless you're comfortable running up and down stairs. Avoid standing behind the big, safe, protective podium. Your audience deserves better!

Get out there and have some fun! Relate to the audience by telling stories. If you can deliver a funny parable directly related to your material, do it. When you're having fun, the crowd will respond. You'll be a hit!

Great presenters rarely walk on to the stage and say "Thank you for having me today." Instead, they walk on to the stage and begin with a story, humor or visuals. These presenters know that those first few seconds are crucial for securing the attention of the audience. Hollow phrases and thank you statements are simply ignored.

A large audience commands a level of preparation and professionalism that's foreign to most demonstrators. A different mindset is required. The projection equipment is no longer yours, so arrive early to practice using it. Move around to relax yourself and by all means, videotape your practice session. You'll be amazed at what you'll learn from reviewing it. It will help you feel more comfortable when you're on stage, live!

Lighting - Room lighting is one of the most important considerations when preparing for your demonstration. Figure out your lighting situation prior to the demonstration. I've found most training and conference rooms designed to house 15 to 75 people have very simple lighting. It usually consists of a hung ceiling with fluorescent fixtures controlled by one or two main switches. There might be windows in the room with little or no control over ambient light that will flood your screen. Considering you probably need a semi-dark area on your screen for projecting images, this excessive light causes problems. Your only solution is to turn off all the lights. If there's excessive ambient light in the room, it still may not be dark enough for a crisp image of your projected screen. While you can *get by* with this type of lighting, ultimately it will have a negative impact on your demonstration. Your audience will get tired! If your prospect wants you to perform your demonstration at their place of business, make sure you understand exactly what to expect. If the room is completely controlled by florescent lighting and the lights can either be on or off, ask if there are any table-lamps available. If there are no window blinds, ask if you can cover the windows. If none of this is possible, push to have the demonstration held at a nearby facility (hotel) that offers adequate lighting.

Electric Power and Cabling Issues - Power requirements can be a challenge. Think about your situation for a second. Your projection equipment is usually placed somewhere in the *middle* of the room. That being the case, your electric power needs to be there as well. An extension cord and power strip can solve most electrical power issues. To complicate matters, the video cable that connects your projection equipment to your laptop is usually 10 feet. Extending the video cable beyond 10 feet is almost always necessary. If you must extend the cable, invest in a gold-plated video connector cable. Not only is the connection better; the resistance in the cable is also lower which reduces signal loss over longer distances. You can buy them in custom lengths on-line. If you have this setup, you can probably move yourself to one side of the room allowing your audience a better view of your presentation.

Room Temperature - We've all been in meetings where the room was either too hot or too cold. It's miserable! It's hard to focus on anything but your discomfort. If you put your prospect in that situation, how do you expect them to concentrate on your message?

So, what's the right temperature? Whatever is comfortable for you is *usually* comfortable for your audience. However, if you're always cold when others are fine (or vice versa), plan on dressing accordingly. Take a "temperature check" about 45 minutes into your presentation to verify the room temperature is OK for them. It's your job to ensure you audience is comfortable.

Room temperature problems are usually caused by:

1. The thermostat is in another room. This is pretty common in commercial facilities. Let's say the people next door (who happen to control the thermostat) have 50 people in their room so they've got the air conditioning cranked. You've got six in your room, and everybody's looking for a sweater. Reverse the situation and everyone in your room is baking.

2. The number of people in a room. If your room is too small for the number of people occupying it, the air conditioning won't cool the room properly. Turning down the thermostat will have absolutely no effect on this problem; the ventilation or air conditioning in this room was not designed to compensate for the body heat generated by too many people.

Your only solution to these two problems is to switch rooms.

Refreshments and Food - Regardless of where you're holding your demonstration, always plan on food and drinks. Everyone *appreciates* someone who provides bagels in the morning, drinks at break and lunch at the proper time. You never want your prospect to be hungry or thirsty. Hunger can be a huge distraction! Offer refreshments, food and breaks at the right time, and you'll have more of their attention for longer periods of time.

There are varying opinions regarding what to feed your prospect. The most important thing: avoid foods containing substances that promote drowsiness. For example, turkey is naturally high in the amino acid L-tryptophane. L-tryptophane is believed to produce a natural calming effect. Milk is also high in this substance, hence the practice of drinking a warm glass of milk before bedtime to promote sleep.

Remember to keep beverages (including water and ice) refreshed throughout the day. Make arrangements for this as part of your preparation. Also, be sure the room is kept clean and tidy throughout the day (empty pop cans, candy wrappers, etc.). Prospects who like to keep their world neat and organized will appreciate this.

The location of a meal is worth discussing. Should you have food catered or should you go to a restaurant for lunch? This depends upon your prospect.

- The more *social* prospects will prefer to go out to lunch. They want to learn more about you on a personal level and like getting out for a break. Capitalize on this social opportunity and do some personal selling. Avoid talking about business and software. Spend this valuable time learning all you can about them as individuals.

- Plan on having lunch in the demonstration room if you have a great deal of material to cover in a short period of time. If this is the situation, your prospect will probably prefer to keep everyone in place. When this happens, I like using the time during lunch to discuss areas of interests besides software functionality, such as implementation philosophy or products futures.

Concerning a lunch menu, less is usually better. Don't overwhelm the prospect with too many choices. Make the menu simple and complete. Good foods for a demonstration lunch include something for everyone:

- Salads.

- Roast beef, ham, and salami sandwiches.

- Hot entrées

- Fruit.

- Sweets.

- Sodas, ice tea, coffee and water.

Room Equipment – Having the right equipment at your demonstration won't be a problem if you use a demonstration checklist (Chapter 6, *Checklists...Preparing for the Demo*). Include your equipment needs for a typical demonstration on this list. Be diligent in using this checklist. Don't show up for a demonstration without an extension cord when you know ahead of time that you always need one!

The following is a discussion of the equipment items that are *most* critical to your demonstration.

Projector - The larger your group, the more sophisticated your projector needs to be. It's really pretty simple:

- The larger the group, the larger the image you need to project.

- The larger the image, the further away from the screen you'll need to put your projector.

- Unfortunately, projection distance has an inverse effect on image intensity. As the projector gets further from the screen, it needs to be more powerful to cast a crisp, clear image.

- The power of a projector is measured in lumens, which is a measure of light intensity. To summarize our earlier discussion:

- A 1200-lumen projector is towards the bottom of the scale and should be considered the minimum acceptable. It will be adequate for groups up to 14 people provided that you can control the lighting. If ambient lighting is high or you cannot control the artificial lighting, then step up to a 1600-lumen or better unit.

- For groups between 15 and 40, depending on room lighting, use a 2400 lumen or greater projector.

- For groups between 40 and 100, you need a projector with a minimum of 3000 lumens and that is assuming you can control the ambient light. More likely a group of this size will be in a brighter room and you will want to move to a more powerful projector.

- For very large groups (100+), you should contract a professional audio-visual firm.

Regardless of the group size, always make sure to isolate your projection equipment on a table or cart. This will keep the screen from bouncing around every time someone moves.

For small groups needing multimedia presentations, many current model projectors offer built-in speakers. This is extremely useful. The sound from your laptop speakers is completely inadequate in a demonstration environment.

When you're team demonstrating, it's common to have more than one laptop in use. If you want to avoid having to unplug and re-connect laptops all the time, some projectors offer multiple input connections. These allow you to connect two laptops and switch between them using a button on the projector or remote control rather then switching cables. These models also accommodate switching between a laptop and a DVD player.

If you need to rent equipment, make sure you clearly communicate your requirements to the audio-visual rental firm. Most important is to specify your lumen (image intensity) requirements. Speakers and number of outputs are other capabilities that might be important. Too often, older trade-ins are used for rental equipment. These are woefully inadequate for most presentations. If you fail to give the rental firm specifications, you'll be disappointed with what they provide.

Get familiar with the operation of the projector you're using *before* the demonstration starts. For example, practice using the controls to adjust the focus, contrast and brightness. If you have two laptops connected to the projector, practice switching between units. If the projector has a remote control, make sure you are comfortable with its operation and the controls on the projector (in case the remote gets lost!). You don't want to be figuring out how to adjust your projector ten minutes into your demonstration.

Network Connectivity - If you'll need an internet connection, always ask your prospect in advance if the room you'll demonstrate in has a network connection that offers unrestricted access to the internet. Quite often the connections in conference and presentation rooms is either limited in what can be accessed or secured through a mechanism that may prevent your software or laptop from working correctly. I bet 50 percent of the time my prospect tells me there's a network connection in the room, but it's not what I need to demonstrate my software. Sometimes there is no connection to the internet, just to the local network. Other times there is access, but it requires VPN software or hardware that I don't have. The opposite can also be true; there is an internet connection, but it will not allow the use of my VPN system.

In other words, you have to test it for yourself. Know your own connection requirements (VPN, no VPN, etc.) and, ideally, test the connection before the demonstration. If you cannot test in in person, arrange a test with your sponsor, using equipment and settings that best simulates what you will need during the demonstration. And then have an alternative in place just in case. If at all possible, avoid wireless connections. Security and settings are often a problem, performance is less predictable, and the possibility of getting booted off is much greater.

If these network connections are a consistent challenge it is time to invest in a high-speed wireless card or tethering your high-speed mobile device to your equipment.

Finally, bring your own long network cable just in case. Sure, there's a network connection. It is at the opposite end of the room from the projector and screen. Is that a problem for you?

Whiteboard, Flipchart or Tablet- It's essential you have one or (preferably) multiple of these items to illustrate a point and personalize your demonstration. If 100 percent of your illustrations are accomplished with PowerPoint, you're making a big mistake. Think back to the "Power-Point Crutch" demo crime (Chapter 4). You need interaction with your audience. Illustrating a point on a flipchart, whiteboard or tablet provides freshness and spontaneity to your demonstration. Whiteboards, flipcharts or tablets are perfect for writing down benefit statements, illustrating points or presenting value statements. Flipcharts are particularly effective because you can return to a point for review or to check it off. That *can't* be done if a point is written on a whiteboard and then erased. If you're demonstrating to a large group, a tablet PC or digitizer is an excellent replacement. Whether my audience is one or 100 people, I use a flipchart, whiteboard or my tablet in *every* demonstration.

Other Equipment Considerations - You're representing a technology company. Make that apparent from the equipment you use. Examples include a wireless keyboard, wireless mouse and a presenter mouse. Obviously, make sure you (and your demonstration teammates) practice with this equipment *before* your demo. These are basic *investments* if you do any product demonstrations to prospective customers.

Even if the prospect tells you they have the items you need, plan on bringing everything you can carry. This includes extension cords, power-strips, tape to secure any cables, and batteries. Bring spare AA, AAA and 9-volt batteries for use in a variety of equipment (laser pointers, remotes, microphones, etc.). There's nothing more frustrating than counting on your remote control for your projector only to learn it won't work because the batteries are dead. I always remove the batteries from all remotes prior to travel to avoid a button being pressed down constantly during transportation and draining the batteries. If you're positive you can use their projection screen, leave yours behind. Otherwise, bring it too! On more than one occasion, I've planned to use my prospect's screen for my demonstration only to learn one of their salespeople needed it for another meeting (guess who had priority). There I was taping flipchart paper against the dark wall in the conference room praying the audience would be able to see something!

Finally, don't forget about room lighting. If your prospect has no window blinds, bring something to cover the windows (with their permission of course). It's better to tape flipchart pages on a window then to let your prospect strain their eyes to see your screen!

CONTINGENCY PLANS

There's nothing more frustrating than showing up for your demonstration only to learn your projector has a burned-out bulb and you don't have a spare. Make sure you have a contingency plan for critical items like your laptop, projector and dial-up modem.

Computer Failure - What would you do if you arrived for your demo and your laptop failed? Here are a couple contingency plans in the event of this catastrophic failure:

- Assuming your software is demonstrated from the laptop itself, have a backup of your software on a portable hard drive so you can load it onto another computer.

It's a plus if you can practice this procedure on a system in your office so it's not totally foreign to you if it happens during a demonstration. If you haven't practiced, chances are you'll be on the phone with your support staff at your office.

- If you use your laptop for a connection to the Internet, ask to use one of your prospects PCs or laptops to do the same thing. It's a good idea during your Discovery visit to test one of their PCs to make sure this option works in the event it's needed during your demonstration.

VIDEO PROJECTION

Your prospect might say, "Hey, you don't need to bring a projector. We've got one here." Bring your projector anyway. Try theirs first. However, if your projector displays higher quality images, use yours. Having both available gives you an option should either projector fail.

Internet Connectivity - All of us take connectivity as a given these days. We connect to check our e-mail, our Facebook profile, and demonstrate our software. Any number of things can fail:

- Access can be restricted at your prospect's site.

- Servers can be down at your site.

- Bandwidth and reliability can be unpredictable or less than expected.

- Security settings can change unexpectedly.

I am sure that each of you have your own demonstration horror story to add to these problems. Again, some software products can operate on a laptop or on the host system. Let's say this is your situation. You're demonstrating on the host system because that's where you've set up the prospect's data (collected during your Discovery). Suddenly the host system goes down. What are your options?

- Because you will be able to deliver a more powerful demo using the prospect's data you set up on the host system, ask if you can reschedule.

- If this isn't possible, make the best of the demonstration data you have on your laptop.

- As a last resort, see if you can connect to a customer's system (pre-arranged of course) and use their training environment for your demonstration.

Software Problems (Bugs) - Hey, they happen. Don't panic. However, don't bang your head against the wall trying the same function over and over again to see if you can reproduce the error. Clear your screen, explain how the function normally works and move on to the next topic.

USE OF PROPS

Demonstrating software products is a "concept sale." You're selling an *idea*, not a tangible object. People like buying and relating to objects because they can touch and feel them. For this reason, I like to use props in my demonstrations. These help the prospect relate to my software, my points, and to me as an individual. There are many types of props you can use, including user documentation, implementation manuals, customer reference letters and value added equipment.

Documentation - If your software includes clear, concise and attractive user and technical manuals, bring an example to the demonstration. Be prepared to show some good examples of your quality by having certain pages tabbed. I like to use the color-coded tapes you can purchase from any office supply store.

The best way to demonstrate the quality of your documentation is to seamlessly *weave* it into your demonstration. For instance, wait until the prospect asks a question you're confident that you can quickly find in the documentation. Use the documentation to answer their question. If your documentation is on-line and context sensitive (it guesses you want help on a screen or field based on where you make your help request), this technique is particularly impressive. You'll seize the moment and connect with the prospect.

User Reference Letters - Most prospects are *risk adverse*. They love to hear about your other satisfied customers. The best way to *demonstrate* satisfied customers is with reference letters. If you don't use reference letters already, I recommend you provide an incentive to your support and implementation staff to solicit them. They're powerful selling tools in a demonstration.

Place user letters in an attractive, professional binder. Encase each letter in a plastic sleeve. Make sure the copy quality of the letter is clean and crisp. If possible, carry original letters or color copies of the original. Organize them in the binder according to subject. For example, have a section of letters that help justify the expense of your product. Another section of letters should discuss your superior service. Letters present a professional image and reinforce the value you place on your customers.

Like any other prop, keep user letters under cover until the right opportunity presents itself to spontaneously bring out the binder and present it. I find that I frequently get that opportunity during a break or at lunch.

A friend of mine, Jack Moore, sold physician billing software. Instead of obtaining user letters from his doctor customers, he convinced them to write a "reference note" on one of their prescription pads. As a prop, Jack would pull out a stack of "software prescriptions" written by his satisfied physician customers.

An alternative to reference letters is to provide your prospect with trade publication articles that are about (or mention) one of your customers. At a minimum, cut out the article and put it in your reference letter binder. If it appears in one of their leading industry trade publications, your prospect probably receives it and may have read the article. However, your prospect may not have been aware it was your customer. Often, you can request nice, brochure quality reprints of these articles from the publisher.

If you have a niche product, your prospects will probably know or recognize some of the companies in your reference letter binder. This familiarity will help your prospects connect with you and your software. It will help them across the Bridge.

White Papers - Consulting firms regularly write research papers they publish and distribute as a service for their clients. These are referred to as "white papers." I think it's a darn good idea for software companies to do the same (hint, hint). They can be used to introduce a business issue and how a particular technology (yours!) solves that issue.

They should be on various subjects related to your software but stop short of being a brochure. Naturally, at the *end* of the white paper, there's a plug for your company and products.

Writing white papers elevates your company above a competitor who focuses solely on marketing literature. In the eyes of your prospect, your company becomes both a consulting firm and a software company. If your prospect is concerned that software companies have a tendency to "develop products in a vacuum," your white papers will help remove that fear as it relates to your company.

If you've written several white papers about various subjects, have copies of each with you for the demonstration. As the opportunity presents itself, pull out a white paper to help illustrate your points and expertise.

Implementation and Training Materials - If you sell a comprehensive software product and follow a structured implementation philosophy, share this information with the prospect. Bring copies of your implementation materials with you for display and discussion purposes. Examples include manuals, checklists, CDs, DVDs or a quick look at your Internet training and support site.

I can assure you that your prospect is fearful of the implementation process. Removing their fear will lead to big steps across the Bridge. The best way to do that is by showing them you have this critical area *nailed*. Something as simple as a well-documented implementation and training process can go a long way toward establishing your credibility.

Equipment Props - If your solution includes third-party equipment such as barcode readers, radio-frequency devices, credit card scanners, smartphone applications, or other pieces of equipment, bring examples. These props don't need to be functional. In fact, I recommend getting a broken unit given to you by a vendor and using it instead of a good unit. You'll make a visual point without having to do an actual live demonstration of the unit (something that you may not have the expertise to do).

Dramatic Props - Sometimes the best way to make your point is to use anything *but* a high tech prop. I like to use children's toys to provide drama and visualization. For example, when I want to illustrate how open my database is to third-party query tools, I pull out a Wiffle® Ball (holes in the ball…get it?). I'll use some Tinker Toys® to help my prospect visualize the flexibility of my order entry system. The use of dramatic props is a controversial one. You know the culture of your prospect. If the organization is very conservative, leave the props at home.

CHAPTER SUMMARY

Your demonstration setting has an important, albeit silent, effect on your success. Don't settle for a sub-standard location or environment. Take the time to think about your needs and plan accordingly. Pamper your prospects with good lighting, comfortable room temperatures, food and refreshments. Make sure your equipment is at the highest professional standards you or your company can afford. By all means, don't forget to bring *anything*. Use a checklist and never again get stressed while you utter the words, "I know I am forgetting something, but I can't think what it is!" Expect problems and have at least one contingency plan for each and every possibility. Finally, have some fun with the prospect. Use props to help them visualize your points by identifying with something tangible.

CHAPTER 9
Team Demonstrating

This form of demonstrating is very prevalent in today's world of complex software sales. It's often necessary for one of the following reasons:

Due to the software's complexity, a single demonstrator can't be expected to learn and demonstrate everything.

Your marketing plan dictates salespeople sell and sales-support people demonstrate. In other words, you purposefully don't want salespeople on the keyboard.

The size of the audience requires more than one person be involved.

The length of the demonstration (one full day or longer) necessitates a second person for sheer relief.

ROLES

The roles of the primary team members in a software demonstration are *very* similar to those you find on an American football team:

Quarterback - In a football game, the quarterback runs the plays on the field. Quarterbacks are responsible for "tactical" aspects of the game. Similarly, in a software demo, somebody has to be on the keyboard, showing the features and functions of the software. The salesperson or a sales-support specialist generally handles this role. (Note that when I refer to a sales-support specialist, I'm talking about the person or position that has comprehensive knowledge of the software and/or the prospect's industry. In some software companies, that's the salesperson, because they are expected to learn their product and industry well enough to demonstrate. In other companies, the salesperson is responsible for orchestrating the sale and calls on a technical resource to actually show the product.)

Coach - On a football team, the coach observes and directs the game from the sidelines. Although he doesn't play in the game itself, he's directly involved in calling the plays. Coaches are responsible for the "strategic" aspects of the game. Similarly, a software demo needs somebody "on the sidelines" directing the action. The salesperson or a sales manager typically serves as the coach.

Special Teams - In football, most of the game involves "regular plays." Players like the quarterback who see action during most of the game execute these plays. However, depending on the game situation, special plays need to be run from time to time. Individuals with special skills are called upon to execute these plays. Examples include kicking a field goal or returning a punt. Similarly, most of a software demo is made up of showing "regular features." These features are typically demonstrated by a salesperson, sales manager or technical sales-support specialist. However, if the demonstrations situation dictates, other individuals may be called upon to address a special need. For example, if a software modification is required, somebody from the development staff may be required to create and show a prototype.

Who's in Charge? - There's only one head coach on a football team. If there are too many people directing the action, the team won't operate as a cohesive unit. The same is true with a software demonstration. There should be only one coach on your presentation team. Before anyone sets foot in the demonstration room, determine who that person is going to be. Identifying the coach is important so you don't confuse your team or your prospect. It will be the coach's responsibility to read the reactions of the audience, determine if the game plan needs to change and relay that information to the quarterback using any number of verbal and non-verbal means.

Don't assume a relationship between job titles and roles. For example, as a sales manager traveling with a seasoned salesperson, I typically assume the role of coach, letting the salesperson play quarterback. While the salesperson directs the agenda and runs the keyboarding, I watch the audience, listen to their questions and make sure they're crossing the Bridge. If I see they're wavering on the Bridge and need a gentle nudge back to the center, I'll interject and attempt to provide clarification. But I don't grab the ball and take over the game. The salesperson (quarterback) stays in charge. Conversely, if I'm demonstrating with a rookie salesperson, I let them coach while I handle the role of quarterback. Why? Because they're new, they simply haven't had time to acquire the product or industry knowledge needed to lead the tactical aspects of the demonstration. However, they should have the observation and communication skills to direct the demo from a strategic perspective. If they don't, I made a hiring mistake!

There are many instances during any given demonstration when the coach and quarterback roles reverse. For example, if you're in a multiple day demo, you're going to want to assign each team member a different section of the demo. Remember that one of the reasons you team demo is because it may be too fatiguing for one. If you tire, you're going to be less effective. So, even though I'm coach for the *overall* demonstration, I might be responsible for a section of the demonstration. During that time, I instantly become the quarterback and one of my teammates becomes the interim coach.

It can be difficult to switch from quarterback to coach. In a football game, do fumbles ever occur when a replacement quarterback takes a snap from center? Sure they do. It happens all the time. Similarly, demonstration fumbles often happen when you transition quarterbacks. As quarterback, you're accustomed to driving forward and demonstrating the software. You're in control. When you hand over the ball to someone else, you're expected to watch and listen. Most good salespeople and demonstrators like to maintain control (as they should), so this role reversal can lead to natural conflicts. In reality, you don't lose control when you move off the keyboard and become the coach. Think about it. How many NFL quarterbacks call every play in a football game anymore? Virtually none! It's difficult to play and strategize the game at the same time. Play calling is usually left to the coach on the sidelines. They have a vantage point that's broad and less pressured than the quarterback's. They can see things unfolding a quarterback participating in the game simply can't.

The Quarterback - This person is responsible for marching the team down the field. He's an offensive-minded player. You can't bridge-demonstrate if you're playing defense. In demonstrating, a good offense will beat a good defense all day long! When someone assumes the role of quarterback, he's in the spotlight. He's on the keyboard or mouse directing the action.

A good quarterback knows the game isn't won on any particular play or any particular series of downs. In order to come out on top, it takes a solid offense the entire duration of the demonstration. He has a solid game plan that was created from the information gathered during the Discovery and knowledge of the competition. Once the game plan is put into motion, the quarterback makes sure the whole team sticks with it, even when faced with adversity. Falling into panic-mode and making broad, general statements in hopes of a quick score is a sure formula for failure.

To avoid being tackled behind the line, the quarterback needs to know how to scramble (asks lots of questions). Again, if he's performed a thorough Discovery, he knows what defenses to expect. He can prepare to face whatever the defense is likely to throw at him in the form of objections, lay-in-the-weeds personalities or competitive traps (blitzes). Before the blitz ever takes place, he's ready to throw an outlet pass and score a touchdown!

The quarterback must also know when to stop play and call a time-out. This happens when he's puzzled by an objection or simply can't provide clarification the prospect is demanding. Not to worry! In a team situation, the quarterback can take some time to think about the question or objection. If he can't formulate a clear response, he asks one of the other team members for a new play. The other team member has the option of either providing the play (answer) to the quarterback or stepping in as a substitute for the next series of downs. If this happens it's *critical* the existing quarterback sits down and *stays on the sideline* until the substitute quarterback has finished. If both people are in front of the prospect at the same time, the prospect will become confused. They'll want to silently signal a "too many players on the field" penalty.

While he's in front of the audience, the quarterback is in charge. He maintains control and vigorously pursues his game plan.

The Coach - Your job is to keep the quarterback informed with new plays and information he needs to score on a consistent basis. You do this by watching the defense (audience) for clues and weaknesses. Your job is *not* to interrupt the quarterback during and after every play. Interruptions break the quarterback's continuity and confidence. If you find yourself constantly interrupting, call a time-out (request a break) so you can review the situation with the quarterback. During the break, refer to the game plan and remind him to stick to it.

A good coach can also substitute as a quarterback on any given play. In order to accomplish this, the coach obviously needs in-depth knowledge of the software, the industry and the prospect. If the coach is expected to be an "on-demand" substitute, it's the salesperson's responsibility to educate them (and everyone else on his demonstration team). To successfully educate your teammates, draft a formal prospect profile document describing the company background, decision criteria and goals for the new system. This document is the natural byproduct of your Discovery. The prospect profile should be in the hands of your team at least three days before the demonstration.

The coach is responsible for managing the prospect and the overall game plan. She does this by sitting somewhere in the room where the entire audience is visible. She also needs a copy of the game plan (agenda, demo script and or Demonstration Plan) in front of her. If a problem develops, the coach spots it early and either picks an appropriate point to interject or makes a note of the problem. The coach waits until a break to bring problems to the attention of the quarterback. After the break, the quarterback should verify the problem with the prospect and then address the issue. This is done even if the answer provided by the quarterback is, "I'll have to get back to you on that." The issue has been noted so the prospect is confident it will be researched and addressed in the future.

In football, coaches have to make the tough calls. For example, when it's fourth down and inches, it's the coach who decides to punt the ball instead of going for a first down. Several years ago, I hosted a demonstration for a prospect at our corporate office. The president of this company was constantly adversarial. He aggressively challenged everything the quarterback (salesperson) did in the demonstration. Eventually, I (coach) called a time-out and pulled the president aside. After a private discussion, I made the tough call and told the president the game was over. Our prospect was sent home! We forfeited the game. As coach, I was faced with two issues. First, the risk of further injury to my quarterback (salesperson) was too great. Second, if this guy had become a customer, our lives would have been miserable!

Coaches have a special role in a web demo. The best situation is to have the coach at the prospect's site, watching the action directly. But if that is not possible, it can still be helpful to have a coach on the conference session. The coach can help drive interaction, anticipate and help in problem areas, and even step in to assist if there are technical problems or delays. Web coaches should have a 'private channel' (private chat, instant messaging, or some other device) to substitute for not being able to visually send signals to the quarterback.

Special Teams - Special team members come in two varieties. The first are deep product specialists from your implementation, support or development departments. They're in attendance because the quarterback or the coach determined prior to the demonstration their specialization was needed to address one of the prospect's special needs. The second are demonstration experts from other product areas that are a part of your overall solution proposal for the prospect. Each type of special team member brings advantages to the game plan, but each also represents risks that you must be careful to avoid. Let's look at each in turn, starting with the 'deep expertise' special team members.

These special team members typically won't have as much demonstration experience as your salespeople, sales managers and sales-support representatives.   Remember this fact. However, that doesn't mean they should not strive to be skilled and professional demonstrators. The prevailing thought toward these special team members is:

- If you put them in the position of quarterback, you're placing your entire game plan at risk. (How many NFL teams would put a place kicker in the game as quarterback?)

- Special team members should be used sparingly and only in certain situations.

- Although these individuals tend to be great typists, resist the temptation to put them on the keyboard, as they tend to fall into teaching mode. For that reason, have your quarterback run the keyboard while the special team member provides verbal support.

All of these points are absolutely true, but not in every situation. You need to determine each special team member's interest in being a quarterback. Many of these folks just don't want to get in front of a prospect. Don't force this issue with them. You still need to involve them, just not in a quarterback role. For example, let's say your prospect wants lots of accounting detail, but your quarterback (salesperson) is unfamiliar and uncomfortable with the topic. Have the quarterback work with the special teams member (implementation specialist who is a Certified Public Accountant) to practice demonstrating debit and credit transactions. Then during the demo, have the quarterback show the software features while your C.P.A. explains what is being done and answers questions.

Now, let's say you have some special team members who *are* interested in taking a more active role in your demo. They would like to be the quarterback for a couple plays (their area of specialization). Here's your warning: if you're not willing to train them to be skilled demonstrators, don't put them in front of your prospects. However, a properly trained special team member is an absolute *gold mine*. Nothing is better or faster at building credibility (especially with a technically oriented audience) than involving a software developer, implementation representative or support specialist *who knows how to bridge-demonstrate*. Some of the best sales-support specialists I have ever worked with came from this background. The reason they are so few and far between is because nobody's willing to help them learn proper demonstration skills. What's the best way to train them? When you're done with this book, buy them a copy to read (a blatant trial-close on my part!). Invite them to any skills development sessions that you hold with your other demonstration teammates (practicing introductions, Elevator Pitches, etc.). If you're willing to be a mentor to these folks, I guarantee you'll find a diamond in the rough!

Now let's turn our attention to the second variety of special team members, those demonstration experts for the additional products that make up the total solution proposal. This group approach is becoming more common for two reasons:

1. The software industry has been through a lot of merger and acquisition activities. The result is a smaller number of vendors with a larger portfolio of products. The goal of these larger organizations is, appropriately, to put more products in more customer environments. To do this, they will often fashion multi-product sales approaches.

2. The customers are becoming more sophisticated. They expect you as a vendor to come in with a total solution, regardless of the number of products involved. And they expect your people to be experts in all of them. All demonstration experts should have knowledge on all of the products in the solution proposal, but naturally there will need to be multiple experts to handle any in-depth demonstration.

So how are we going to run this game plan without creating the disaster of having two quarterbacks? Here are a few guidelines:

1. There does have to be one quarterback. One product needs to be at the center of the solution, with the

other products playing supporting roles. This means one quarterback runs the show, calling in the other 'backs' to help win the game.

2. The products and the total demonstration need to build to and support a single overall message (*see Demo Theme in Chapter 3*). You do not want to confuse the prospect with competing messages.

3. In multi-expert situations, some experts mistake this all-critical game for team try-outs. They try to outshine the quarterback, and move their product to the center. At best, that confuses the prospect. More often it makes them mad.

4. Everyone needs to remember it is a team, not eleven individual players. The demonstration and the products must appear as seamless as possible to the prospect. Terminology, messages, benefits, and integration points should be as consistent as possible.

The best way to emphasize this last point is to give you an example of where the players did not understand their role and fumbled the ball – badly. I was working in a multi-product company that sold infrastructure products. In that mix we had both database products and integration products. A retail prospect in South Dakota wanted to use the two products together to share customer and product information between store locations. It seemed like a pretty straightforward request and we had a slick solution for making it work. We sent out a presales person from each of the two groups with instructions to come back as the favored vendor. It did not quite work out that way.

I didn't need to call our sponsor. He called me right after the demonstration, and he was *not* happy. It seems that as our integration specialist was doing his part of the demo, he was asked about a particular detail concerning how the database worked with the capability he was demonstrating. Our 'expert' answered by saying that he really had never worked with the database and had no idea how it worked. He then looked at the database expert and asked "can you answer that?" to which the database expert said, "I'm sorry, I wasn't listening to the question. Can you please repeat it?" The decision maker was in the room and immediately called a halt to the whole proceedings. It was his opinion that if we could not even coordinate a two-product demonstration properly, we would never be successful in implementing a two-product solution. What the integration expert should have done instead is to cut his eyes to the database expert to get his attention while he asked for clarification of the question. The question you might have is how would the integration expert know he needed to get clarification to the question? He would know because the database expert did not <u>stand</u> and take the question when the integration expert looked at him. This is a silent signal that shows the team is working well together. Once the integration expert got the question clarified, now the database expert has had time to think of a response. He would simply rise and respond. They would have looked like they were working together!

Regardless of their role or purpose, it is the job of the quarterback to manage special team members. While your special team members wait to present, have them spread out in the room. Don't allow them to sit together in the back of the room. I like to assign their seating strategically. For example, in the situation above, where we brought in our C.P.A., I'd have her sit next to the prospect's controller.

Similarly, I would position that integration specialist (the good one, not the one from the story) next to the prospect's integration specialist.

Special team members play a key role in your game plan. Use them in special, predefined situations. If they're apprehensive about being in front of a group or they are not properly trained, use them in a supporting role. If you find that special technician who also wants to be a quarterback, take them under your wing. Help them learn the concepts in this book. Under the proper circumstances, they could be what you need to push a deal over the goal line!

Quarterback	Lead person on the keyboard. In charge of the flow of the demonstration. Must have excellent product knowledge, prospect knowledge, demonstration skills and command of the audience.
Coach	In more complex demonstrations this is often the person watching the audience and not on the keyboard. They give cues to the quarterback when the demonstration needs to be adjusted to better fit the needs of the audience.
Special Teams	Technical specialists who are not necessarily demonstration professionals. Usually domain experts. They offer commentary and expertise and occasionally demonstrate a particular function of the software.

PREPARING YOUR COLLEAGUES

Prior to the demonstration, you need to hold a meeting to:

- Define the roles of the people involved. If the players are unfamiliar with the concept of defined roles in a demonstration, take the time to thoroughly explain each role (quarterback, coach and special teams).

- Stress the importance of sticking to their roles.

- Discuss the game plan (agenda) and seating.

- Make sure each team member understands why they're in attendance and what you do, and do not, want them to say during the demonstration. This is especially true for special team members.

Each team member should have updated copies of the prospect's Feature Survey Forms, Demonstration Attendee Checklists and Discovery Log (Chapters 4 and 5). They need to know and practice the process flows they're responsible for *before* the demonstration. Everybody should also be familiar with the demo participants (name, title and interests). If one of your teammates has worked with similar customers in the past, make it a point to remind them to mention this experience in the demonstration. Prospects always appreciate and value real-life testimonials. Finally, share with your team who the competitors are and the overall selling strategy you're implementing.

STRATEGY

Every good salesperson has formed a strategy for their prospect. There are many books and courses available on this subject. A good strategy helps identify the prospect's decision-makers, recommenders, blockers and coaches. Although the demonstration may be the most critical component in the strategy of a software sale, it's not the only one. For that reason, it's important to understand the entire strategy because it will provide your teammates with a high-level road map for your demonstration. Your strategy will also help clarify the agenda and highlight the critical areas that need to be demonstrated. Team members, especially the coach and any quarterbacks, should spend time with the salesperson to review the strategy for this prospect. Keep this strategy in mind throughout the day.

NON-VERBAL SIGNALING

During a team demonstration, members of the team need to communicate effectively with each other in a non-verbal way. Assume you're the quarterback in a demonstration. Your colleague Bill is acting as the coach. A question is posed by the prospect that you don't know the answer to. What's the natural thing to do? "Bill, do you know the answer to that question?" If he doesn't know the answer to your question it will make your entire team look uninformed. Besides, it puts him on the spot. If I was Bill and you did this to me, I'd shoot you!

Here's a better way to handle this situation. Catch Bill's attention by making eye contact. This is Bill's cue you need help. If Bill knows the answer, he can step in. If he returns your stare, you know he doesn't have an answer either. You have two choices: probe the prospect for clarification or write the question down and get back with them.

Now let's say Bill does know the answer to the question. Rather than giving you the blank look, he gives you some type of non-verbal signal (wink, gentle nod of his head, etc.). The method I prefer is to have Bill slowly rise out of his seat and face the quarterback. If this happens, the quarterback knows he has the answer and is prepared to step in. Now that Bill's given you the green light, you pass him the ball ("Bill, do you know the answer to that question?"). Then you sit down to make sure the prospect is focusing attention on Bill. Another alternative is to use the pen on the table. If your teammate moves the pen to the middle of the table, she has something to say, can help you or can answer the question. If she pulls the pen back, she has decided not to say anything.

Non-verbal signals provide transitional continuity during your demonstration. Your prospects don't see or feel the bump in the road. Consequently, they proceed across the Bridge with little or no hesitation.

RELIEF

If you're a coach, be on the lookout for this problem: quarterbacks run out of mental or physical steam from time-to-time during long demonstrations. A properly planned agenda that spreads out the workload can help prevent this situation. However, even with proper planning, a team member may still become fatigued. Classic clues of fatigue include the quarterback's:

- Inability to answer a relatively simple question.

- Lack of physical movement.

- Committing the "Field by Fielder" demo crime (Chapter 4).

- Sudden loss of enthusiasm.

- Anger or frustration

If you notice any of these signs, call a time-out from the sideline and meet with the quarterback. If she can't *effectively* continue and you're capable of substituting, do it! A short break to regroup and re-energize her may be all that's needed to get her back on the field making big plays again.

READING THE AUDIENCE

As quarterback, it's easy to get absorbed in your keyboard work and miss audience cues. Although it's primarily the job of the coach, anybody who's not running the keyboard (quarterback) should be looking for these cues. There are two types of cues to watch for:

1. Clarification Cues - These include whispering, fidgeting, furrowed foreheads, excitement, and of course, raised hands. After sensing one of these cues, I'll take the first appropriate moment to stop my quarterback and ask the audience if they need clarification on anything. Having brought this to the quarterback's attention, they can now circle back and address any issues.

2. Keep Your Mouth Shut Cues - If your audience is nodding their agreement, pointing at the screen and smiling, keep your mouth shut! Your quarterback is doing her job and you don't want to interrupt her flow and rhythm. She's moving people across the Bridge. Don't get in her way!

WHEN AND WHEN NOT TO INTERRUPT

There are few things more damaging than a poorly timed interruption in your demonstration. I've been in situations where I was on the keyboard, rockin' the audience. They were smiling, nodding and whispering to each other as they pointed toward the screen. I had them eating out of my hands. Just as I prepared to summarize and complete this section of the demonstration, a teammate stood up and said, "Not only can the software do that, it can also..." The entire room turned away from me (and the powerful closing message I was about to deliver) and looked at him. A flood of questions began and we were suddenly defending our position. I was forced to watch the excitement in the room evaporate! *Never* make the mistake of interrupting your teammate when they're on a roll, as good as your intentions may be. Interruptions never have the positive impact you anticipate. More often than not, they take you backwards.

What's the right way to interrupt? Let's say Sharon is your quarterback and you want to get her attention. As was described earlier, I recommend standing up and moving away from the audience. Again, in a smaller setting, have a signal like setting a pen out in front of you. These gestures are an indication to her that someone in the audience needs clarification. When she turns the floor over to you, your response should be something like, "Sharon, I think perhaps Bill has a question." *Sharon* (very important) should now ask Bill if he has a question. In this example, the coach (you) signaled a situation but the quarterback (Sharon) remains in control. Your job is simply to bring the situation to her attention. If you had grabbed control by answering the question, you'd have eroded your quarterback's credibility, which could have far-reaching consequences. Don't submarine your quarterback. Unless, that is, you plan on carrying the day from that point forward!

NOTE TAKING

Lots of new information comes out during a demonstration. Obviously, if you're demonstrating alone, it's your responsibility to take good notes. However, if you're in a team demonstration, somebody who's not the quarterback should handle this crucial task. Make sure this responsibility is assigned during your pre-demonstration team meeting.

I like to take notes in one of two places.

1. For detailed notes that require adequate space, I use the same log I started for this prospect during my Discovery interview. The demonstration notes take over where the Discovery notes left off. This keeps all the information together in one place.

2. For abbreviated notes, I use the Demonstration Plan (see below).

Like note taking during the Discovery, it's helpful to code your notes. Codes make your note-taking more efficient so you have more time to listen. For example, use **AI** to denote an *action-item*. **A*** might signify an *A-item* (most important). "**B**" could mean the prospect really connected with a specific *benefit*. It's also important that each entry in your notes has a person associated with it. For example, next to an action item, enter the name or initials of the person who asked the question that will require follow-up. This information can help in a couple ways. First, it allows you to retrace the question if you need clarification, either during or after the demonstration. Second, it provides a reason to follow-up with the key members of your audience.

In a team-demonstrating environment, there's no excuse for committing the "Write it Down" demo crime. Here are some other suggestions:

- In some cases, take notes on your laptop during the demonstration. The gentle clicks on the keyboard can be very annoying to the audience so be sure to get permission to do so from the Prospect.

- Write important questions and issues on a flipchart. Leave it in view for the prospect. Doing so allows the prospect to let go of their question and move on to additional material.

- Have more than one laptop running the software at the same time. When a question stumps the quarterback, another member of the team can quietly research the question after it was written down on the flipchart. If an answer is found during the demonstration, the quarterback should present it and *always* go to the flipchart and put a big checkmark next to the question. The checkmark gives the audience a sense of closure. If there are a number of checkmarks by the end of the demonstration, you'll leave a positive impression with your prospect.

DEMONSTRATION PLAN

Leading up to your demonstration, you and your team members need to jointly develop a Demonstration Plan. This document will help you organize your team and stay on track during the demo. You might want to show the plan to your audience and review with them how you will be updating it during the course of the demonstration. I sometimes share an updated version of the plan as a follow-up item after the demo. In addition to ensuring that you cover the topics that are important to your prospect, proper use and development of a Demonstration Plan will make you look thorough and professional in their eyes.

Below is an example of a plan I like to use:

Topic from Agenda	Functions to demonstrate	Demonstration / Key Notes	Modification Specs	Cheat Sheet
Demo Opening	Dashboards	* Pres was excited at metrics shown		Dashboards
Consumer Financing	Customer credit rules	AI - need credit rating field	CF-101	Credit setup & processing
	Revolving charge	* AI loved simplicity		
	Balloon payments	* CFO worried about exposure		
Dining room sale	Inventory status	* John want better visibility of cost at other locations	OE-101	Order Entry
	Price negotiating capabilities	* Sales manager loved this! Said it would help reduce unceccesary negotiating.		

Some characteristics to incorporate and procedures to follow as it relates to your Demonstration Plan include:

- Place your agenda items on the far-left column. These should be a direct byproduct of your Discovery.

- Orient agenda items towards process flows.

- Enter reactions during the demonstration in the Key Notes column. The entries you make here should be brief. Use your full notes to record extended detail (see Note Taking above).

- If a modification is required, note that in the Modification Spec column for the corresponding topic. If your technical department provides modification-tracking numbers, and you will be using the updated Demonstration Plan as a follow-up piece, place the corresponding modification tracking number in the column.

- Use the Cheat Sheet column to note the name of any step-by-step process flow document you'll be using for this topic. Cheat sheets are helpful for keeping organized throughout your demonstration. An example is provided below.

I. **Dashboards**
 A. **Signon – Executive Role**
  1. Financial Snapshot
  2. Investigate
  3. Declining Margins
  4. Top 10 Customers
 B. **Signon – Sales Management**
  1. Forecast Picture
  2. CRM/Sales Process Drill Down
  3. Salesrep Top 10 Prospects
 C. **Signon – Operations Manager**
  1. Ship Volume Review
  2. Error/Return Analysis
  3. Safety Analysis

PRIVATE JOKES

There's almost nothing more uncomfortable and annoying than feeling like others are having fun and you are not. Never tell jokes only you and your demonstration team will understand and appreciate. These private jokes will make your prospect feel left out. Though they probably laugh along with you, I can assure you the prospect doesn't find them amusing. They're only doing this to alleviate their own discomfort. Poking friendly fun at your teammates is acceptable in limited fashion, but private jokes are always in poor taste.

RESPECT FOR AUTHORITY

If one of your team members is in a position of authority, provide them the proper respect. Some prospects may view a company that doesn't display respect in its ranks as disorganized and improperly focused. It can be difficult predicting how a prospect will react to this issue. If respect for authority isn't important to them, but you provide it anyway, nothing is lost. However, if it is important to them, and you don't show proper respect, there is a lot to lose. Why gamble?

PHYSICAL CONTROL

If more than one of the presenters is standing at any one time it can be distracting in a demonstration.
- Who's in charge?

- Who's going to speak next?

- Who should I be paying attention to?

- Who should I direct my question to?

These are all questions that could be running through the audience's mind. Keep it simple. Stand when you're addressing a group of three or more people. Sit when you're not.

TEAM IMPROVEMENT

A team debriefing is an important final step in your quest to improve. I like to break this process down into several steps.
1. Meet with everyone involved in the demonstration immediately following the conclusion of the demo.

The closer the meeting is to the event the more fresh the ideas will be that are discussed. During the meeting, plan on discussing the following four areas of the demonstration:

   a) Preparation – What should we have done differently in preparing for the demo?

   b) Demonstration Technique – What demo crimes were committed?

   c) Product Knowledge – Where did you feel we were struggling?

   d) Teamwork – How can we improve the operations of the team?

2. The debriefing process will include six steps per person. These steps must be completed in the order presented below:

   a) Presenter provides positive reflection of what they did that worked well.

   b) Peers provide positive observations of the presenter.

   c) Meeting leader provides positive observations.

   d) Presenter provides constructive reflection of what did not work well.

   e) Peers provide constructive observations.

   f) Meeting leader provides constructive observations.

   g) Presenter discusses summarizes their plan for improvement.

3.   To avoid offending a team member (which defeats the whole purpose of this exercise), here are a some suggestions:
   - Before the demonstration, ask each individual if they want to receive comments on their performance. They will almost certainly tell you "yes" which disarms them before the meeting starts.

   - Also, before the demo, confirm with each individual that they're OK with a public discussion. If not, meet with each person in private. Human Resource experts will support private constructive criticism over a public setting. I agree. The challenge is one of practicality.

   - During the positive reflection steps (a-c), the word "but" is NOT allowed. For example, you don't want the demonstrator to say "I thought my opening tells were good **but**, my benefit statements need some improvement." The word 'but' eliminates the benefits derived from discussing the positive aspects of their demonstration. It is easier to improve upon your strengths than it is to eliminate your weaknesses. Completely separate the positive from the negative and you'll see a substantial difference someone's overall improvement.

   - Be very specific with your comments (positive or constructive). Ask yourself this question. "How can I improve upon a mistake if I don't know exactly what I was doing when I made the mistake?"

   - Be willing to discuss the positive or negative impact of an observation. If there is little impact, the comment is probably not worth discussing.

CHAPTER SUMMARY

Team demonstrating is crucial in larger, complex demonstrations. Synergy among team members is the key to a successful team demonstration. If your teammates know the rules ahead of time and execute their roles, you're in control. You'll put yourself in a better position to win the game!

CHAPTER 10
"Yes But,..."

The 2WIN! Global team has had the great pleasure of conducting over a thousand workshops in over 40 countries around the world, reaching a very large audience of professional presenters and demonstrators. Personally, I have been thrilled at how well the techniques in this book and in our workshops have been received by such an experienced and dedicated group of professionals. I have been humbled that so many have been willing to share their experiences with prospects and customers, both before and after the training. Their stories would fill another book!

The 2WIN! Global instructors have assisted a tremendous number of workshop participants as they begin using Tell-Show-Tell, work on their presentation techniques, and re-work their demonstrations to eliminate crimes. The work is very gratifying for us and very rewarding for workshop participants. I will never forget one such experience. At the end of the first day of a workshop, I like to ask people what they have learned. It gives me a better idea of what to look for and adjust for the second day. In one memorable case, a woman that entered pre-sales with a consulting background responded this way: "I've learned that everything I've done has been wrong!" We all laughed, but truthfully, she was already a good demonstrator with over 6 years of experience. She just had not been exposed to what she could do to be even better! A few weeks later I received an e-mail from her saying that at the end of her most recent demonstration, people had actually stood and applauded! It is hard to get a better endorsement than that.

I have an 18-year-old son. He is a fantastic young man with great intellect, athletic skills and personality. However (you knew this was coming), when it comes to receiving constructive suggestions, the first words out of his mouth are often "Yes but…" Let me give you an example. As my son Trent is getting ready to go to a friend's house I'll say "Trent, I realize that you are being overwhelmed by your schedule and thus forgetting some of your follow up items like sending an email to your coach about missing next Tuesday's practice." Trent replies with "I know. I'll do it tonight." "Sure thing." I reply. "Trent, have you considered putting a reminder into your mobile? Mobile reminders and electronic calendars are great ways to help your remember tasks like the email and appointments." Trent replies with "**Yes but**, I don't have time to put all those reminders in my mobile." I happen to know that he's able to enter 30 text messages a minute so the suggestion that he doesn't have time to enter these items is absurd!

As you might imagine, we have also heard a few dissenting voices over the years when we ask the question at the conclusion of the workshop, "Can you begin implementing these techniques next week?" A rare dissenter replies with "*Yes but*, …". Why does this happen? People have been involuntarily put into one of our workshops. A small percentage of these attendees have had any number of seemingly legitimate reasons why the techniques I have outlined in this book will not work in a given situation. Now I am the first to say that any technique must be 'tuned' to the expectations of the audience, the culture of the audience and the nature of the environment. That being said, I thought it was worth writing just one more chapter to highlight a few of these different situations and how the Demo2WIN! techniques are effective in almost every demonstration situation and environment.

WEB DEMONSTRATING

Many people seem to treat web demonstrating in the same manner as that old saying about the weather: Everybody complains about the weather (web demonstrating), but nobody does anything about it. It is true; demonstrating your solution over the web can be less satisfying and less effective. It is hard to connect to people, you cannot read their reactions, and there is often no feedback or questions. But that doesn't mean you should just give up and bore your audience! Throughout this edition of the book I have provided you with best practices for web demonstrating that we have created, witnessed or experienced around the world. Here is a summary of what I have learned about web demonstrating:

- If Tell-Show-Tell is valuable in a standard demonstration, it is critical in a web demonstration. Without Tell-Show-Tell, you are left with an hour or more of 'feature/feature/feature', each one passing by on the screen with no interaction, no natural conversation, and no change in routine. Imagine being on the other side of that demonstration! It would be like watching a boring television show with one actor, no action, and no commercials, but with the ability to change the channel. What do you think you would do with the remote control?

- On the web, Tell-Show-Tell provides for variety, pacing, and interaction. Every opening and closing tell provides an opportunity to re-engage your audience, switching their focus from the software on the screen to you and your message. Use the features of your web presentation system to change views, bring up slides, and drive interaction. Use a high definition web camera so that you actively move the audience's focus between you and the software.

- Speaking of interaction, have you ever wondered what is happening on the other end of the line while you are going from screen to screen, feature to feature? At some point, usually fairly early in a web demo, someone in the audience will have a question. If you haven't explained to your audience how to use chat or emoticons, you may never know they have a question. There is no natural place to ask a question. Within a few minutes our inquisitive audience member will probably just give up. As you wait for everyone to log in, show them how to use the interaction tools. Interactions are another reason for Tell-Show-Tell: Each opening and closing tell provides a natural interaction point for the audience and a natural place for you to ensure that there are no lingering questions from the audience. Consider enhancing your interactions with polls, white boarding on the screen, and using the highlighter that is included in most web platforms.

- Themes and props are just important in a web demo as they are for one in person. If you have a web camera, you can still use props by holding them up to the camera. If you have no camera, use an image of the prop that is embedded in your presentation.

- If your web tool supports VOIP and the connection speeds support smooth video and voice, use a digital quality microphone and headset connected to your computer. Have the prospect connect their computer to speakers or a headset and you will sound like you are in the same room together. If your competitor uses standard telephone headsets and you leverage VOIP/Video, you'll gain an advantage before you show any software.

- Elevate your energy by standing when you perform a web demo. Raise your keyboard/mouse and monitor to a comfortable level and get excited! Use your hands, raise your voice, and move around. You need to be able to transmit your passion for your solution over the web because you don't have as much personal presence.

- As I have discussed in the preceding chapters, a great demonstrator builds a Bridge and helps audience members across that bridge. I have seen some great examples of that in live demonstrations, but remarkably few in web demonstrations. People that excel at presenting from the prospect's perspective in a live demo suddenly revert to canned non-Bridging demos on the web! When you are doing a web demo, work carefully on all of the Bridging techniques you learned in this book. Use people's names, and use them often. Use the prospect's process descriptions, terminology, and information. Make it as easy as possible for them.

- Which brings me to crimes: Many of the crimes that are misdemeanors in a live setting become felonies when committed in a web setting. Crimes such as Teaching vs. Demonstrating and Field by Field just take a potentially boring environment and make it mind-numbingly boring. The alienation crimes are particularly important to avoid, as you cannot depend on your natural charm and your ability to read your audience to save you. It is an environment where it is easy to blunder and hard to recover, so my best advice is to just avoid the crimes in the first place.

When the first edition of Demonstrating to WIN was written, demonstrating software over the web was rare. Today it is common. All of the concepts and techniques in the book are important in live demos, but critical in web demonstrating. A few may require minor adjustment, but all are applicable.

SHORT DEMONSTRATIONS

Most of my career has been spent selling Enterprise Resource (ERP) Systems. ERP demonstrations are often complex, long, and grueling. The techniques I have covered in this book are very important in situations where you will be in front of the audience for long periods of time, covering many subjects in great detail with a large number of people. But are they appropriate when selling a smaller solution, one that might require perhaps just a one-hour demonstration? The overarching answer is, "Of course!" We have trained thousands of people who sell niche solutions, business intelligence solutions and middleware. All of these demos are 1 hour or less. Some of the items being discussed might not be as relevant (break management, for example), but the fundamentals apply particularly well to short demonstrations.

Think about everything that you need to accomplish in a short demonstration:

- The prospect needs to understand the relationship between your software and their needs or processes.

- You need to establish a trust relationship with the prospect, showing them that you understand and can help them in their endeavors.

- The prospect needs to understand the value of your solution and begin the process of differentiating you from your competition.

- All of the audience participants need to start (and hopefully complete) their journey across the Bridge.

Given all that you need to accomplish, you don't have a minute to waste! You need to give a highly organized, easy to comprehend demonstration. The best way to do that is by avoiding all technobabble, always working from the prospect's perspective, and making each feature or capability easy to understand by using concrete examples in a Tell-Show-Tell approach.

There is often a perception that Tell-Show-Tell takes up valuable time that should be spent exposing the prospect to as many features as possible. I suppose that in theory, you could cover more features in the same amount of time without Tell-Show-Tell, but have you ever suffered through such a demonstration? It is painful! It is like trying to learn physics by speed-reading the textbook! If you are faced with too much to cover and too little time, do not revert to a speed-feature approach. Spend more time learning the issues around which the prospect will make their decision and use the techniques we have discussed to really focus on those parts of your software.

If you do a good job, they will come back for more (regardless of what they say at the outset).

THE 'NO DISCOVERY' DEMONSTRATION

Lack of Discovery has a definite impact on your ability to create and deliver a great, customized demonstration. But it should not be an excuse for jettisoning all of the good work you have done in creating better demonstrations. Let me suggest a three part approach to these situations:

1. Prepare a good, solid demonstration using Tell-Show-Tell techniques. Pay attention to your benefits and the prospect's industry terms and information. Try to anticipate the process steps and benefits that will be most important to the prospect based on your knowledge of their industry and your experience with other customers.

2. If possible, open the demonstration by showing them what you believe is the most relevant, exciting and differentiating Tell-Show-Tell you can think of. Then stop your demo and begin asking Discovery questions. If it is too risky to guess on the relevance of your hot demo example, use the opening part of your demonstration to conduct a 'mini-Discovery'. Before you ever get into the software, spend a few minutes asking questions about important processes, current limitations, and desired goals. Use this time to establish trust, uncover any company information and terminology, and prioritize the capabilities to emphasize in your mind.

3. As you begin the main section of the demonstration, use your Tell-Show-Tell technique to ask questions,

validate your ability to meet their needs, and emphasize key benefits. Your professional background, combined with this approach, gives you the best opportunity to find the elements that will take your audience members across the Bridge and will help them start the journey.

When faced with a 'No Discovery' situation, our first temptation is to show as many features as possible and hope that some of them hit the target. This is fully dependent on the prospect understanding and seeing the benefit in what you are showing. This approach rarely works. A little time spent in Discovery at the beginning and throughout the meeting more than makes up for any time lost in the demonstration. Remember, you will always perform Discovery on prospects. Sometimes the demo IS the Discovery.

"WE ARE TECHNICAL. NO SELLING PLEASE"

Any prospect can make the 'no selling' request, but you will most often hear it from technical audiences. When you do, be very careful. Technical people are absolutely convinced that they can make decisions on complex software choices by just looking at every feature, reviewing every specification, and asking every technical question they can think of. They are wrong.

Think of it this way: You and I are in the solutions business. We sell solutions every day. We know our product and the problems that it addresses. We study the issues of the industry, we know the strengths and weaknesses of our product, and we have experience with a variety of customers. Prospects make software purchasing decisions only occasionally; every few years or less. They may know what they don't want based on their current systems or processes, but that doesn't mean they know what to look for or how the right solution will benefit them.

So how do we solve this 'no marketing' demand and still show our solution properly? It's simple: Just stick to your plan! Use Tell-Show-Tell. Use the prospect's terminology, processes, role definitions, and information. Frame your demonstration around their processes, procedures or job roles. Emphasize benefits with closing tells and properly set up each demonstration vignette with good opening tells. Learn everything you can during Discovery and reflect it back during the demonstration. But there are a couple of points to consider in a 'no selling' demonstration:

- You are going to have to be at your best, because all of your opening tells, stories, benefits, terminology references and the like will have to be done without Power-Point or other presentation software. It all has to come out of your mouth or placed on a flipchart or whiteboard, not be shown on the screen. As soon as you put up a slide you will be accused of 'selling' – a dirty word to this audience. One of our clients faced a challenge just like this when presenting their solution to the IT department of a prospect. They had a slide deck prepared to support their message, their differentiators, and their benefits. The business leaders of the organization loved it. Before the demonstration started, the IT director made her feelings quite clear. As the client was setting up the projector, she walked in and said, "No slides. My guys are smart and will see through any attempts at selling." At first the client was concerned with this last minute change. But then, they realized that they knew everything that was on the slides and could verbalize it as easy as show it. The stories and messages went into their opening tells, the benefits went into their closing tells, and they scribbled key words, figures, and diagrams on a whiteboard as they went through the demonstration. Their prospect loved it and the IT manager thanked them for avoiding the 'selling s!@&'. They never suspected that they got the same demonstration they would have received with the slides.

- 'No Selling' doesn't mean you can't use visuals. Technical audiences love whiteboards, and there are bound to be whiteboards in the room where you will meet. Use them! Not only can you jot down key points and lay out key diagrams, you can get them involved! Ask questions, and then ask audience members to draw out processes, systems, networks – anything that you can use to help emphasize your benefits. In fact, whiteboards give you the opportunity to associate your benefits with their environment. There is no better way to build that Bridge and start people across it. The answers are right there in front of them.

There is an interesting paradox about technical people, particularly system engineers and administrators. One of our 2WIN! Global faculty members has led teams of engineers during his career and he pointed this out: While most engineers are absolutely convinced that they can make good product decisions based on features and specifications only (no marketing), they also tend to be the people that have the least imagination and the least ability to see beyond the feature to the benefit! So they are actually the people that are most in need of the work that you do to add perspective, value, and benefits to your demonstration.

THE SCRIPTED DEMONSTRATION

There is nothing worse than a scripted demonstration. You have likely seen them – page after page of feature-by-feature requirements that must be demonstrated exactly as described, exactly in the order of the document. Unless you wrote the script, this will be a challenging situation for you and will be a remarkably unproductive experience for the prospect. Getting through this requires a lot of planning on your part and courage on the part of the salesperson. This is probably why so many people give up and do the demonstration exactly as requested.

Is it possible to do something better? Can we break the rigid demands of this format? Very often the answer to these questions is "Yes"! It requires coordination between the salesperson, the pre-sales person doing the demonstration, and your champion within the prospect's organization.

Our goal is to meet the requirements of the script without demonstrating to the script. This can usually be accomplished by reorganizing the order of the script into process flows or role definitions. For example, the script items in order processing can be re-arranged into the particular tasks needed to build an order, fulfill an order, and invoice an order. Here is a very important point: Even if the script is (in the mind of the prospect or consultant) written in processes and process steps, it will be written to the prospect's current definition of those processes or some consultant's definition of such a process in a perfect world. Do not fall prey to these definitions. They won't match the definitions as expressed in your solution. Demonstrating 'by the script' will lead to nothing but confusion and frustration. Your software will appear incomplete and overly complex. So what should the demonstration look like?

1. Start with a non-software description of the processes or roles that will be satisfied during the demonstration. Indicate that these have been built based on the information and feature requirements of the script. Make it clear that you will be showing these processes as they will be used in the live environment, and that each process will be presented in a clear, consistent manner to help the audience manage the information and understand the flow of the software. Make it very clear that you will provide a cross-reference to the script prior to the start of the demonstration.

2. Before each process, summarize what will be shown. In some instances, explain the process, the steps, and the tasks that you will be performing. This is basically a process-level opening tell that prepares the audience for what they will see. In other instances, give them an *opening tell* that paints a scenario that the upcoming show will solve. Reference the appropriate sections in the script, assuming that the script is laid out by process.

3. During your Tell-Show-Tells follow the natural flow of the process or role as it is implemented in your software. Call out particular capabilities or features that you know are in the script, but do not follow the script point-by-point and do not cross-reference every feature to the script while you are trying to show the software. You want the audience to be following your process, not focusing on the script.

4. At the end of every process (and perhaps at the end of certain Tell-Show-Tell loops on difficult or complex tasks), stop and provide a cross-reference back to

particular items on the script. This meets the requirement of checking off every item on the script, but more important it provides one more place for you to review your capabilities and the benefits of those capabilities. This approach avoids the disjointed, confusing situation of trying to show software and keep up with a checklist at the same time. If the script or script section is particularly detailed or complex, hand out a guide that shows every requirement met as the result of a given process or area. But don't pass it out until after you have demonstrated that particular area. If you pass it out too soon, you'll 1) invite challenges and 2) put their eyes on the handout rather than your Tell-Show-Tell.

5. If you have been involved in a consultant-controlled script before, you'll recognize this decry. "Don't deviate from the script. If we determine that you are deviating from the script you will be disqualified and asked to leave." Bold words from that spindly little consultant! The problem is that if you don't deviate in certain key areas, you won't be able to differentiate yourself from your competition. So, here's what you do. Stick to your newly cross-referenced script per the consultant's specifications. Once you've established a rhythm to the script and trust with the audience, have the courage to sneak in a key competitive differentiator. Make sure it is one that is 100% applicable to this prospect's needs. The audience will love it. As soon as you break, the consultant will call you over and scold you for deviating from the script. Apologize! Call over the person that you directed this feature to and apologize to them

in front of the consultant. Nine times out of ten that person will say "Oh, don't worry about it. I thought what you demonstrated was really useful!" If you are in a situation where you know the demo is scripted, do everything you can to demonstrate late in the process. If you've been demonstrating to scripts long enough you've probably heard a prospect say, "Look, just skip the script and show us how your software works. We've tried the script and it just isn't working." If I had been the first to demonstrate, they would have made me stick to the script and I would have been the one that proved that it didn't work! What are the chances of getting the deal in that situation?

Scripted demos are a real challenge. However, if you think of them in a different way, they can work to your advantage. Bend the rules just like a good attorney works a judge and jury and you'll improve your win rate.

"THIS MATERIAL IS TOO AMERICAN"

If you are from outside of North America, you have probably been forced to read enough U.S. style selling books to realize that the U.S. style does not universally apply to your culture. I completely agree! At 2WIN! Global, 60% of our business over the past 10 years has been outside North America. We understand the cultural business differences between two countries as close as Belgium and The Netherlands or two countries as distant as Japan and South Africa. However, if you take a core concept like Tell-Show-Tell, it has universal, cross-cultural, global applicability. A crime like Data Dump confuses prospects in Dubai as much as it does in Beijing!

Cultural differences most certainly apply to the more creative aspects of what I've presented in this book. For example, a theme in Germany should be short, crisp and business oriented whereas a theme in Australia can be quite creative. That stated, a theme in a U.S. conservative company such as Nordstrom's Department Stores would look very much like the aforementioned German theme.

When it comes to Discovery, cultural adaptation is critical. For example, a salesperson in Japan who is working a deal where the C-Suite will determine the viability of a project will rarely interview a C-Level executive due to the respect the Japanese have for higher authority. However, that does not mean the C-Suite should be avoided during Discovery! If the deal is important, the salesperson needs to invite someone within their organization with respectable authority to perform those interviews.

Please don't let culture get in the way of how you apply the majority of these tactics. Make your own cultural adjustments to Demonstrating To WIN! and you'll find great success throughout your career.

"I DO NOT HAVE TIME TO DO IT THIS WAY"

This is the most common objection I get to the ideas, techniques, and checklists in the book. From one perspective, I understand. Many companies have cut back on resources but are still pursuing all the business they can find. Because your time is limited, you need to be as productive and efficient as possible. The techniques I've presented in this book are crucial if you want to improve your overall efficiency and win rate. You simply can't afford not to do it this way!

It is true that there is a 'transitional' cost in the Demonstrating To WIN approach. There is work to do in defining common processes, creating reusable opening tells, clarifying benefits, and substituting prospect perspectives for technobabble and product-speak. Learning to conduct a productive Discovery session takes time, as does the practice needed to eliminate crimes from your demonstrations. But these time costs are truly transitional – once you regularly incorporate them into your discoveries and demonstrations, your time preparation time will decrease. Further, your preparation time will be more productive and efficient.

The real time gain in the Demonstrating To WIN approach is productivity. In software sales, the only demonstration that really matters is the one that sooner or later results in a closed deal. Demonstrations that don't ultimately end in a sales transaction are, from a productivity standpoint, wasted time! So every demonstration should do everything possible to advance and increase the possibility of a sale. Ultimately, that is why I wrote Demonstrating To WIN and why the entire 2WIN! Global team is dedicated to helping individuals around the world implement the concepts and techniques found in this book.

CONCLUSIONS

As you've learned throughout this book, a successful demonstration contains certain common elements. You need product, prospect and competitive knowledge. This will allow you to build the Bridge from their old software to yours. Practice, research and planning are required prior to *every* software demonstration.

Conduct a thorough Discovery whenever possible. Remember the refinishing process for a fine piece of antique furniture. The preparation is what ultimately produces a beautiful result, not the final coat of varnish.

Dedicate yourself to eliminating crimes from your demonstrations. How? Practice your demonstration with colleagues who can spot demo crimes.

Pay attention to details. This includes the proper layout of your room, equipment for the job, props to illustrate your points and even the food your serve. Never ignore the details when it comes to a demonstration.

Finally, take responsibility for your continuing professional improvement. It doesn't have to be difficult. For example, organize a group of colleagues (don't forget your special team members). Choose three crimes from Chapter 4, *The Demo Crime Files*. Together, go in a room and practice demonstrating a feature in your software; first while committing the crime and then by doing it correctly. Lead a group discussion on ways to improve. Make a video recording of your sessions and review the tape in private. You'll be your best critic.

Demonstrating software is not an art. It's a blend of the proper preparation, demo techniques and attention to detail. Follow these simple principles and you'll quickly find that your prospects will start following you across the Bridge. Your new demonstration skills will lead to more business. You'll be demonstrating to WIN!

If you'd like information on training workshops, consulting or continuing education programs to improve your software demonstrations, call, write or email:

2WIN! Global
P.O. Box 50108
Colorado Springs, CO USA
80919-0108
www.2WinGlobal.com
bobr@2WinGlobal.com
+1 719.594.9959 tel

I N D E X

28999519R00184

Made in the USA
Lexington, KY
09 January 2014